D0871846

Discarding Images

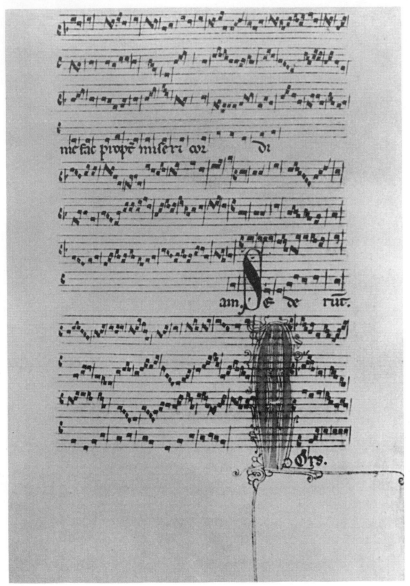

A final *clausula* appended to Perotinus' *Sederunt principes* in Florence, Biblioteca Medicea Laurenziana, plut. 29. 1. fo. 7ᵛ. Reproduced by permission

Discarding Images

*Reflections on Music and Culture
in Medieval France*

CHRISTOPHER PAGE

CLARENDON PRESS · OXFORD
1993

Oxford University Press, Walton Street, Oxford OX2 6DP
Oxford New York Toronto
Delhi Bombay Calcutta Madras Karachi
Kuala Lumpur Singapore Hong Kong Tokyo
Nairobi Dar es Salaam Cape Town
Melbourne Auckland Madrid
and associated companies in
Berlin Ibadan

Oxford is a trade mark of Oxford University Press

Published in the United States
by Oxford University Press Inc., New York

© Christopher Page 1993

British Library Cataloguing in Publication Data
Data available

Library of Congress Cataloging in Publication Data
Page, Christopher.
Discarding images: reflections on music and culture in
medieval France / Christopher Page.
Includes bibliographical references and index.
1. Music—France—500–1400—History and criticism.
2. France—Civilization—1000–1328. 3. France—
Civilization—1328–1600. 4. Civilization, Medieval.
I. Title.
ML270.2.P22 1993 780'.9'02—dc20 93–8142
ISBN 0–19–816346–0 (cloth: acid-free paper)

Set by Hope Services (Abingdon) Ltd.
Printed in Great Britain by
Biddles Ltd.
Guildford & King's Lynn

For Malcolm Gerratt

Amice, ascende superius

Preface

IN a review, Liane Curtis has described a previous book of mine in words that I am glad to apply to this one: 'It is not a book on music but rather a social history illuminated by its interest in music as an essential part of human experience.' The chapters gathered here form a series of essays, united by their concentration on music and culture in France between the thirteenth century and the fifteenth. They all attempt to examine images of musical life in medieval France, and they are designed to be brisk and suggestive.

In writing them I have incurred many debts. John Stevens read the entire book in a previous version and returned it with the usual wealth of subtle but searching comment. John Caldwell, Tess Knighton, Daniel Leech-Wilkinson, Ann Lewis, and Régine Page did the same. Jill Mann provided vital help when I was trying to trace the excellent study by David Aers, cited in the notes to the Afterword. Chapter 5, in an abbreviated form, was read at the Twentieth Annual Conference on Medieval and Renaissance Music held at the University of Newcastle in July 1992, and I am grateful to several delegates for their comments, especially David Fallows and Reinhard Strohm. Parts of Chapter 3 were aired informally when I had the pleasure of being *respondedor* at a session entitled 'Words and Music in the Medieval Motet', chaired by Margaret Bent and held at the meeting of the International Musicological Society in Madrid, 1992.

I owe a special debt to Bonnie J. Blackburn and Leofranc Holford-Strevens for their meticulous work on the typescript and their many pertinent comments. Duane Lakin-Thomas provided the essential technical help and advice as always.

I offer special thanks to Malcolm Gerratt, who has done so much to encourage musicologists in Britain during the last few years and to whom this book is dedicated.

C.P.

Cambridge

Contents

List of Illustrations

List of Music Examples

xii

. . . the old Model delights me as I believe it delighted our ancestors. Few constructions of the imagination seem to me to have combined splendour, sobriety, and coherence in the same degree.

C. S. Lewis, *The Discarded Image*

Introduction

The idea that a 'medieval' period intervened between Antiquity and the Renaissance has long been part of the Western cultural tradition. It is such a familiar idea, indeed, that we forget its deficiencies. To define nearly a thousand years of mankind as 'an age lying between two other ages', both of which are implicitly judged to be more important, shows a certain want of sympathy, not to say a poverty of ideas.

The Humanists who first distinguished the 'medieval' centuries and gave them a name were not lacking in ideas; when they began to evoke a 'middle time' (*media tempestas*) that seemed to separate them from Antiquity they were building an arch of historical imagination that reached across more than a thousand years towards the Ancients; that vault has been lovingly restored and buttressed ever since; no one has ever seriously attempted to dismantle it.

The Humanists did lack sympathy, however. Their feeling for the culture of the Ancients was highly selective and cannot be called a passion for *Antiquity* as such; they admired the Greece of Pericles, not Crete or Mycenae; they esteemed the Rome of Augustus, not the civilization of the Etruscans. Their image of the *media tempestas* was also selective, but it was also intensely negative, as the ambiguity of the word *tempestas* ('a period of time', 'a tempest') reveals.

Some modern scholars, granting all this, will argue that the Humanists' idea of a 'middle time' has now become harmless, at least in the specialized usage of medievalists, and that colloquial parlance, where the adjective 'medieval' is usually pejorative, is none of their concern (though it may irritate them from time to time). Musicologists, in particular, might further declare that there has never been facile agreement as to what makes 'medieval' music as opposed to 'Renaissance' music,[1] and that these concepts have inspired so much

---

[1] For a spirited instance see Wolf, 'The Aesthetic Problem of the "Renaissance" '.

valuable discussion that their usefulness is obvious—quite apart from the vivid meaning which they impart to certain facts of musical history.[2]

We may have sympathy with all these positions, and if the truth be told, we have no choice but to endorse them. A new interpretation of Western history may eventually emerge that nullifies the idea of a *media tempestas* (and such a new interpretation has been passionately called for in the past),[3] but it is far in the future.

We do have the option, however, to ask ourselves whether the concept of a 'middle period' has endured for five hundred years because it expresses truths which cannot be denied—certain truths in the history of music among them. Without hoping entirely to satisfy the advocates of that view, one might reply to their suggestion with another. The Middle Ages have certainly endured, but there is considerable scope for disagreement about the reasons for their tenacious hold over the Western imagination. Brian Stock, for example, has argued that the 'Middle Ages' have not survived because they define the past but because they serve the present:[4]

The Renaissance invented the Middle Ages in order to define itself: the Enlightenment perpetuated them in order to admire itself; and the Romantics revived them in order to escape from themselves. In their widest ramifications 'the Middle Ages' thus constitute one of the most prevalent cultural myths of the modern world.

In many ways the endeavours of modern scholars have reinforced what Stock provocatively calls the 'cultural myth' of the Middle Ages. It is the principal claim of this book that scholarship, musicology included, has long shown a tendency to homogenize and to monumentalize the 'medieval' period. This is done with the aid of certain mental schemes which, for all the ingenuity that may be deployed in acting upon them, are simple in themselves. I refer to antinomies such as efflorescence/decay, élite/popular, literate/non-

---

[2] Such as the firm view of Tinctoris that a 'new art' had arisen in the first half of the 15th c. with Dunstable and, in France, Dufay and Binchois. See the passage from his *Proportionale* in *Opera theoretica*, ed. Seay, iia. 10 and below, Afterword.

[3] For a penetrating discussion of the emergence of the 'Middle Ages' as a concept, see Burrows, 'Unmaking the Middle Ages'. Compare W. K. Ferguson, *The Renaissance in Historical Thought, passim*; Halecki, *The Limits and Divisions of European History, passim*; and Robinson, 'Medieval, the Middle Ages'.

[4] Cited in Aers, 'A Whisper in the Ear of Early Modernists', 192.

literate, learned/unlearned and urban/rural, most of which will surface repeatedly in these chapters. No doubt these contrasts are essential, in some form, if we are to make any sense of what we find; I do not suggest that they be abandoned. My proposal—and much of this book is concerned to illustrate it—is that they sometimes lead to simplistic and stereotyped reasoning.

It is understandable that musicologists should have adopted the concept of a medieval period followed by a Renaissance, albeit with some vigorous protest along the way, for musicology is a young discipline and all young things are dependent at first. The immense task of devising a history of musical forms and styles between the origins of Christian chant and the fifteenth century has been attempted many times in the last fifty years and could not have been accomplished without the aid of categories borrowed from historians, the Middle Ages and Renaissance among them. The polyphony of the Ars Antiqua, for example, has long been conceived in terms of themes such as systematization (the rhythmic modes), centrality (the Parisian region), and university learning (represented by the University of Paris and its links with the cathedral of Notre-Dame). These themes reflect the entrenched view of the thirteenth century as the great age of the Gothic: supposedly a time of scholastic rigour, of piety, of clerical élitism, and of rational (yet intensely spiritual) cathedral architecture. As brought to bear upon medieval art, this is the Middle Ages we meet in the great tradition of medieval architectural history, initiated by Émile Mâle (Pl. 1) and continued by Erwin Panofsky, Otto von Simson, and others.

In contrast, the secular polyphony of the fourteenth and even of the fifteenth century is apt to be regarded as an art of the Gothic in decline—of the 'waning' Middle Ages of the great Dutch historian Johan Huizinga. In various forms, this view has been held almost since 1919 when Huizinga's immensely influential study *The Waning of the Middle Ages* was first published in its original Dutch edition. The chansons of the Ars nova, for example, have sometimes been presented as luxuriant but wilful and almost mischievous compositions. It has been proposed that the leading composer of the French Ars nova, Guillaume de Machaut, sometimes writes 'a *perverse* accompaniment to a charming melody' (my italics).[5] The tradition to

---

[5] Caldwell, *Medieval Music*, 177.

Pl. 1. Émile Mâle

which Machaut made such a substantial contribution has been interpreted as one doomed to decay by a process as inevitable as the passage of the seasons, finally going to seed with the so-called 'mannerists' of the later fourteenth century who are often judged to be wayward and, in the words of a recent critic, 'pretty unmusical'.[6] The stylistic changes of the earlier fifteenth century may be welcomed and much admired, but as we shall see in Chapter 5, a 'waning' model of a decadent and declining Middle Ages has repeatedly been evoked to provide a cultural context for the secular polyphonic art of composers such as Dufay, Binchois, and Busnoys. This is the Middle Ages of Huizinga, Cartellieri, Stadelmann, Tuchman, and of countless textbooks, articles, and exhibition catalogues.

In recent years, however, as musicology has become progressively more enterprising, some old ideas have begun to dissolve. Painstaking research on English music has uncovered not just the vigour but also the abundance of polyphonic musical traditions in medieval England, and it is becoming as unfashionable to regard these repertories as 'peripheral' to developments in the 'central' Parisian region as it is to

---

[6] Milsom, 'Recent Releases', 116. Milsom makes this remark in the context of an accomplished and comprehensive review of recordings of medieval music. The question naturally arises whether it is the 'mannerist' pieces themselves or the performances they have received which are 'unmusical'.

regard English Gothic as a provincial version of a style forged at Saint-Denis.[7] Intensified work on the cultural context of major composers such as Busnoys is producing results that seem to owe little to the inherited schemata of Middle Ages/Renaissance and which are invigorated by a draught of recent developments in the New History (in this case women's history).[8]

Medieval studies have begun to take a direction that is particularly noticeable in the spheres of literary history and art history. This might be described as the move towards a more fragmented Middle Ages in which the very concept of a 'middle period' as a coherent construction of the modern mind is implicitly or explicitly questioned. In a recent article of exceptional interest, David Aers has taken issue with the specialists in Renaissance literature who, searching for the beginnings of interiority in English texts, interpret the Middle Ages as the 'other': the blank space before the supposed development of introspection and interiority in the later sixteenth century. Aers is quite right to maintain that this dismissal of the Middle Ages rests upon an ignorance of the complexity and variety of medieval thought, a debility that is enforced by patterns of university specialization in English literary studies dividing the 'medievalists' from the 'early modernists' or 'modernists'. For Aers, the Middle Ages are not 'the medieval world with its quiet hierarchies' that generations of scholars have used as the target for their generalizations; he describes them as 'centuries of Christian tradition, an extraordinarily diversified, complex and profoundly adaptive culture of discourses and practices'.[9]

Among art historians, Michael Camille has recently surveyed

[7] For a recent example of musicological revisionism see Bill Summers's review of general histories of medieval music in *Plainsong and Medieval Music*, 1 (1992), 101, and for the architectural historians see Wilson, *The Gothic Cathedral, passim.*

[8] Higgins, 'Parisian Nobles'. To the extent that the New History has made any impact upon musicological writing in the medieval field, studies written from a feminist perspective are already treating the concept of the Renaissance with great scepticism. See Macy, 'Women's History and Early Music'. For a most striking (and successful) attempt to find an alternative to traditional methods of narrative history for a well-defined project, see Knighton, 'A Day in the Life of Francisco de Peñalosa'. She presents a wealth of information about the duties and lives of Spanish composers *c.*1500 in the form of a letter, of her own devising, from Peñalosa to a colleague. Compare some recent experiments described in Burke, 'History of Events and the Revival of Narrative'. It may be doubted whether any male contributor to the volume in which Dr Knighton's essay appears would have dared abandon traditional methods for such a technique.

[9] Aers, 'A Whisper in the Ear of Early Modernists', 178.

attitudes to idols in the Gothic period and finds himself 'chipping away at the neatly organized foundations' of Émile Mâle's famous study, *L'art religieux du XIIIᵉ siècle en France*, first published in 1898 and widely known in the English-speaking world by one of the two titles chosen for various editions of the English translation, *The Gothic Image*. For Mâle, initiating the modern tradition of scholarship on iconography and the meaning of medieval ecclesiastical architecture, the Gothic cathedral is 'a coherent *summa* in stone' to be interpreted in close and faithful relation to texts such as the *Speculum historiale* of Vincent of Beauvais. In contrast, Michael Camille examines medieval images and discovers 'realms of intervisual and not just intertextual meanings, where images do not just 'reflect' texts innocently but often subvert or alter their meaning'.[10]

I share the view, expressed by Aers and Camille, that the most exhilarating project for the medievalist is now to investigate the variety and complexity of the Middle Ages and to question the received generalizations that are habitually used to constitute the 'medieval' period in our minds. This is the process referred to in the title of this book as one of 'discarding images'.

The primary inspiration for these chapters has been provided by performance. The chance to hear medieval music in recorded performances of increasingly high quality is one of the most obvious ways in which the musicological opportunities available to the modern scholar exceed those of previous generations. Recordings are sometimes superseded by advances in knowledge, and are often vanquished by changes in taste, yet innovative or challenging performances can none the less disturb a wide range of preconceptions that we may unwittingly hold about the interest and scope of a repertory. One may surely go further than this, however. In 1982 I addressed this issue in general terms, arguing that the sound of medieval music, as interpreted today, has the power to influence our aesthetic and intellectual apprehension of the Middle Ages, just as a visual experience of paintings by van Eyck shaped the conceptions of Johan Huizinga:[11]

This . . . is what makes the revival of interest in the performance of medieval music significant for our entire grasp of the Middle Ages and not simply of its musical life. The images that excite the imagination [in medieval manu-

---

[10] Camille, *The Gothic Idol*, p. xxvii.   [11] Editorial in *Early Music*, 10 (1982), 426.

script illumination and sculpture] have the power to form constellations with
a truly astrological influence over the doings of our minds. Sounds can do
the same . . . Our decades are the first in which it has been able to happen.

In recent years changes in our conception of performance practice
in later medieval France have undermined (almost without our realiz-
ing the fact) some ideas that support the notion of a Renaissance in
music as conventionally interpreted. Attempting to give substance to
that concept, Gustave Reese wrote that[12]

The small total range that characterized medieval polyphony, and which
helped to bring about frequent crossing of the voices, had made desirable a
sharp differentiation of the individual parts—whether in rhythm, in melody,
or in the timbres of the performing media. But as a wider total range came
into use in the Early Renaissance, crossing became less frequent and differentiation between the voices less sharp. The growing homogeneity of the
voices eventually resulted in the establishment of imitation as a standard
technique of the Late Renaissance.

It should perhaps have been plain long ago that this view involves
certain contradictions. If the lines of medieval polyphonic compositions were already differentiated, either in rhythm or in melody, then
it would surely have been in the Renaissance, when the voices became
more homogeneous, that some differentiation in the timbres of the
performing media would have been required, not in the Middle Ages.
Be that as it may, recent research into the performance of late
medieval music suggests a rather different picture of medieval sonorities and one that makes a comparison with Renaissance sonorities
much more difficult to draw in these sweeping terms.[13]

At bottom, this book has been written because I could not reconcile
the sound of much medieval music, and the aesthetic experience of
hearing it, with some conventional judgements about its imaginative
properties, its cultural meaning, or its intended audience. It is in the
nature of things that these judgements should often derive from
authors writing many decades ago. A great deal of recent interest in
medieval music has been (quite properly) philological and historical
in character, concentrating upon sources, transmission, composer
biography, and institutional history. Ideas about the aesthetic properties of medieval music, of its creative processes, and of the milieux in

---

[12] *Music in the Renaissance*, 4.
[13] For a recent review of this issue see Page, 'Going Beyond the Limits'.

which it was performed have been very slow to change; those ideas lie in our minds like a sediment where some venerable things—some almost a century old—have gradually come to rest for want of anything to stir them. They represent the deposit of many years' work in the humanities: art history, architectural studies, iconography, literary criticism, and more besides.

This book offers a sequence of essays, some of them (such as the first and fifth) devoted to very broad issues in our interpretation of the Middle Ages, and others devoted to narrower questions which (it may be hoped) possess a wider significance. In various ways, the chapters presented here ask the following questions, all of which are designed to explore suppositions about what is medieval, and which may be stated here in their barest essentials:

What is distinctly medieval? Some of the most influential writing about the distinctive character of medieval civilization is characterized by a reluctance to consider post-medieval conditions in either an erudite or an intuitive fashion. The belief that the Middle Ages formed a kind of sublime anomaly in the history of Western culture has become so strong that no reference to modern experience is deemed necessary (or legitimate) to test the validity of what is said about the medieval period.

What is the nature of medieval critical language? In our determination to reconstruct a distinctively medieval aesthetic which meets scholarly standards by being based upon written evidence, we fall into the trap of mapping medieval perception in terms of contemporaneous written expression. Medieval ways of describing the materials and effects of the 'arts', music among them, have a tendency to carry the discussion of artistic materials no further than basic matters of form and structure, and their language of praise, like the things which they can identify for praise, are governed by convention.[14] In some cases (the reaction to Chaucer's poetry in the fifteenth century provides an example), it is clear that we shall form a very distorted impression of medieval susceptibilities to art if we found our judgements upon what medieval writers themselves declare. Musicologists are particularly vulnerable in this regard since very little medieval writing has yet been discovered which records a personal or impressionistic reaction

---

[14] The outstanding guide to these tendencies as manifest in medieval writing about *ars musica* and *ars poetica* is now Stevens, *Words and Music*.

to music. Throughout most of the period covered by this book, the earlier thirteenth century to the mid fifteenth, the principal authors who wrote about musical matters (that is to say, the 'theorists') resembled their counterparts in the sphere of medicine. Like the physicians who studied their Galen and Aristotle, the music theorists were constantly drawn by the 'seductive distractions of scholastic elaboration';[15] they were often inclined to treat their material in a scholastic or philosophically oriented manner because 'the ability to do so was a skill that both made individual reputations and also helped to secure for medicine [and music] a position of respect'.[16] At the same time, the music theorists shared a large body of authoritative material; as with the physicians, 'adherence to a learned tradition expressed in a body of authoritative . . . writings constituted a guarantee of the separate identity of rational enquiry about the human body [and music] . . . as an authentic intellectual enterprise, distinct from natural philosophy'.[17] For a great deal of the Middle Ages the composition and study of medical texts bore no simple or direct relationship to clinical practice and experience; so it was with music. This problem surfaces throughout the chapters of this book.

What is the evidence of modern performance worth? The reluctance of some musicologists to draw upon the evidence (if it may be so called) of modern performance can be explained in various ways.[18] At the present time research in this field is moving so rapidly that recordings—which would be a vital part of the 'evidence' if we admitted it— are soon out of date. Furthermore, it might be argued that to perform medieval music in the twentieth century is to abandon the caution required of any scholar when evidence is sparse, and to do so in a fashion that must be brazen if it is to be effective. This is not the

---

[15] Siraisi, *Medieval and Early Renaissance Medicine*, 79.   [16] Ibid. 80.   [17] Ibid. 81.

[18] Despite advances in the performance of medieval music during the last thirty years, little attempt has yet been made to assess the influence—constructive or otherwise—which modern performance can bring to bear upon musicological enquiry. For a fascinating hint of what performance may contribute to the editing process, see the prefatory remarks by Fallows to his completion of G. Thibault's edition of the chansonnier of Jean de Montchenu, p. xi: 'Enfin je dois témoigner d'un privilège extraordinaire, qui constitue en vérité un rêve devenu réalité. Grâce à l'appui d'Anthony Rooley, la société Decca a eu le courage d'entreprendre l'enregistrement sur disque du chansonnier tout entier. Rooley et ses musiciens du Consort of Musicke m'ont permis d'assister à toutes les répétitions et séances d'enregistrement. Beaucoup de leurs idées, exprimées soit verbalement soit musicalement, ont amélioré de façon sensible le commentaire.' It would be of the greatest interest to know *how* the remarks and interpretations of performers contributed to Fallows's work.

place to debate whether there is ultimately any qualitative difference between the speculations of the scholar on one hand and of the performer on the other; what I wish to suggest is that sustained exposure to the sound of medieval music contributes to a vital sense of proportion (in the colloquial sense of those words), not only in the analysis of specific musical details and effects but also in conceiving what the music may have meant. As an academic study, performance practice embraces more than what performers do; it asks who performed where, for whom, to what effect, and upon what occasion. The second chapter of this book is a modest contribution to the history of performance practice in this sense, for it endeavours to suggest a broader social and artistic base for the motet and its audience than has hitherto been acknowledged. The third continues this theme, concentrating upon a famous remark by Johannes de Grocheio which is usually construed—mistakenly, in my view—as a reference to the 'élite' or 'intellectual' audience of motets *c*.1300. These two chapters, together with Chapter 5, have drawn much of their inspiration from the experience of listening to motets and chansons in performance during the last ten years and developing an *ear* for them.

How are medieval people to be described? Terms such as 'élite', 'intellectual', 'learned', and 'popular' are often used by medievalists, and are freely employed by musicologists when discussing the audience for secular polyphony. It is by no means certain what such words can be taken to mean in a medieval context; the answer will not be the same for the tenth century as it is for the twelfth, nor will it be the same for a thirteenth-century friar as it is for a thirteenth-century monk. The danger of such words is that they carry associations that are generally comforting to the modern scholar (who belongs to an intellectual élite) but which may be irrelevant and therefore deceptive.

I

Cathedralism

I

SINCE the Renaissance, the Western imagination has been inclined to picture the medieval period as a kind of odyssey: an exhilarating but enforced journey, taking mankind to a strange country and ending in the Renaissance with his homecoming and the restoration of his inheritance. Medievalists may deny that they see their period in these terms, and they invariably take professional pride in rejecting a view of the Middle Ages that seems so authoritative to the general mind and yet so erroneous to theirs. None the less, the concept of a medieval odyssey is easier to denounce than to displace.

Great churches are prominent in the musicologist's map of that journey. Indeed, scholars have frequently employed 'the Gothic cathedral' as an ideogram for medieval culture. It expresses a certain flamboyance, at least when applied to the later Middle Ages, but the principal meanings assigned to that ideogram now are perhaps these: piety, asceticism, rationality, and illumination, both literal and metaphorical. For Hans Tischler, surveying the early layers of the Ars antiqua motet repertoire, the driving principle of medieval art, including polyphonic music, can be discerned in 'the portal of a Gothic cathedral' and is essentially a 'rationalistic attitude'.[1] For Ernest Sanders, the medieval motet is 'like [a] cathedral . . . a Summa', both of which follow rigorous plans and represent a triumph of design.[2] For Nino Pirrotta, searching for relationships between scholasticism and music, there is 'a spiritual congruity and cultural continuity' between the Notre Dame polyphony of Leoninus and 'a Gothic cathedral'.[3]

---

[1] *The Style and Evolution of the Earliest Motets*, i. 11. For the debate about Gothic 'structural rationalism', so closely associated with Viollet-le-Duc, see Abraham, *Viollet-le-Duc et le rationalisme médiéval*, and Mark, *Experiments in Gothic Structure*.

[2] 'The Medieval Motet', in Arlt *et al.*, *Gattungen der Musik*, 528.

[3] 'Dante *Musicus*: Gothicism, Scholasticism and Music', 245.

It is understandable that musicologists should so often have chosen the cathedral to express the aesthetic and intellectual tendencies of the Middle Ages. Scholars usually look outside their own discipline for such comprehensive metaphors, and we shall see that some literary historians have invoked the cathedrals (as some architectural historians have turned to music). Musicologists have a close interest in them, for the communities serving a bishop or archbishop sheltered many major composers, including Guillaume de Machaut (in later life) and Guillaume Dufay (at various times). Furthermore, a cathedral is sometimes the only obvious sign in a European city that the Middle Ages ever happened, a fact which gives the spires of these great churches an emblematic force in the mind to match their material presence in the landscape. They have always possessed that strength. Medieval maps, usually drawn by clerics, reveal that these impressive buildings were of paramount importance in evoking a city, although extensive fortifications might rival them for interest (Pl. 2). It might also be suggested that the cathedral ideogram has a special importance today because cathedrals provide an enduring testament to values in medieval civilization that most detractors can be persuaded to admire (not to mention most university students, prejudiced by the infantile ideas that Régine Pernoud has denounced).[4]

An ideogram works by stylizing its subject. What is so striking about the cathedrals of the Middle Ages, however, is that they are not in the least stylized; the tremendous diversity of design attests to the

---

[4] *Pour en finir avec le moyen âge, passim.*

Pl. 2. A map presenting an itinerary, in graphic form, compiled by Matthew Paris, monk of St Albans, in the mid-thirteenth century. The journey begins at London (bottom left) with the cathedral of St Paul's dominating the urban landscape in which the Thames, Westminster, the Tower, Lambeth, and the major city gates are represented. The journey continues up the left-hand column to Rochester and the Medway, to Canterbury (with the cathedral as the only urban feature shown), and then to Dover. The waves at the top of the column represent the sea journey to Calais, Boulogne or Wissant. Beginning again at the bottom right, the chart gives routes from Calais to Reims via Arras and Saint-Quentin, or from Boulogne to Montreuil (represented by what is probably the Abbey of Saint-Saulve), to Saint-Riquier (represented by its abbey) to Poix and finally to Beauvais, with its cathedral placed in the centre of the area enclosed by the ramparts. London, British Library, Royal 14 C. vii, fo. 2ʳ. Reproduced by permission

le chastel de Doure lentree e la clef
de la riche isle de engletere

Benun̄ee

Reins

labbeie seī
augustin

pois

Seir quin

Cantrebire chef de iglises de engletere

ken

Seint Richer

leuue de

Rouecestre ki est euescfie

Arraz

MVSEVM BRITANNICVM

garnī chastroil

la cire de lundr ki est chef denglere
Brutus ki prim̄ enhabita engletere
la funda. e lapela troie la nuuele

Westm̄

Clateif

N̄redame de
Boloine

la tur
la grāt
Riue de tamise
lambech
la f. pūt
entre
la ieglise pol
Seint maur

Wisant port
de mer entre
Doure

mcdieval architects' freedom from any detailed intellectual or symbolic schemes that clerics, working far from the mason's bench, might have wished to impose upon them. If there is a pervasive symbolism or ideological force in cathedrals (beyond the devout purpose for which they were constructed) it is a variable one, each building being a response to the dynamism of the town that supported it.[5] One might also argue that there is a sinister meaning conveyed by cathedrals; whatever modern scholars such as Otto von Simson may propose about their symbolism,[6] those great buildings represented a bishop's effective control over his diocese;[7] they expressed, with sheer weight of stone, the power of a Church newly conscious in the twelfth and thirteenth centuries of the value of concerted action against its enemies:[8]

Leprosy had long been identified with enmity to the church . . . The analogy between heresy and leprosy is used with great regularity and in great detail by twelfth-century writers . . . Jews were also held to resemble heretics and lepers in being associated with filth, stench and putrefaction . . . And so it might go on, well beyond nausea and towards infinity.

The bishops and chapters for whom the cathedrals were built possessed an authority whose power was manifest in the lives of many lepers, whose disease, having not yet succumbed to scientific understanding, generated intense metaphors of decay as such incurable diseases generally do; it was also apparent in the lives of many Jews, housed in Jewries and compelled to wear distinctive clothing. This is not to deny the sublimity of cathedral design, which cannot be denied; it is only to isolate a strain of idealism in our apprehension of 'the Gothic', whether it be viewed as an architectural or, more broadly, as an aesthetic or even an intellectual style. The roots of that idealism lie in the nineteenth-century respect for Gothic piety and self-effacing craftsmanship, fostered by Viollet-le-Duc, among others, and by Émile Mâle, who saw the medieval sculptor as 'un modeste artiste'. Such views have been reinforced in the twentieth century by the symbolic and intellectual dimension given to the Gothic style by Otto von Simson and Erwin Panofsky, among others.[9] In the musico-

---

[5] Bourin-Derruau, *Temps d'équilibres*, 285.   [6] *The Gothic Cathedral, passim.*

[7] Murray, *Reason and Society*, 201.

[8] Moore, *The Formation of a Persecuting Society*, 62–5. Some recent studies, concerned with day-to-day relations between Jews and Christian laymen, have presented a much milder picture of relations between the two communities. See especially Shatzmiller, *Shylock Reconsidered*.

[9] Simson, *The Gothic Cathedral*; Panofsky, *Gothic Architecture*. For the influence of this

logical sphere, this is the kind of idealism that inspires Ernest Sanders, citing both Simson and Panofsky, to propose that 'medieval man' produced his musical compositions by moulding music 'as numerus sonorus, into a composite whole . . .'.[10] Sanders seems to be situating the art of composition within an intellectual and . almost ascetic context which is no more convincing as an evocation of the actual human experience of composing in the Middle Ages than the invocation of 'medieval man' that introduces it.

Until quite recently, medievalists in many fields of enquiry have found the concept of a still Middle Ages most enticing, especially when it is the stillness of the library. This attraction has been so great, indeed, that the title of this book draws attention to it, alluding to *The Discarded Image* (1964) of C. S. Lewis. A handbook designed to explain some of the ideas that may puzzle a modern reader of medieval texts, *The Discarded Image* evokes a Middle Ages of credulous but tidy—indeed pedantic—minds:[11]

There was nothing which medieval people liked better, or did better, than sorting out and tidying up. Of all our modern inventions I suspect that they would most have admired the card index.

Lewis would probably have sympathized with a recent tendency in musicological writing (almost entirely the province of university academics) to elevate the composers of medieval polyphony to positions of academic dignity. Craig Wright, in his bid to identify Leoninus,[12]

scholarship upon some musicological writing see especially Sanders, 'The Medieval Motet', 502 (and n. 16), 525 (and nn. 98–9), 526 (and n. 101), 527 (and n. 114), Tischler, 'Coordination of Separate Elements', and compare the comments of Pesce, 'The Significance of Text in Thirteenth-Century Latin Motets', 91. A thorough critique of Simson's book—one extending beyond the doubts of some initial reviewers—seems long overdue. See Kidson, 'Panofsky, Suger and St. Denis', 10 n. 32, where it is emphasized that Simson's view of Suger as the creator of Saint-Denis urges its case 'to the limit of credibility'.

[10] 'The Medieval Motet', 528.

[11] *The Discarded Image*, 10. Cf. Burrow, 'The Alterity of Medieval Literature', 386: 'even that remarkable man [C. S. Lewis] . . . displayed the disadvantages of having a relatively accessible Middle Ages'. Compare also the remark of Menache, *The* Vox Dei: *Communication in the Middle Ages*, 4: 'The prevailing approaches to medieval communication assume, in one way or another, the stability and conservatism of medieval society as a whole. A more dynamic perspective of medieval society is still missing.'

[12] Wright, 'Leoninus, Poet and Musician'. Wright's fluid hypothesis is already congealing into fact. See Fassler, 'The Role of the Parisian Sequence', 349: 'New research shows that he [i.e. Leoninus] was born around 1135, that he studied in Paris, and that he wrote poetry as well as music.' In Robertson, *Service-Books*, 48, the process goes to an extreme and we read of 'Canon Leoninus . . . of Notre Dame . . .'.

emphasizes that composers of the fourteenth and fifteenth centuries were often learned individuals—university men, no less—and many scholars would probably now agree that the art of polyphonic music was fostered by a clerisy in the later Middle Ages.[13] Some will object that it is not because many musicologists are university teachers that this image of 'the medieval composer' has emerged: to the extent that we have any information about the education and attainments of medieval composers of polyphony (and we have very little of substance before the later fourteenth century) this picture seems to be accurate. The problem is that a vast amount of medieval polyphony (virtually all Ars antiqua motets, for example, and most polyphonic conductus) was composed by persons about whom nothing is known and little can be confidently surmised. It might also be added that a survey of the individuals who composed monophonic chant for new liturgical feasts in the Middle Ages would perhaps produce a similar profile to the one evoked by Wright for composers of polyphony.[14]

It is too early to comment extensively upon this sociology of the medieval composer, but it may be salutary to notice that the master masons and architects of the cathedrals were once elevated in this way but are now being stripped of their degrees, so to speak. In 1948 Erwin Panofsky saw the thirteenth-century architect Hugues Libergier 'in something like academic garb' on the front of his tombstone;[15] four decades later, however, Christopher Wilson identified that garb as a costume worn 'by the rich burgesses of the northern French towns' when they commissioned such monuments for themselves.[16] It remains to be seen whether a revisionism of this kind will

---

[13] Wright, 'Leoninus', 3–5. On p. 5 he says: 'They [medieval church composers] had the training, acquired in the cathedral schools, to write liturgical and ceremonial polyphony, and they had the intellectual perspective, gained in the fledgling universities, to fashion it in a way that was harmonious with the educational and philosophical systems of the day.' In general this is a perceptive passage and surely correct, but it explicitly refers to composers of sacred music and little or nothing can be said for certain about the musicians who composed, adapted, and otherwise developed the repertoire of Ars antiqua French motets. We may also be left wondering whether Wright somewhat overstates his case in declaring that the composers of liturgical polyphony knew how to compose in a way that was 'harmonious with the educational and philosophical systems of the day'.

[14] Such a survey would include Julian of Speyer and Stephen of Tournai, neither of whom would cause any surprise if it were discovered that they were composers of polyphony.

[15] Panofsky, *Gothic Architecture and Scholasticism*, 26.

[16] Wilson, *The Gothic Cathedral*, 143. It is revealing, in this context, to briefly survey the changing views of Villard de Honnecourt, whose famous 'sketchbook' in Paris, Bibliothèque nationale, MS fr. 19093 has attracted so much attention for more than a century. The history of

eventually overtake the two composers whose enterprises have so often been compared to the emerging Gothic edifice of Notre-Dame, namely Leoninus (about whom little is known for *certain*) and Perotinus (about whom almost nothing is known at all).[17]

The concept of an intellectual and ascetic Middle Ages owes much to the widespread belief that symbolism and allegory were the characteristic modes of medieval understanding and expression.[18] A brief excursion into the realm of art history will show how sweeping such an interpretation of medieval thought can be when it moves from precise illustration to broad generalization. In his *Landscape into Art* Kenneth Clark attributes the scarcity of landscape painting in the Middle Ages to 'the symbolizing faculty of the medieval mind'.

Villard scholarship is marked by a tendency to elevate him to the rank of a learned master mason, but in recent years that trend has generally been reversed as scholars have looked afresh at the evidence with a dash of scepticism. In 1943 Nikolaus Pevsner, in common with numerous authors before him, called Villard an 'architect' and his manuscript a 'textbook' (*An Outline of European Architecture*, 94). As late as 1977 one could still find Villard being spoken of as a 'master mason' and his manuscript described as a pattern-book (Kostof, 'The Architect in the Middle Ages', 89). A turning-point came with a review essay of 1973 by Branner, asking whether Villard was really an *architect*; could he not have been 'a lodge clerk with a flair for drawing'? More recently, Bucher has suggested that Villard belongs with the 'petits architectes du peuple' who built bridges, fountains, cisterns, and other such projects ('L'Architecture vernaculaire', *passim*), while Kidson has continued his excellent and in many ways iconoclastic work on medieval architecture, questioning the traditional thesis that Villard was a Gothic architect-mason. See the excellent survey by Barnes, *Villard de Honnecourt*.

[17] See e.g. Yudkin, *Music in Medieval Europe*, 363. Compare Sanders, 'Consonance and Rhythm', 268 n. 8: 'I add here the suggestion that Leoninus "made" the *Magnus Liber* around 1180, since the choir of the new cathedral of Paris was finished in 1177—except for the roofing—and the high altar was consecrated in 1182. It is difficult to imagine suitably stimulating conditions prior to that time.' The magnetism which Paris has come to possess for the minds of musicologists working on the Ars antiqua is remarkable, and would make a fascinating study in its own right. For examples of it at work see Hoppin, 'A Musical Rotulus', 132; Levy, 'A Dominican Organum Duplum', 206; Yudkin, *De Musica Mensurata*, *passim*, and Norwood, 'Evidence Concerning the Provenance of the Bamberg Codex'.

[18] The literature on this topic is vast, the classic study being de Lubac, *Exégèse médiévale*. See also Eco, *Art and Beauty in the Middle Ages*, *passim*. It would be hard to find a more influential (and controversial) discussion of the medieval fondness for allegorical interpretation than D. W. Robertson's *A Preface to Chaucer*. Robertson's claim, familiar to all students of Middle English literature, is that the only orthodox interpretation of a literary text in the Middle Ages was one that read it allegorically in terms of the Augustinian doctrines of *cupiditas* and *caritas*, the former denoting the love of things for their own sake and the latter the love of things for the sake of God. In recent years Robertson's views have come under attack from many quarters. A case in point, of particular interest to musicologists, concerns the interpretation of the lyric *Maid in the mor lay*, recently reconstructed in both words and music (somewhat adventurously perhaps) in Harrison and Dobson, *Medieval English Songs*, 188–93; on the competing interpretations of this poem see Wenzel, 'The Moor Maiden'.

When artists of the period looked upon nature, Clark argues, their view was frozen by 'the icy winds of doctrine', so that a flower or a tree became a stylized image.[19] Ideas of this kind have a noble pedigree, especially amongst those who are seeking to demonstrate what they take to be the innovations of Renaissance civilization; we think of Burckhardt (to name no other). Friedländer has offered a more sympathetic version of the same argument, commenting upon the tendency of later-medieval artists to associate skill of execution with firmness of line and not with the 'informal, hazy, or indistinct' qualities that have been associated with so much landscape painting in recent centuries.[20]

Recently, however, Walter Cahn has emphasized that this view embodies a 'hieratic and drastically simplified picture of the Middle Ages', and that many find it 'either wrong or at least one-sided . . .'.[21] He cites Pächt's study of landscape depiction in the fifteenth century as an example of research which finds in the art of the later Middle Ages 'much that foreshadows or prepares the ground for the apparent innovations of the Renaissance' (Pl. 3).[22] The observation might be made that medieval artists, whatever their medium, were almost invariably concerned with narrative subjects and that narrative usually requires human figures; there was accordingly a powerful tendency in the visual arts of the Middle Ages for landscape to be presented as token scenery to contextualize the figures at the centre of visual and narrative interest. It is striking that François Avril finds one of the first post-classical landscapes in a manuscript of Guillaume de Machaut's poetry where an illumination shows an enchanted region with no human inhabitants.[23]

Musicology has been affected by the 'hieratic and drastically simplified' image of the Middle Ages that Cahn mentions. An article by a distinguished scholar, whose work continues to influence studies of medieval performance practice and musical life, provides an example. In a seminal study entitled 'The Role of Musical Instruments in Medieval Sacred Drama' (1959) Edmund Bowles declares that from the time of the Church Fathers to the schoolmen[24]

---

[19] Clark, *Landscape into Art*, 1–31; see also Cahn, 'Medieval Landscape', 12–13.

[20] Friedländer, *Essays über die Landschaftsmalerei*, 16 ff.; Cahn, 'Medieval Landscape', 12.

[21] Cahn, 'Medieval Landscape', 13.   [22] Pächt, '"La Terre de Flandres"'.

[23] Discussed in Huot, *From Song to Book*, 244.

[24] Bowles, 'The Role of Musical Instruments in Medieval Sacred Drama', 67. In this article Bowles attempts to devise principles of instrumentation for medieval liturgical drama on the

Pl. 3. The Flanders countryside. London, British Library, Cotton Augustus A. v, fo. 345^v. Franco-Flemish, late fifteenth century. Reproduced by permission

the belief prevailed that behind each concrete object or event lay a hidden meaning related to the Scriptures . . . the physical world had no reality to medieval man except as a symbol, a shadow of the real, spiritual realm beyond.

It would hardly be possible to attribute a greater asceticism to the Middle Ages than this. Bowles cites Otto von Simson's study of numerical design in the Gothic cathedral, a book which has done so much to direct scholars in fields outside architectural history towards a hieratic and 'symbolist' Middle Ages. He also cites H. O. Taylor's monumental treatise *The Medieval Mind* (1911), another influential work that is deeply committed to the idea of a medieval consensus: the 'mighty bases of conviction' which supposedly define the Middle Ages. Taylor spends many pages on the subject of symbolism and allegory, and it is this section of his book that is cited by Bowles. Viewed from the perspective of the 1990s, however, *The Medieval Mind* contains little to suggest why some critics regard Geoffrey Chaucer, for example, as a poet who 'expresses a fragmented and problematic outlook [and] an uncertainty about fundamental truths . . .'.[25] Regardless of whether one agrees with such critics (and in general I do not), the tendency of Taylor's book to turn medieval culture into a great nave, formed by massive pillars of certainty, is disturbing. The schoolmen were more Aristotelian than Platonist, so why should their symbolic interpretations have denied physical reality? In the sphere of textual interpretation their complex allegorical senses did not nullify the literal meaning of words. The passage quoted above from Bowles's article shows where such thinking as Taylor's may lead, for it would surely be inadvisable to accept the claim that 'the physical world had no reality to medieval man except as a symbol, a

basis of the symbolism of musical instruments in patristic and later medieval scriptural commentary. He does not raise the question of whether instruments should be used in such works as the *Play of Daniel*, thus revealing how research on performance practice is often unwittingly directed by contemporary fashions in performance and by other pressures of a non-academic kind, for that is surely the first question to settle. The subject has received very little attention since Bowles's essay, but recent scholarship has come increasingly to favour an *a cappella* hypothesis for all liturgical chant and for any music (such as liturgical drama) in some way appended to it. If this hypothesis is correct, then the symbolism of musical instruments, surely a bookish matter for the most part, was clearly not sufficiently powerful or vivid in the minds of contemporaries to warrant the emergence of such practices as Bowles attempts to reconstruct. Once again, we are prompted to question the supposedly 'symbolic' mentality of the Middle Ages.

[25] Jordan, *Chaucer's Poetics and the Modern Reader*, 2.

shadow of the real, spiritual realm beyond'. Was every keen lover of illuminations, figured windows, or motets such a philosopher?[26]

Medieval treatises on the materials and techniques of arts such as poetry and music are mostly rudimentary and technical; the aesthetic elements of those arts, if discussed at all, are usually treated in a conventionalized or impressionistic way. Just as a theorist of poetry like Geoffrey of Vinsauf does not prepare us for Chaucer's ironic humour, so a theorist of composition like Aegidius de Murino does not broach the experimental character of Machaut's harmony. The absence of informal or critical writings on music from the Middle Ages is particularly damaging. To compile a commentary upon Scripture, a sermon, a scholastic *questio*, or any of the genres that dominate medieval writing was to move into a frame of mind where Christian conscience and a respect for conventional exposition went hand in hand. The result was usually a surface of biblical (or other) authority in which the author was safely encased, like a tortoise in his shell, but whose rigidity he did not always completely share—in a manner that can never be fully defined but which becomes apparent in some texts, as we shall see.

II

The principal evocation of what might be called the 'medieval consensus' in musicology is the Pythagorean model of musical thought. Pythagoreanism in this context implies a belief that numerical proportions are the fundament of all nature and the source of all beauty.[27]

[26] The position taken by Bowles seems to deny what a hundred years of research into medieval science have established, namely that it was in the 12th c. that 'men of philosophic temperament began to turn away from the vision, given them by St Augustine, of the natural world as a symbol of another, spiritual world, and to see it as a world of natural causes open to investigation by observation and hypothesis' (Crombie, *Science, Optics and Music*, 94).

[27] The bibliography on this topic is extensive. The major studies include Bower's translation of Boethius, *Fundamentals of Music*, pp. xx–xxiv; Chamberlain, 'Philosophy of Music'; De Bruyne, *Études d'esthétique médiévale*, i. 3–26 and 306–38; ii. 108–32 (where, on p. 108, it is boldly stated that 'l'époque romane et même l'époque gothique n'apportent rien de neuf à la vision musicale du monde'), and iii. 227–38; Sanders, 'The Medieval Motet', esp. 525–8; Stevens, *Words and Music, passim*. De Bruyne and Stevens provide by far the most richly documented surveys. As pointed out by Wimsatt and Cable ('Introduction' to Baltzer *et al.* (eds.), *The Union of Words and Music*, 9–10), the study by Stevens is a nuanced and meticulously guarded exposition of a view whose essentials have sometimes been argued in a brisk and uncompromising manner. Seay, *Music in the Medieval World*, 21, gives what is perhaps the most abrupt statement

Some medieval texts reveal that minds were not completely settled on this issue. An example is provided by a passing reference to music in the encyclopaedic *De universo* by William of Auvergne (d. 1249), a Master of Theology and Bishop of Paris. At one point William turns to consider the sources of musical pleasure:[28]

Non immerito vero perscrutandum est quid sit quod delectet animas nostras in vocibus musicalis seu melodiacis, et forsitan videatur alicui non irrationabiliter quod non voces ipse delectent eas sed magis numeri et proportiones musice qui nullatenus audiuntur sed interius solummodo cogitantur. Iudicium autem huiusmodi non leve est quoniam videmus aliquos absurdissime canentes et iniucunda percussione aures audientium offendentes, suis cantibus non mediocriter delectari.

It is not otiose to study what it is in musical or melodious notes that delights our souls, and perhaps it will seem to someone—and not without reason—that it is not the notes themselves which delight our souls but rather the numbers, and the musical proportions, which are not audible but which are only perceived within us. But it is not easy to rule in such matters, for we see some who get great delight from their songs but who sing completely out of tune and who offend the ears of those who listen with an unpleasant, jarring sound.

William endorses a Pythagorean position here, but he has an enquiring mind. He observes that the subliminal effect of numerical proportion is a good hypothesis if one wishes to explain music's power to give pleaure, but it does not completely decide the issue. He introduces his Pythagorean proposal with a 'perhaps' (*forsitan*), which lends the writing a tone of reasoned rather than dogmatic authority, signalling the need for circumspection: 'it is not easy to rule in such matters . . .'. We should not be misled by the mildness of William's tone; in a few lines he has journeyed to the border of a traditional explanation and is looking over the edge.

With the recent work of Albert Seay, Ernest Sanders, and John Stevens,[29] among many others, the Pythagorean model has become established as a means to interpret what medieval authors habitually

of a Pythagorean viewpoint, declaring that the primary purpose of sounding music in the Middle Ages was 'the concrete demonstration of the fundamental ratios . . .'. This is counterintuitive and has been most ably challenged by Treitler, 'Troubadours Singing their Poems', 16–17.

[28] The text and translation are taken, with slight modifications, from Page, *The Owl and the Nightingale*, 142–3.

[29] See above, n. 27.

say about the technical, aesthetic, and moral aspects of music. Stevens's work offers a comprehensive interpretation of the medieval view of music married to words, arguing that number was perceived in aesthetic and intellectual terms by medieval musicians and was the essence of their art.[30] (The 'intellectual terms' in this context include a commitment to ideas that are essentially metaphysical, such as the belief that numerical proportions have their origin in the mind of God.) Stevens draws extensively upon the 'explicit' theory presented in treatises on music and poetry,[31] and as an interpretation of what *musica* meant in the Latinate and essentially pedagogical traditions of the Middle Ages his account is never likely to be superseded. How completely does it convey the medieval experience of music? A question of this kind can be asked about any theory founded upon medieval writing that purports to describe the materials of an art, in this case the *ars musica*, *ars rithmica*, and *ars metrica*; as we have already observed, the written language for describing such things rarely went beyond the inventory of rudiments and basic principles.

This is a vast problem which cannot be investigated here in relation to arguments as extensive as those of Stevens. It may be useful, however, to consider a brief but none the less sweeping presentation of a Pythagorean position. This is to be found in James Wimsatt's recent discussion of Guillaume de Machaut's attitude to music, as expressed in the *Prologue* to his poetic works:[32]

As a line of distinguished scholars has noted, for medieval theorists music was an expression of mathematical ordering. Its abstract numerical quality generated St. Augustine's influential statement 'Musica est scientia bene modulandi' ('Music is the science of good measurement'). The conception of music as the most exact of the mathematical sciences led to its being seen as a principle of creation, for God's mode of action was conventionally seen as mathematical, based in the biblical text 'Thou hast ordered all things in measure and number and weight' (Wisdom of Solomon 11:20). Thus music worked by cosmic principles and was inherent in the perfectly harmonious movement of the heavenly bodies.

This is a resonant description of what many scholars now associate not just with the medieval view of music but also with the medieval experience of it. It is well known that Machaut's *Prologue* describes

[30] *Words and Music*, 13–47.   [31] Ibid. *passim*.
[32] 'Chaucer and Deschamps' "Natural Music" ', 134.

13

music as an art 'which makes one want to laugh, sing, and dance'; noting this passage, Wimsatt argues that Machaut attributed the pleasurable effects of music to the exactitude of its *mesure* and to its abstract virtues, not to 'a lilting melody or a spirited rhythm'.[33] Even allowing for the subjective nature of observations about these qualities in any music, we may react immediately to Wimsatt's claim with the observation that Machaut's music possesses so much animated melody and rhythmic verve that the cardinal importance of those qualities to Machaut can scarcely be doubted.

Wimsatt's view illustrates the way in which interpretations of medieval art and culture often generate counter-intuitive arguments that have a tendency, in the context of a prevailing assumption about medieval 'otherness', to shed their counter-intuitive appearance and begin to seem duly objective and historical. It may be true, of course, that Machaut would indeed have explained his art in such terms to anyone who questioned him; tradition provided him with no other way of being profoundly serious about the sources of musical pleasure and its influences upon the human constitution. He may even have explained his art in those terms to himself. None the less, Machaut's music leaves no doubt that his sensations when composing were as indifferent to moral or intellectual persuasions as those of any composer at any period in history when genuinely engrossed.

If we approach the Pythagorean model with an open mind then several brisk observations can be made. First, it is not an exclusively medieval model. Scholars who work on the sixteenth and seventeenth centuries are inclined to believe—and with some justification—that Pythagoreanism 'came to full bloom in the Renaissance'.[34] Secondly, the tendency to conceptualize in terms of gradations—a quality of 'medieval thought' which is fundamental to Pythagoreanism—is found in the ratiocination of many periods before Romanticism. Paul

---

[33] 'Chaucer and Deschamps' "Natural Music" ', 135. Compare Moyer, *Musica Scientia*, 48–9, who cites Burtius (who is following earlier authors) on the effects of each mode: 'the second mode is heavy and doleful and fit for lamentations . . .', etc. Moyer comments: 'The logical support for this passage must come from the Pythagorean arguments about macrocosm and microcosm which Burtius presented in the first treatise . . .'. This seems very wide of the mark; Burtius' remarks belong in a tradition of medieval reflection about the *sound* and aesthetic properties of the plainchant modes as configured in the common melodic formulae of each mode.

[34] Kuntz, 'Pythagorean Cosmology', 253. The articles of faith that Kuntz attributes to the Renaissance Pythagoreans will sound familiar to every medievalist: 'an ordered cosmos, the chain of being, God and the cosmos, man as microcosm, nature as a paradigm for the discovery of the eternal law, the primacy of numbers, harmony in music and in nature . . .'.

G. Kuntz has made this point with welcome directness. 'What seems to me so permanently right about medieval philosophy', he remarks, 'is that in reflecting on order of degree or hierarchy one begins from common sense . . .'.[35] None the less, many medievalists of the twentieth century have believed in a distinctively Gothic amalgam of reason, piety, and Pythagoreanism. Here is Ernest Sanders in a famous essay devoted to the medieval motet,[36] completed at a time when scholars in various fields (especially literary history) were influenced by Otto von Simson's account of the Gothic cathedral as a symbol of order and the key to an aesthetic of light.[37] In more than seventy pages, and with copious musical examples, Sanders traces the evolution of the motet from the Notre Dame clausulae to its fifteenth-century manifestations in the work of composers such as Guillaume Dufay. His discussion is of superlative quality, not only for its mastery of detail but also for its lofty generalizations about the meaning of the motet:[38]

The intrinsic necessity of [the motet's] existence is self-evident, because, inspirited by divine laws, it is that species of musica instrumentalis which optimally fulfills man's obligation to fashion approximate audible images of musica mundana.

This is a remarkable passage whose diction rises to the greatness of its theme. Evoking the language of taut philosophical argument ('the intrinsic necessity of its existence is self-evident . . .'), Sanders claims authority through a delicate use of archaism ('*inspirited* by divine laws . . .') and through the solemnity of Latinate diction where an Anglo-Saxon lexis would have conveyed the intended meaning but not the desired tone ('that *species*/kind of musica instrumentalis which *optimally*/best fulfills . . .). It makes for an imposing passage, and many have been rightly impressed by it. Dolores Pesce, for example, airs the suggestion that the motet[39]

may even have possessed a metaphysical significance in its time, in much the same way as a Gothic cathedral: each projects a perceptible spatial or temporal order, which in Gothic architecture relies on the fundamental proportions

---

[35] Kuntz, 'A Formal Preface', 5. [36] 'The Medieval Motet', *passim*.
[37] Simson, *The Gothic Cathedral: The Origins of Gothic Architecture and the Medieval Concept of Order*. For references to this book in Sanders's article see above, n. 9.
[38] 'The Medieval Motet', 557.
[39] 'The Significance of Text in Thirteenth-Century Latin Motets', 91.

seen within a building's dimensions, and in the motet on the rhythmic and harmonic coordination of two or more apparently disparate vocal lines. The motet could thus be viewed as a symbolic representative of a higher order, perceived consciously or unconsciously by its listeners.

This is an admirable summary, notable for its caution as well as for its clarity. No doubt it is true, as John Milsom has recently maintained, that certain kinds of verbal and musical complexity in the Ars nova motet were 'best savoured through the contemplation of the work as an ideal object, outside the experience of sounding music',[40] but that is not quite the same as acknowledging the presence in such motets of elements liable to carry every listener into a realm where aesthetic pleasure and metaphysical belief coalesced in some supposedly medieval manner of admiration. It is possible that some motet composers were drawn to a hyperbolized and even transcendentalized conception of the materials of composition; such attitudes have been too common among the composers of the twentieth century for us to deny them to those of the fourteenth. However, it is unlikely that such Ars nova composers always met with listeners fully sympathetic to their own assessment of what the art of composition involved, or that elaborate motets were written exclusively for such listeners by composers contemptuous of any other kind. The encyclopaedic *Speculum musice* (*c*.1325) by Jacques de Liège is overwhelmingly concerned with number and proportion, but if we search the seventh book of the work (concerning polyphony) for a passage where Jacques seems to sanction Sanders's elevated conception of the motet, then we find little. A passage at the end of Book III, concerning the mental exhilaration to be derived from advanced arithmetical problems as applied to the theory of music, shows that Jacques regards numerical complexity as a purely intellectual challenge for men with a *purum et clarum ingenium*.[41]

If we are interested in the differences between vanished minds as well as in the similarities between them, then it is invigorating to discover that Sanders's essentially Pythagorean model of music's higher meaning was not thought to supply an answer to every question. We have already encountered William of Auvergne's reflections on this matter (see above, p. 12). A second, more pointed, illustration leads us to Johannes de Grocheio. In his *De musica* of *c*.1300, Grocheio gives

---

[40] 'Recent Releases', 114. [41] *Speculum musicae*, ed. Bragard, iii. 163.

an accurate (if somewhat brief) account of the three categories of music, inherited from Boethius. *Musica mundana*, says Grocheio, designates 'the harmony caused by the motion of the heavenly bodies', while *musica humana* is 'the balance achieved in the human body through the best mixture of elements in it'. Finally, *musica instrumentalis* is 'that music which is caused by the sounds of instruments, natural and artificial'.[42] These three categories were vital to the Christianized Pythagorean notion that the numerical verities which God held in His mind were first manifest in the constitution of the universe, then manifest in the constitution of the human body, and finally expressed in the music of voices and instruments. It is precisely because this threefold conception was so potent that Grocheio's rejection of it is so striking:[43]

Qui vero sic dividunt, aut dictum suum fingunt, aut volunt Pythagoricis vel aliis magis quam veritati oboedire, aut sunt naturam et logicam ignorantes . . . Corpora vero caelestia in movendo sonum non faciunt, quamvis antiqui hoc crediderint . . . Nec etiam in complexione humana sonus proprie reperitur. Quis enim audivit complexionem sonare?

Those indeed who divide [music] in this way are either dissembling in what they say or they wish to obey the Pythagoreans, or others, more than the truth, or they are ignorant of nature and of logic . . . Celestial bodies in movement do not make a sound, although the ancients may have thought otherwise . . . Nor also is sound innate in the human constitution. Who has heard a constitution sounding?

Elated by the advances in cosmology and medicine that were made during his generation, Grocheio has missed the Pythagoreans' point about *musica humana*: Boethius does not say that the human constitution has audible sound located within it. Indeed, he speaks cautiously of this matter and in similitudes. None the less, Grocheio's rejection of the Pythagorean classification of music is final. Whatever his commitment to the conventional (yet potent) notion of numerical harmony underlying all Creation, Grocheio, on the verge of the Ars nova, sweeps the Pythagorean taxonomy aside in favour of a classification that is rational and empirical, based upon the characteristic audience for each type of music and its effects upon them. His

---

[42] Text from Rohloff, *Die Quellenhandschriften*, 122, corresponding to Grocheio, *Concerning Music*, trans. Seay, 10.
[43] Ibid.

dismissive reference to those who follow the 'Pythagoreans . . . more than the truth' casts a shadow over Sanders's proposition that the motet was perceived as an 'approximate audible image of musica mundana'. That is consistent with what a medieval author might say about the motet, but to the best of my knowledge no such author actually says it, and Johannes de Grocheio, who admired the motet as a form, seems to deny the possibility of ever wishing to say it.

III

It has been suggested that the imagination and aesthetic of the later Middle Ages were essentially architectonic in character. This idea can be illustrated with particular clarity by the work of several literary critics writing in the 1960s and 1970s. All were seeking, among other things, to qualify the claims of the 'Human Comedy' school of Chaucer criticism represented, above all, by George Lyman Kittredge in *Chaucer and his Poetry* (1915).[44] Gathering strength from some magisterial pages by Curtius about numerical construction and number symbolism,[45] and further invigorated by Otto von Simson's study of the Gothic cathedral as a symbol of order,[46] scholars such as D. W. Robertson Jr.,[47] R. M. Jordan,[48] and Elizabeth Salter[49] began to approach Middle English literature with the aid of suggestive analogies drawn from the visual arts. Panofsky's *Gothic Architecture and Scholasticism* was at hand to provide a stimulating example of how architectural history and the history of thought could flow into a common stream.[50] D. W. Robertson Jr., whose main purpose was to propose an intensively 'allegorical' aesthetic for the entire Middle Ages, opposed Kittredge's interest in psychology and character with the argument that it was anachronistic to bring such interests to texts of the fourteenth century because the minds of the period did not work in ways amenable to that approach. Medieval writers, he

[44] Even the most recent Chaucer criticism still continues the dialogue with Kittredge here and there, such is the influence of his ideas. See, for example, the excellent study by Mann, *Geoffrey Chaucer*, 150.

[45] Curtius, *European Literature and the Latin Middle Ages*, 197, 367–70, 501–9.

[46] Simson, *The Gothic Cathedral: The Origins of Gothic Architecture and the Medieval Concept of Order*.

[47] *A Preface to Chaucer, passim*, but especially 3–51.

[48] *Chaucer and the Shape of Creation, passim*.

[49] 'Medieval Poetry and the Visual Arts'.   [50] On Panofsky's study see below, 30–4.

claimed, thought in terms of 'symmetrical patterns, characteristically arranged with reference to an abstract hierarchy', and he contrasted this with a Romantic tendency to think in terms of 'opposites whose dynamic interaction leads to a synthesis'.[51] According to this interpretation, medieval thought can be described as essentially cumulative and aggregative, an ordonnance of harmonious but separate parts. In 1967, R. M. Jordan extended this approach, proposing that a historical understanding of the writings of Chaucer depends upon the critic's sympathy with Gothic principles of construction, especially those of the great cathedrals. Deriving much of his understanding from Otto von Simson, Jordan went so far as to suggest that 'Chaucer approached the materials of his art much in the manner of a builder approaching bricks', manipulating 'inert, self-contained parts, collocated in accordance with the additive, reduplicative principles which characterize the Gothic edifice'.[52]

This architectonic view is consistent with the conceptions of musical structure expressed in Ernest Sanders's celebrated essay on the motet, dated 1967 and therefore contemporary with the work of Jordan and other critics with similar interests.[53] Sanders too cites Curtius and Otto von Simson,[54] and he shares with Jordan a sense of Gothic artistic procedure which owes much to the example of the great cathedrals:[55]

It has been pointed out that 'mathematical formulae underlie nearly all medieval architecture and indeed most medieval art', and that the ratios of the primary intervals—symbols of eternal truth—can at times be demonstrated to have determined the basic dimensions and details of Gothic cathedrals . . . Optimally, the teleological meaning of the motet is to be an image of the divine order, and its composition is a joyous science . . . Like the cathedral, the motet may be termed a Summa . . .

(I am puzzled by the reference to motet composition as 'a joyous science' here, since the motet seems far removed from the fourteenth-century perpetuation of the troubadour art in Toulouse, where the phrase *lo gai saber* was coined.) Like Jordan, Sanders welcomes any clear sign that the medieval art which concerns him was conceived by contemporaries in architectonic terms:[56]

---

[51] *A Preface to Chaucer*, 6.   [52] *Chaucer and the Shape of Creation*, pp. xii and xi.
[53] 'The Medieval Motet'.   [54] See n. 9 above and 'The Medieval Motet', 526 n. 100.
[55] Ibid. 525–8.   [56] Ibid. 526.

Just as much architecture is thought of in the Middle Ages as a visual manifestation of musical proportions, music, i.e. measured discant, is by the end of the thirteenth century described in architectural terms: *Tenor autem est illa pars supra quam omnes alie fundantur quemadmodum partes domus vel edificii super suum fundamentum. Et eas regulat et eis dat quantitatem.* [The tenor is the part upon which all the others are founded, like the parts of a house or edifice upon its foundation. And it governs them and gives them extent].

Compare Jordan once more:[57]

Augustine understood the visible world to be a sign of invisible truth, and knowing that God had disposed all things in 'measure and number and weight' Augustine employed the musico-mathematical language of the *Timaeus*—as did Boethius, Macrobius, and other major thinkers—to elucidate the rational order of divine creation. My discussion of Gothic architecture views that great achievement as a literal realization, structured in stone and glass, of the principles of Creation, principles which had been formulated in the pagan language of proportion and revered by Christians for more than a millennium as the language of God.

For musicologists, an architectonic view of Gothic aesthetics has its attractions. Treatises on measured discant consistently speak of composition as a collocative rather than a holistic procedure with part being added to part, an aspect of their writing that is conspicuous in what Régine Pernoud has called 'notre époque d'analyse structurale'.[58] Many Ars antiqua motets were produced by supplementing or otherwise modifying pieces that already existed in a complex process of composition and adaptation that is neatly expressed in the language Jordan uses to describe Chaucer's 'Gothic' procedure.

Let us examine this attitude as it is manifest in Sanders's analysis of a specific piece. In his essay of 1967 Sanders praises a short four-part setting of *Sederunt*; 'evidently', he writes, 'the composer envisioned a piece demonstrating the number 12 in various ways'. His transcription is given in Ex. 1. In his article it is preceded by the following quasi-algebraic diagram presenting the number of longs in what Sanders considers to be each complete phrase of each voice (without explanation, he omits the first note of the piece, presumably regarding it as *ultra mensuram*):

---

[57] *Chaucer and the Shape of Creation*, p. xi.   [58] *Pour en finir avec le moyen âge*, 15.

Ex. 1. A final *clausula* appended to Perotinus' *Sederunt principes* in Florence, Biblioteca Medicea Laurenziana, plut. 29. 1, fo. 7^v. The transcription is from Sanders, 'The Medieval Motet', 521. Sanders indicates the incise-marks of the original notation by a bar through all staves (as after the first duplex long), or by a comma above the stave (*a*) when the incise-mark cues a change of syllable and (*b*) when the incise-mark appears at a point where there is no change of syllable and where the musical phrase does not seem to require (or even to allow) a rest, as in the fourth measure of the Quadruplum. He represents other incise-marks by rests followed by a barline. Plicas are not indicated. This method of transcription succeeds admirably in conveying the complex phrase-structure of the counterpoint. (Here, and in the following musical examples, roman numerals indicate tenor repetitions.)

| Triplum and Quadruplum | 2L+4L+4L+2L | +4(3L) |
| Tenor and Duplum | 6L+4L+2L | +5L+4L+3L |

Commenting upon the piece, Sanders reiterates his view that 'it is hardly possible to demonstrate the number 12 in a more tightly packed composition'. His presentation of this point involves a subtle visual rhetoric. This four-part setting of the word *Sederunt* is appended in *F* (fo. 7ᵛ) to Perotinus' celebrated *Sederunt principes*, and is presumably designed to provide an abbreviated polyphonic setting for the solo portion of the chant after the Psalm verse. Quoted by itself, however, the setting seems highly concentrated and self-sufficient; we can hardly avoid the impression that a specific compositional project is being undertaken and completed before our eyes by a miniaturist. The diagram given above intensifies our sense that this is indeed a composition that may be viewed in quasi-architectural terms as an edifice built upon a rigorous floor-plan.

In the event, this interpretation is difficult to accept. A cantus firmus of seven notes, such as the one employed here, seems an odd choice for a piece supposedly designed to demonstrate the number 12, while the scribe's presentation of the Tenor in *F*, which deserves to be regarded as a thirteenth-century assessment of the structure which the composer has created, is not obviously duodecimal in character (see Frontispiece). Even allowing for the variable function of the incise marks which the scribe has deployed (the second and third indicate the placement of syllables), the notation of the tenor hardly demonstrates the number 12. Furthermore, the floor-plan which Sanders offers for the piece rests entirely upon his transcription of a notation which leaves some details uncertain: none of the final four longs of the tenor is a *longa duplex*, and yet one or more of them must clearly be extended if the Tenor is to accommodate the material in the upper voices. Sanders's interpretation produces a result with twenty-four longs (that is to say 2 × 12), but that is one of several possibilities; it might be argued that the very beginning of this piece and the very end—places where there is particularly wide scope for varying interpretation—are not to be counted in the central concern of the piece, which is to decorate a cantus firmus of seven notes that is extended by repetition.

The weakness of the view which regards collocation and aggregation as the essence of creation in the Gothic era deserves a study to itself, and one which could become nothing less than a comprehensive survey of medieval music theory and compositional practice. That is out of the question here, but the fundamental suppositions of such an approach can be illustrated with the aid of Hans Tischler's recent work on the Ars antiqua motet. In the first volume of his exhaustive survey of the formal characteristics of the motet repertoire, *The Style and Evolution of the Earliest Motets*, Tischler proposes to set the thirteenth-century French motet in its cultural context.[59] This section of his book owes something to an earlier article of his published in 1968,[60] but goes far beyond that study in its interpretation of the motet as the reflection of a quintessentially Gothic mentality. Tischler finds the essence of that mentality in a 'rationalistic attitude' which seeks to co-ordinate individual elements into a 'higher unity' using hierarchic organization. He discerns it in the Ars antiqua motet:[61]

The harmonic unification of several individually phrased voice parts, each carrying its own text and often using different languages, reflects the period's tendency toward coordinating several individual activities so that they form a higher unity as . . . in the feudal system.

Is this really a description of something that is characteristic of the medieval period? The significant labours of most periods before Romanticism can be described in terms of individual elements arranged to achieve a 'higher unity', relying upon a hierarchic organization

---

[59] *The Style and Evolution of the Earliest Motets*, i. 5–13.
[60] Tischer, 'Intellectual Trends'.
[61] *The Style and Evolution of the Earliest Motets*, i. 10.

which is loosely comparable to structures of political power. Here is Tischler once more:[62]

The arts furnish striking examples of this drive [to co-ordinate separate elements in a higher unity]. The portal of a Gothic cathedral . . . presents numerous statues, each in its own niche, self-contained, not interacting with each other and therefore easily replaceable . . . Yet in each group, all the figures or reliefs are conceived as portraying a common idea: the virtues or vices, the patron saints or the patriarchs . . . giving them an external unity. Moreover, they are all arranged in symmetric architectural patterns that confer an externally imposed order on them. Often the various groups are further differentiated and hierarchially ordered by size.

We may visit a garden laid out for a patron with classical tastes (perhaps an English gentleman of the eighteenth century) and see statues of Graeco-Roman deities, 'each in its own niche, self-contained, not interacting with each other and therefore easily replaceable'. Furthermore, such statues are often 'arranged in symmetric architectural patterns that confer an externally imposed order on them'. We may wonder, therefore, whether Tischler's passage sheds any light upon the Ars antiqua motet. While every medieval theorist acknowledges the primacy of the tenor part in a polyphonic composition, it is perhaps not quite accurate to say that the voices of a motet (or of any medieval polyphonic composition) are 'hierarchically' arranged. To employ a metaphor used by some theorists, the tenor is certainly the foundation of the musical edifice, but that is not the same as a hierarchy—a gradation of status—for the parts of a house are structurally, not hierarchically, arranged. Taking a broader view, we may grant that motets co-ordinate individual entities (the separate voices) into a higher unity (the complete piece), but the same might surely be said of any contrapuntal music or indeed—with some definition of terms—of any musical structure. It is true that motet melodies and texts are often replaced, recalling Tischler's descriptions of Gothic statues in their niches, but that is because motets existed in a generally fluid state and were constantly attracting fresh attention. In that sense they were not in the least monumental, and to imply that the voices of a motet are 'self-contained, not interacting with each other' would be to ignore the many ways in which duplum, triplum and quadruplum may be bound together by a structure of

[62] *The Style and Evolution of the Earliest Motets*, 11

consonance and by repetition and imitation, both verbal and musical. We shall return to this subject in Chapter 3.

Does this 'cathedralism' embody an accurate perception of what is distinctively Gothic about the Gothic cathedral? As an example of the imprecision that has sometimes bedevilled discussion of these matters, even at the highest level, we may cite a passage by the doyen of French medievalists, Georges Duby. Duby has called the later Middle Ages 'Le temps des cathédrales', and an important section in his book of that name is headed 'Dieu est lumière: 1130–1190'.[63] These titles evoke a familiar (but still potent) image of the Gothic cathedral as a temple of light, literal and spiritual, but Duby's dates of 1130–90 are quite misleading in this context: the great churches of that period are not always infused with illumination. Indeed, they are often tenebrous, invoking Milton's 'dim religious light'. John Gage has described the experience of entering by the West Door of Chartres, and his words cut deep into our stereotyped perception of the Gothic cathedral:[64]

When we enter Chartres Cathedral, even on a bright spring morning, we enter a twilit world. Although our eyes become adapted to the gloom—and it may take a matter of several minutes—we still tread warily, for the interior is not so much lit as suffused with a muffled glow that seems only remotely associated with the stained-glass windows which remain difficult to locate precisely, in some indefinite space, like hanging screens of luminous colour . . . The glass of Chartres acts, indeed, less as a conductor of daylight, than as a fine-meshed filter against it; and light-levels inside the cathedral may be some hundreds of degrees lower than those outside . . . And yet for those modern commentators who have sought to interpret the meaning of stained glass beyond the narrowest bounds of style and iconography, light has seemed to be the key throughout the whole span of the Gothic centuries . . .

Gage explains that a major change in the aesthetics of stained glass took place during the course of the later thirteenth century; Chartres may be crepuscular, but the Chapter House of York Minster, glazed in the late 1280s, is bathed in light 'even on a dull Yorkshire day'.[65] It is clearly necessary to be cautious if we are tempted to read the Gothic period by the light of cathedral windows. More precision is required before even the most general analogies may be safely drawn.

[63] *Le Temps des cathédrales*, 121–62. Compare Bourin-Derruau, *Temps d'équilibres*, 285: 'Si la cathédrale résume le XIIIᵉ siècle . . .'.
[64] Gage, 'Gothic Glass', 36.   [65] Ibid.

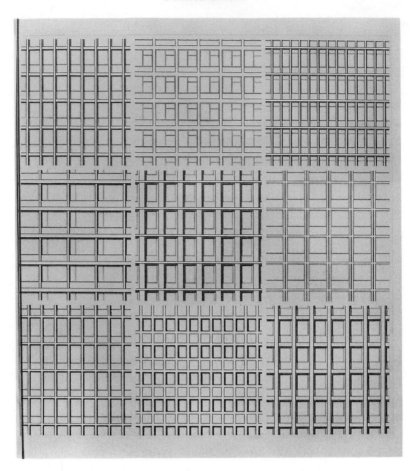

Pl. 4. Skeletal structures from Siegel's *Structure and Form in Modern Architecture*, published in 1962. Reproduced by permission

Let us turn from the windows to the nave itself. It may be convincing to speak of a Gothic cathedral as composed according to 'additive' or 'collocative' principles in certain respects, but with some definition of terms these principles can surely be discerned in much later-twentieth-century architecture. Allowing for differences of style, there seems to be as much addition and collocation in some twentieth-century skeletal structures (Pl. 4) as in the thirteenth-century 'sketch-book' of Villard de Honnecourt (Pl. 5).[66] Indeed, the structural and

[66] For full details of Villard and a critical bibliography see Barnes, *Villard de Honnecourt*.

Pl. 5. A design for a clocktower (*orloge*) from the 'sketchbook' of Villard de Honnecourt. Paris, Bibliothèque nationale, fr. 19093, fo. 6ᵛ. French, c.1230–5. Reproduced by permission

27

aesthetic relationship between the Gothic cathedral and some forms of modernist architecture are very striking. By the same token, there is nothing exclusively medieval in the belief that a fine building should be laid out according to 'mathematical formulae', nor that it should embody musical relationships and speak 'the language of proportion' (to quote from Jordan). These ideas can be found in the pages of Vitruvius' *De architectura*, where, we may be sure, many medieval authors encountered them.[67] Of course, Vitruvius does not associate the language of proportion with what Jordan has called 'the language of God', and it would be possible to maintain that Christian theology intensified (or at least spiritualized, which may not always be the same thing) the perception of architectural patterns in the minds of some men disposed to think in such terms. However, it has long been known that medieval descriptions of the magnificence of cathedrals do not always speak in terms of divine harmony and order.[68] In cathedrals and other great buildings some medieval observers saw bright colours and costly objects, and they did not always transmute the base metal of their impressions into the gold of pious joy.

The greatest problem with what we are calling cathedralism is that it rests upon certain very simple but far-reaching suppositions about medieval culture; these suppositions tempt the modern interpreter to find meanings of a correspondingly simple but pervasive kind, whether the medieval materials in question explicitly invoke those meanings or not. If they are explicit, then the matter is closed; if they are not explicit, then the 'symbolic mentality' is evoked and the meanings are assumed. Christine Smith's recent discussion of Leon Battista Alberti's *Della tranquillità dell'animo* provides a case in point. That treatise, composed in 1441 or 1442 at the end of an extended sojourn in Florence, contains a remarkable description of the city's cathedral. Alberti and Nicola de' Medici, strolling in the cathedral, are joined by Agnolo Pandolfini who, glad to find them there, proceeds to rhapsodize about the great building in which they walk:[69]

[67] Vitruvius, *De architectura*, i. 1. 8, where it is said that an architect must have a knowledge of music and associated mathematical relations. In the rest of this chapter, some of which is relevant here, Vitruvius refers, *inter alia*, to the collocation of bronze vessels as echo-chambers under the circles of seats in theatres according to the ratios of fourth, fifth, and octave.

[68] Schapiro, 'On the Aesthetic Attitude in Romanesque Art', *passim*.

[69] Smith, 'Della tranquillità dell'animo', 107.

Cathedralism

And certainly this temple has in itself grace and majesty; and, as I have often thought to myself, I delight to see joined together here a charming slenderness with a robust and full solidity so that, on the one hand, each of its parts seems designed for pleasure, while on the other, one understands that it has all been built for perpetuity. I would add that here is the constant home of temperateness, as of springtime: outside, wind, ice and frost; here inside one is protected from the wind, here mild air and quiet. Outside, the heat of summer and autumn; inside, coolness. And if, as they say, delight is felt when our senses perceive what, and how much, they require by nature, who could hesitate to call this temple the nest of delights? Here, wherever you look, you see the expression of happiness and gaiety; here it is always fragrant; and, that which I prize above all, here you listen to the voices during mass, during that which the ancients called mysteries, with their marvellous beauty.

Offering the translation that I have just borrowed, Christine Smith comments:[70]

Agnolo's words express his direct visual observations, and communicate his personal feelings. But, at the same time, they describe the soul's equilibrium through the allegory of the architectural style of the church and the interior ambient which it encloses . . . In a second series of images, Agnolo depicts an antithesis between the constancy of the Cathedral interior and the extremes of nature outside its walls, that is, the opposition between spiritual tranquility and the variability of fortune.

This is not very convincing as an interpretation of Agnolo's words. In the passage quoted (which is all that Smith gives) Agnolo does not 'describe the soul's equilibrium', nor do the last lines of his speech depict 'the opposition between spiritual tranquillity and the variability of fortune'. Rhetorical style apart, there is little in Agnolo's encomium of Florence Cathedral that would surprise a modern visitor to the same building. A twentieth-century tourist might well note that the Cathedral is slender but robust; that it is cool inside whatever the weather; that it is exhilarating and, above all, that it is even more sublime with the voices of a choir echoing through it. Smith's remarks provide a striking example of the way modern historians, in many fields of study, sometimes take it for granted that medieval utterances which are not overtly satirical or scatological must express a grave meaning, missing an element of common humanity in the process.

[70] Ibid.

29

Where does this leave the 'architectonic' metaphors that are occasionally used by music theorists? Here is the passage from Johannes de Grocheio's treatise that Sanders interprets as an example of architectonic thinking, quoted as he cites it in his article:[71]

Tenor autem est illa pars supra quam omnes alie fundantur quemadmodum partes domus vel edificii super suum fundamentum. Et eas regulat et eis dat quantitatem.

The tenor is the part upon which all the others are founded, like the parts of a house or edifice upon its foundation. And it governs them and gives them extent.

This is misleading because something has been omitted. The last sentence should read 'eas regulat et eis dat quantitatem, quemadmodum ossa . . .' ('it governs them and gives them substance, as bones do . . .').[72] Grocheio's observation about the tenor giving *quantitas* (a difficult term to translate) is therefore not only an architectonic comparison but also an anatomical one. To be sure, there is an architectonic image in this passage (*partes domus vel edificii*),[73] and it is not the only one to be found in the theorists, but is it any wonder that the music treatises contain such metaphors? We still say that some kinds of tonal music are constructed upon a 'bass' part, where the spelling of Modern English 'bass' does little to conceal its origin in Latin *basis*, whose fundamental senses (I have just used an architectonic metaphor) include the base of a pillar. Such conceptualizing is ubiquitous in the language of every age.

IV

Cathedralism owes something to Erwin Panofsky (Pl. 6), whose *Gothic Architecture and Scholasticism* is cited by all the scholars whom I have mentioned, both literary historians and musicologists.[74] Ernest Sanders has made notable use of the book. First published in 1951, having begun as lectures in 1948, Panofsky's essay was to provide the cutting edge of what Kidson has called a 'full-scale art-historical

[71] 'The Medieval Motet', 526.

[72] Text from Rohloff, *Die Quellenhandschriften*, 146, corresponding to *Concerning Music*, trans. Seay, 27.

[73] See 'The Medieval Motet', 526, citing Coussemaker and corresponding to Jacques de Liège, *Speculum musicae*, ed. Bragard, vii. 9.

[74] See e.g. Sanders, 'The Medieval Motet', 528.

Pl. 6. Erwin Panofsky

counter-offensive . . . against the excessively technical views about Gothic associated with the name of Viollet-le-Duc'.[75] The main thrust of such an offensive, Panofsky believed, had to lie with a recognition of the cultural and intellectual significance of Gothic architecture. His thesis is that the Gothic style and scholasticism were developed in the same period and in the same place ('the 100-mile zone around Paris'), and that they reflect a common 'mental habit'.[76] The essentials of this habit, as Panofsky discerns them, are a passion for an explicitly hierarchical ordonnance of parts, rigidly disciplined, patterned, and repeated. To this suggestive argument, which is capable of being presented (as I have just done) in a summary fashion, Panofsky brings a wealth of reference to theological and philosophical thought. Sometimes, indeed, he raises the discussion to pinnacles of abstraction that challenge the reader's head for heights:[77]

. . . the mystic depends on his senses as purveyors of visual images and emotional stimuli, whereas the nominalist relies on them as conveyors of reality;

[75] 'Panofsky, Suger and St. Denis', 1. For analyses and explorations of Panofsky's views about Gothic architecture, taking in both *Gothic Architecture and Scholasticism* and his *Abbot Suger on the Abbey Church of St. Denis and its Art Treasures* (1946), see also Holly, *Panofsky and the Foundations of Art History*, 158–60 *et passim*; Price, *Medieval Thought*, 138–41; Radding and Clark, 'Abélard et le bâtisseur de Saint-Denis'; and Wilson, *The Gothic Cathedral*, 9–10.
[76] *Gothic Architecture and Scholasticism*, 21. [77] Ibid. 15.

and the *intuitus* of the mystic is focused upon a unity beyond the distinction even between man and God and even between the persons of the Trinity, whereas the *intuitus* of the nominalist is focused on the multiplicity of particular things and psychological processes.

This is vertiginous indeed, especially since the foundations of *Gothic Art and Scholasticism* are not as solid as one might wish, given the imposing edifice that is set upon them. It is misleading to claim that 'in the 100-mile zone around Paris . . . scholasticism possessed what amounted to a monopoly in education'.[78] What of the monasteries? There was not always a welcome for the schoolman's *questio* in the cloister. Panofsky's tendency to see the influence of a few decisive individuals behind any change in the philosophical preoccupations of the learned is a version of the 'great man' theory of history. Arguments which present medieval thinkers as having acted in conscious relation to trends of thought which have become clear with the benefit of hindsight can rarely carry conviction, especially since that clarity may be an illusory one produced by the simplifying effect of distance. It may even make us anxious, and perhaps justifiably so, to find such trends reduced from their contemporary complexity to the point where they can be succinctly named in textbook fashion ('the conflict of faith and reason'). Panofsky's evocation of far-reaching and rapid intellectual changes occurring within less than a generation and finding a response in architectural styles does not carry conviction in every particular. We may question, for example, whether there was a specific period in the later twelfth and thirteenth centuries when 'a decrease of confidence in the supremely synthetic power of reason . . . may be discerned'.[79]

It is in this context that Panofsky takes a quasi-academic view of the Gothic 'architect', recently challenged by Christopher Wilson, among others.[80] It will be worth pausing over this part of Panofsky's argument, if only in order to reveal the means by which one modern interpretation of an art other than music has become impregnated with suppositions about scholastic and university influence which are comparable, in some ways, to those that obtain in Ars antiqua studies. The nearest thing that Panofsky finds to a forum in which master masons could have encountered the professional discursive tech-

---

[78] *Gothic Architecture and Scholasticism*, 21–2.   [79] Ibid. 9.
[80] Wilson, *The Gothic Cathedral*, 142–3.

niques of the schoolmen is the *disputatio de quolibet*, a kind of lecture (invariably in Latin) which was devoted to 'what you please' because it was free to range beyond the immediate concerns of the university textbooks. Glancing down the lists of Parisian *questiones de quolibet* as they are presented in the invaluable guide to *La littérature quodlibétique* by Glorieux, it is difficult to imagine that the occasions for these lectures had really become 'social events not unlike our operas, concerts, or public lectures', as Panofsky states.[81] When we add the powerfully (and no doubt necessarily) subjective element in Panofsky's observations upon the 'gentle animation'[82] of early Gothic figures and other points of Gothic style, interleaved between his arguments and offered in illustration of them, we may be tempted to admire his essay as a cathedral in its own right and then to leave, with due reverence, by the West Door.

Of the recent scholarship which has been devoted to Panofsky's legacy, Peter Kidson's critique of Panofsky on Abbot Suger and Saint-Denis, birthplace of the Gothic, is outstanding.[83] Kidson repaints Panofsky's portrait of Suger; gone is the great patron seeking a defence of his expensive tastes in terms of what Panofsky calls a 'neo-Platonic light metaphysics', supposedly culled from the pages of Pseudo-Dionysius' *De caelesti hierarchia*, a book that looms large in cathedralist works such as Otto von Simson's volume, prominently cited by Bowles, Sanders, and many others.[84] Kidson concedes that Suger probably read the *De caelesti hierarchia*, but he also shows that Suger's writings never mention Pseudo-Dionysius by name and contain no identifiable quotations from his work. Kidson also argues that Suger's writings, so often regarded as a classic exposition of Gothic architectural symbolism, are about matters of no conceivable interest to anyone outside the Abbey of Saint-Denis, a fact clearly reflected in the very limited manuscript transmission of Suger's treatises.[85] Furthermore, the *De consecratione*, written after 1144 'when the choir was finished and the whole operation had been brought to a splendid conclusion', contains 'hardly anything about symbolism'.[86] Kidson

---

[81] *Gothic Architecture and Scholasticism*, 23.   [82] Ibid. 6.

[83] 'Panofsky, Suger and St. Denis'.

[84] *The Gothic Cathedral*, 52–3, 103–7, 120–3, *et passim*.

[85] 'Panofsky, Suger and St. Denis', 9.

[86] Ibid. Kidson's article is cited in the bibliography of A. W. Robertson, *Service-Books*, but is not apparently used in the text since she explains various aspects of the Saint-Denis liturgy, including the notable absence of polyphony, in terms of a Pseudo-Dionysian imagery of light

interprets Suger as an enthusiastic patron, eager for results but ignorant of the technical means, his conception of his own doings bearing more relation to pride in himself and in his community than to 'neo-Platonic light metaphysics' or the intellectual activities of the schools. The implications of this position reach beyond Saint-Denis to the whole question of architectural meaning in the later Middle Ages; once again, Kidson is excellent value:[87]

by its very nature medieval architecture involved mysterious operations that were excluded from the conspectus of the liberal arts and therefore beyond the understanding of even the most highly educated ecclesiastical patrons. So while it may be granted that any symbolism present in Gothic architecture was the contribution of the clergy rather than the craftsmen, at best it can have been no more than a partial and superficial factor in the design procedure.

The essentially unprofitable influence of Panofsky's *Gothic Art and Scholasticism* upon musicology can best be illustrated by a study that freely acknowledges its influence: Nino Pirrotta's 'Dante *Musicus*: Gothicism, Scholasticism and Music'. This is how he begins:[88]

In recent years I have spoken several times on the subject of 'Notre Dame, University, and Music', without ever committing my ideas to paper. The fact is that I had found it quite easy to stress the coincidence of date and purpose that existed between the building of the new Parisian cathedral begun in 1163 and the composition of a polyphonic cycle for use there during the liturgical year . . . But it was clear to me that I was avoiding the more difficult and necessary task of recognizing the spiritual congruity and cultural continuity that must have existed between those expressions of a single society, a Gothic cathedral, a scholastic approach to knowledge and faith,

and dark without drawing attention to the important correctives offered in Kidson's study. In the event, Robertson's meticulously documented survey illustrates the danger of drawing analogies between musical structures or practices and cathedral architecture and aesthetics. For Pirrotta, as for many other scholars, the emergence of the organum of Leoninus is almost a projection in sound of the emerging Gothic edifice of Notre-Dame; for Robertson, the *absence* of polyphony and Leoninus' organum from the liturgy at Suger's church is a projection of the Gothic edifice of Saint-Denis. Cathedrals, it would seem, are like statistics: one may prove anything with them.

[87] 'Panofsky, Suger and St. Denis', 2. Compare Wilson, *The Gothic Cathedral*, 9: 'visual diversity [in cathedral design] reflects the huge margins of creative freedom which architects were allowed when giving physical form to what remained after all very general symbolic concepts', and 10, referring to the 'virtual impossibility' that 'non-expert contemporaries would have been able to gain any intellectual purchase on Gothic great church architecture'.

[88] 'Dante *Musicus*', 245.

and the then new style of music now variously labelled Notre-Dame polyphony or *Ars antiqua*.

Pirrotta clearly believes in a 'spiritual congruity and cultural continuity' uniting music, Gothic architecture, and scholasticism. He proceeds with his attempt to find this congruity, graciously acknowledging Panofsky as his guide,[89] but he does not find it. What he finds—and this is quite a different matter—is a sustained cathedral metaphor. Sometimes it is elegant but fanciful:[90]

As the architectural plan of a mediaeval cathedral was oriented with intentional symbolism toward the rising sun, similarly the plan of the musical cathedral opens with the season of Nativity and encompasses the year according to the cycle of the liturgical, not merely seasonal, calendar.

At other times it is felicitous enough, but does not demonstrate the 'spiritual congruity' which Pirrotta set out to discover:[91]

We may say—if I am allowed to continue my metaphor—that Perotinus expanded the ideal musical apse by doubling the *circulus anni* and raising its vaulting higher.

In one instance the cathedral metaphor is unhelpful, and is no sooner raised up than demolished:[92]

Should we want to push our architectural metaphor further, we might compare the troped *clausulae* to windows in which stained-glass figurations were inserted, were not the transparency of those figurations clouded by the fact that, while the basic plainchant remained untroped, different tropes were added to each of the other four voices of the polyphonic composition.

The question of whether a supposedly Gothic, architectonic structure can be discerned in the musical compositions of the later Middle Ages is a subject too vast for this or indeed any other one book. I therefore restrict these remarks to certain broad observations. Numerous troubadour and trouvère songs may be cited which, for all the scrupulous calibration of syllables which they display from line to line and stanza to stanza, possess organic melodies where motifs of varying length are repeated and exchanged (Ex. 2). In recent years, as the 'modal' interpretation of trouvère song has gradually lost ground, the important stylistic and registral differences between songs in the High Style (like the one quoted in Ex. 2) and simpler songs, perhaps

[89] Ibid.   [90] Ibid. 249.   [91] Ibid. 250.   [92] Ibid. 251.

Ex. 2*a*. The melody of *A penas sai don m'apreing*, a *canso* by the troubadour Raimon de Miraval (fl. 1185–1213), as preserved in MS G (Milan,
Biblioteca Ambrosiana, R.71 Sup.). From Switten, *The* Cansos *of Raimon
de Miraval*, 148

for dancing, in a strict measure, have become increasingly clear. In
part, the difference lies in the way High Style songs may seem upon a
hearing of the first verse to be relatively 'blank' and even unstruc-
tured, but prove, as the verses pass by, to possess many points of
internal cohesion which the ear gradually discerns (not always at a
conscious level) in the flow of melody. Something similar may be said
for many of the monophonic *cantiones* composed during the twelfth
and thirteenth centuries.[93]

Numerous Ars antiqua motets also leave us uncertain about the
importance of layered and architectonic planning. These pieces are
perhaps the quintessential examples of musical architecture in the
medieval repertoire, for the treatises consistently refer to the creation
of motets voice by voice and to the role of the tenor as the 'foundation'. As far as vertical sonorities are concerned, it may be granted

---

[93] See e.g. the analyses in Switten, *The* Cansos *of Raimon de Miraval*, 15–41, and the discussion of the Latin *cantio* in Stevens, *Words and Music*, 63–79 and 484–91.

Cathedralism

Ex. 2b. An analysis of repeated or varied material in *A penas sai don m'apreing*. From Switten, *The* Cansos, 26

Ex. 3. The Motetus and Tenor of the three-part motet *Res nova mirabilis/Virgo decus/ALLELUYA*. Adapted from Anderson, *Compositions of the Bamberg Manuscript*, 129

Vir-go de -cus ca - sti - ta - tis, Vir - go re - gi - a, Vir - go

ALLELUYA

ma-ter pi - e -ta - tis, Vi - ri ne -sci - a, Vir - go tem -plum

tri - ni - ta - tis, Ce - li do -mi - na, Vir-go pu -ra,pra-vi - ta -tisDe - le

vi - ci - a, Nos e -mun -dans a pec - ca - tis Per suf -fra - gi -

a; Per te no -bis pe - ne da - tis De -tur ve - ni - a,

Ne dam -pne - mur pro pec - ca - tis In mi -se - ri - a,

Sed fru - a-murcum be - a -tisCe -li glo - ri - a.

that some motets reveal a purist's determination to begin each perfection with a perfect consonance, and this obviously requires a measure
of architectonic design. The two-part texture shown in Ex. 3 displays
this kind of scrupulosity, with almost every perfection (three quavers
in the transcription) beginning with an octave or a fifth. The highly
calculated approach to consonance in this piece is reflected in the
earliest layer of the treatise known as the *Discantus positio vulgaris*,
where the compiler refers to the placement of consonant and dissonant intervals according to whether the notes on which they are
placed are odd (*impar*) or even (*par*). Counting a long-short pattern
in mode 1 as comprising two numbered positions, he describes the
impar notes (1, 3, 5, etc.) as more suited to consonance than the *par*
ones (2, 4 etc.).[94]

Other motets, however, reveal a more synthetic and melody-
dominated conception. The Ars antiqua motet repertoire is protean,
and we should perhaps be wary of commenting too precisely upon the
aesthetic or formal properties of any given 'piece' (if that term is
appropriate). None the less, it may be observed that the Tenor and
Motetus of *Mout souvent/Mout ai esté/MULIERUM* (Ex. 4) do not

Ex. 4. Extract from the Motetus and Tenor of the three-part motet *Mout
souvent/Mout ai esté/MULIERUM*. Adapted from Anderson, *Motets of
the Manuscript La Clayette*, 46

---

[94] Original text in *Scriptores*, ed. Coussemaker, i. 95. The motet shown in this example was
known to the compiler of the treatise, who cites it, albeit in another connection.

show the same constructivist determination to make a texture with a perfect consonance at the beginning of each perfection—or, as Johannes de Grocheio puts it, 'to sound a fifth as often as possible' between tenor and motetus.[95] Studying this piece, and hearing its finely formed motetus, we do not immediately sense the justification for Sanders's observation that the superstructure of a motet 'is designed proportionately to unfold, demonstrate, and articulate the fundamental numerical theme given by the tenor'.[96] The texture of Ex. 4 recalls Franco's dictum that the composer of a conductus, free from any constraints imposed by pre-existing material, should compose 'as beautiful a melody as he can'.[97] In the passage quoted the composer has clearly been concerned to invent a melody of 'four-beat' phrases that is not primarily defined by its compliance with the architectonic strictures of the theorists or of the tenor part.

As we shall see in Chapter 3 below, when Ars antiqua motets are considered as joint creations in words and music, it can be established that some pieces can only have been put together in a synthetic or holistic manner, the composer-poet progressing through his work in all parts (save the tenor) at once, maintaining a vigilance on many fronts—for points of fleeting imitation, perhaps, for textual echoes or, occasionally, for timed contrasts of meaning.

The trend of some recent thinking would make the admittedly architectonic approach to composition advocated by fourteenth-century theorists such as Aegidius de Murino less amenable to a 'Gothic' interpretation than might be first thought.[98] The composition of polyphonic pieces (especially motets) in successive layers, voice by voice—admittedly an additive and collocative process—may have been adequate for the beginners to whom treatises such as those by Aegidius de Murino are principally addressed. To some extent, that process is inevitable when a piece is constructed over a cantus firmus which the composer, to borrow Grocheio's distinction, must *ordinare* before he begins to *componere* and invent the new voices.[99]

[95] Text in Rohloff, *Die Quellenhandschriften*, 146–9, corresponding to *Concerning Music*, trans. Seay, 28.

[96] 'The Medieval Motet', 527.

[97] Franco of Cologne, *Ars cantus mensurabilis*, ed. Reaney and Gilles, 74: 'primum cantum invenire debet pulcriorem quam potest'.

[98] See, for example, Leech-Wilkinson, 'Machaut's *Rose, lis*'.

[99] Text in Rohloff, *Die Quellenhandschriften*, 146, corresponding to *Concerning Music*, trans. Seay, 28.

Here there is only room to emphasize Daniel Leech-Wilkinson's important observation that these methods do not explain the artistry of advanced composers such as Guillaume de Machaut.[100] He proposes that Machaut was capable of hearing four-part chord progressions in his mind's ear and that much of the celebrated *Messe de Nostre Dame* is musical art of a synthetic kind. His conclusions run parallel with the recent trend in modern performances of Gothic polyphony towards blend and a projection of the harmony, rather than a multi-coloured individuation of lines, that also represents a searching examination of traditional views.[101] It is here, more than anywhere else, that an additive, collocative conception of medieval polyphonic composition has a direct effect upon sound and therefore upon the aesthetic apprehension of the repertoire. The 'linear' conception of Gothic polyphony, expounded by Gilbert Reaney, among others,[102] advocates an additive conception of the music as a collaboration of individuated parts rather than a synthetic conception which emphasizes the succession of sonorities. The epitome of this view can be found in Reaney's declaration that Machaut heard two superimposed fifths as a consonance. Machaut's treatment of this sonority shows that he was prepared to treat it as a sharply dissonant one (Ex. 5).[103]

There is no need to deny the value of the many insights that Jordan, Sanders, and others have offered into the artistic procedures of the Romanesque and Gothic eras. The concept of art is not immutable but varies from one civilization to another. A special effort of historical imagination is clearly required in order to understand the various ideas of art that existed before galleries, collectors, connoisseurs, and the concept of art for art's sake.[104] However, cathedralism goes too

[100] Leech-Wilkinson, 'Machaut's *Rose, lis*', and id., *Machaut's Mass, passim.*

[101] Discussed in Page, 'The Performance of Songs', and id., 'The English *a cappella* Heresy'.

[102] Reaney, 'Voices and Instruments', 6: 'providing one adheres to the principle of contrast, almost any vocal-instrumental combination common to the fourteenth century may be utilised in performing the music of the period . . . Whereas in modern times blend is the acme of the orchestral textbook, in the Middle Ages every instrument stood out from its neighbour, as was fitting in a period when individual, contrapuntal parts were valued more than unity of texture.' For Reaney's later thoughts, see his article 'The Part Played by Instruments in the Music of Guillaume de Machaut'.

[103] Reaney, 'Fourteenth Century Harmony', 137; see also Leech-Wilkinson, 'Machaut's *Rose, lis*', 23 n. 2.

[104] Alsop, *The Rare Art Traditions*, 5–8, 56–8, *et passim.*

Ex. 5. Extract from the ballade *Seur toute creature humeinne* (text omitted) by Guillaume de Machaut. Adapted from the edition by E. Keitel accompanying *Early Music*, 5 (1977)

far. There is evidence for an appreciation of beauty in the Romanesque and Gothic centuries that is not touched by religious exaltation; the supposedly architectonic character of Gothic thought and aesthetics can be exaggerated, and there are signs that serious thinkers did not regard the question of why music pleases the ear as entirely settled.

2

The Rise of the Vernacular Motet

I

THERE is a consensus that the audience for medieval motets comprised 'an educated élite',[1] 'the intellectual élite',[2] 'the educated',[3] or 'men of letters',[4] and that motets were enjoyed in 'very exclusive social circles'.[5] It is apparent that these observations are basically the same, and the next chapter will be concerned with the evidence upon which they are based. For the moment, let us look in a slightly different direction. The author of one text in the Montpellier codex says that he has 'often found many a clerk, cowl set aside, who doesn't insist that there be a debate on logic',[6] and it is generally accepted that the Ars antiqua motet is connected with the recreation of masters and students in the University of Paris.[7] Finn Mathiassen has emphasized the recreative quality of motets to the point of claiming that the motet was 'more closely related to . . . chess or cricket than to the art of music when considered from a modern point of view'.[8] This carries a certain conviction, but it also raises a question: how does this view of the motet consort with the idea that its audience characteristically comprised 'the intellectual élite' moving in what Mathiassen himself calls 'very exclusive social circles'? There is little reason to believe that either chess or cricket (in its various medieval forms) were particularly exclusive or élitist pastimes in the thirteenth

[1] Huot, 'Polyphonic Poetry', 262.

[2] M. Gushee, 'The Polyphonic Music of the Medieval Monastery, Cathedral and University', in McKinnon (ed.), *Antiquity and the Middle Ages*, 166.

[3] Hoppin, *Medieval Music*, 341.   [4] Gallo, *Music of the Middle Ages*, 25.

[5] Mathiassen, *The Style of the Early Motet*, 34.

[6] Text and translation by Stakel and Relihan, in Tischler (ed.), *The Montpellier Codex*, no. 33 (Motetus).

[7] See e.g. Gallo, *Music of the Middle Ages*, 25–7, and Mathiassen, *The Style of the Early Motet*, 33–42.

[8] Mathiassen, *The Style of the Early Motet*, 37.

century. The argument of this chapter is that there was a broader
base for the materials and ethos of at least the vernacular motet than
has sometimes been acknowledged, and that the modern tendency to
associate these pieces exclusively with 'the intellectual élite' is mis-
guided. It will explore the inherently light tone of many vernacular
motets in the earlier layers of the repertory when considered in relation to thirteenth-century musical culture as a whole.

Our investigation begins with a question that deserves to be boldly
stated: why did motets with Old French secular texts ever emerge?
To put the same point in rather more guarded terms: why did it occur
to clerical musicians that discant clausulae (or sections thereof) could
be extracted from liturgical organa and stripped of their Latin texts,
if they had received one, to be given texts, often decidedly secular, in
the vernacular? The question seems worth asking because the emergence of such secular motets from the clausula matrix is often presented as if it were inevitable, requiring no explanation. Yudkin, for
example, declares that the Latin motet was developed when composers began to trope the upper voices of clausulae, and that 'soon . . .
the added texts began to be written in the vernacular, in French, and
to take on a decidedly secular slant'.[9] Why did this happen?

Ernest Sanders has provided one convincing answer to this question. He proposes that by giving vernacular texts to melismatic
clausulae composers were able to create a mensuralized art of written
polyphonic song at a time when there was no notation in existence
that could record a melodic line that was both measured and texted;
with a textless clausula model available for consultation, recorded in
modal notation, the rehearsal of a motet derived from that clausula
could proceed, Sanders argues, even though the motet was notated in
a manner that did not indicate rhythmic values.[10] This carries conviction, but there may be more to the question than a deficiency in the
nature of contemporary notation *cum littera*.

Plate 7 shows a section from a two-part setting of *Alleluya:*

---

[9] *Music in Medieval Europe*, 395. Throughout the course of this chapter I accept the prevailing view that the first motets were produced by troping the upper voices of pre-existing two-
part clausulae. This is a view that has been challenged both in specific and in general terms,
most recently by Frobenius ('Die Motette'). Even if it were true that the clausula did not generally precede the motet, it would not greatly modify the central hypothesis of this chapter,
namely that the coexistence of vernacular two-part motets and melismatic clausulae, many
apparently for liturgical use, would sometimes have lent a festive, parodic tone to the motets, at
least during the early decades of the form's existence.   [10] 'The Medieval Motet', 508–9.

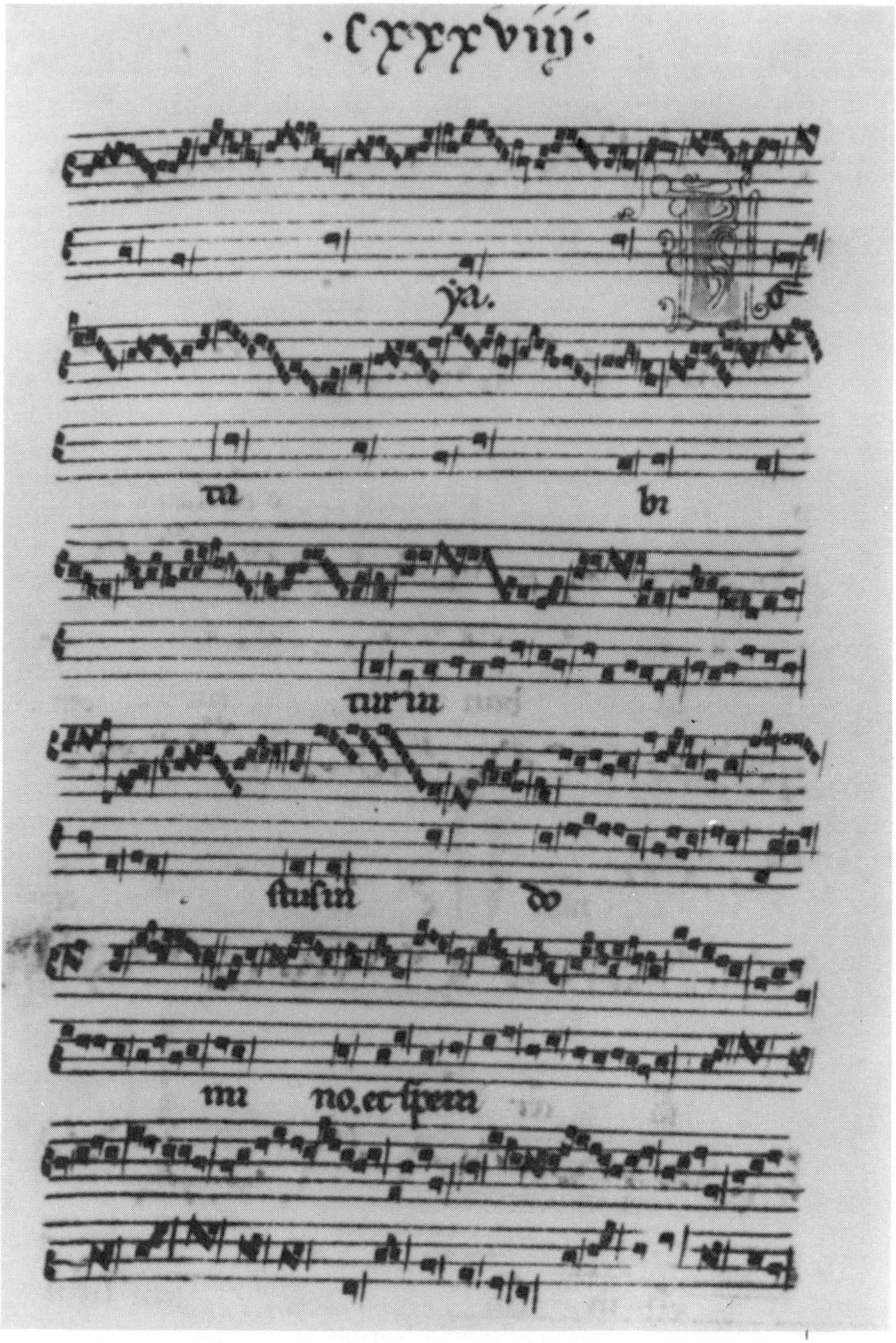

Pl. 7. A section of *Alleluya: Letabitur iustus in domino*. Florence, Biblioteca Medicea Laurenziana, plut. 29. 1, fo. 138^r. Reproduced by permission

Letabitur iustus in domino from the major Notre-Dame source, *F*. The first word of the verse, *Letabitur*, beginning at the end of the first system, is set in *organum purum*, the Duplum moving in a florid, quasi-improvisational manner over the sustained and unmeasured notes of the Tenor. For the next word of the verse, *iustus*, the composer breaks into discant, the Tenor immediately forming itself into a series of perfect longs beneath the measured Duplum. This discant section is the one with which we shall be directly concerned. Taken as a whole, this page has the icy seriousness that Bakhtin has associated with 'official' culture in the Middle Ages.[11] With its plainchant notation and staves ruled in red, it gives the appearance of an authoritative and highly specialized liturgical book—a scion of the 'Great Book', the Magnus Liber. It is dense in appearance and severe in its demands, for it requires the highest musical expertise for its interpretation. Uttering the word of ecstatic praise, *Alleluya*, and proceeding with the words of the Psalmist, it asserts all that is[12]

stable, unchanging, perennial . . . It [is] the triumph of a truth already established, the predominant truth that was put forward as eternal and indisputable. This is why the tone of the official feast was monolithically serious and why the element of laughter was alien to it.

When we perceive the page of *F* in this light (always bearing in mind that *F* is a very diversified manuscript), it seems all the more remarkable that anyone should have appropriated a section of discant over the syllable *iu-* of *iustus* to make a two-part vernacular motet. That theft took place, however, and the result is preserved in the tenth fascicle of *W2* (Ex. 6). This is the text:

> A grant joie
> Chevauchoie
> L'autrier
> Par .i. bois, [MS: boais]
> Si trovoie
> Simple et coie
> A mon chois
> Pastorele
> Gent et bele;
> La vois
> Sor mon roncin Norrois.

[11] *Rabelais and his World*, 73.   [12] Ibid. 9.

Ex. 6. The two-part motet *A grant joie/IU[stus]*. Adapted from Tischler, *The Earliest Motets*, no. 164

The other day I was riding in the highest spirits through a wood, and there I found a shepherdess, modest and shy, fair and beautiful, at my disposal; I saw her from my horse Norrois.

So many Ars antiqua motets have survived that it is easy to over-look what bewildering pieces they are. We might familiarize this one a little by employing an analytic approach, drawing attention to the combined repetitions of melodic and rhythmic patterns in both parts, 'one of the most significant innovations of the Notre Dame school',[13] and to do so would probably be to identify qualities which con-tributed to a contemporary musician's impression that this section of the source clausula was somehow separable from its context, contain-ing a latent song. However, it was not in the least inevitable that this clausula should be taken from its context and given secular French words; if there had been any inevitability about such a process of ver-nacular contrafaction then there would surely be more Old French contrafacta of polyphonic Latin conductus in existence.

---

[13] Hoppin, *Medieval Music*, 231.

Nor can the creation of a motet like *A grant joie/IU[stus]* be wholly explained in terms of a desire for a new kind of measured, polyphonic song repertoire in the vernacular, developing and expanding the resources of the contemporary monophonic tradition. It is important to remember Ernest Sanders's useful observation that 'for a good part of the [thirteenth] century the motet frequently was on the point of transforming itself into another genre, viz. the polyphonic cantilena',[14] but the motet *A grant joie/IU[stus]* is a very strange thing when viewed in terms of the monophonic tradition represented by the chansonniers. Indeed, its strangeness underlines the danger of regarding all Old French motet texts as 'more or less indistinguishable from the texts of trouvère songs'.[15] *A grant joie/IU[stus]* is a pastourelle that stops at exactly the point where pastourelles were designed to become interesting: the moment when the scene has been set and the encounter between the speaker and the girl (usually a shepherdess) is about to begin. As a poem, the Duplum does much to claim that it is a pastourelle but little to substantiate the claim. It is almost a parody of a pastourelle in the sense that it creates expectations of that literary form and then disappoints them, possibly for the sake (among other things) of the humour that arises from the distortion of expected conventions.[16]

At the same time, *A grant joie/IU[stus]* is very brief, like many other motets from all layers of the repertory. The shortness of such a motet sets it in the mind as something removed (almost stripped away) from a larger context, in this case its organal matrix. The brevity of *A grant joie/IU[stus]* would have been obvious to thirteenth-century listeners familiar with trouvère songs performed in full,[17] with conductus, and with expansive liturgical compositions

---

[14] Sanders, 'The Medieval Motet', 533. [15] Yudkin, *Music in Medieval Europe*, 402.

[16] Bayless, *Parody in the Middle Ages*, 8.

[17] Modern recordings of trouvère songs in full suggest average times for the five-stanza *grand chant courtois* of around 4–5 minutes, but this may not be long enough since few modern performers have explored the possible implications of Grocheio's statement that the *grand chant* should be sung in a manner that makes it seem to be composed entirely of perfect longs. See Rohloff, *Die Quellenhandschriften*, 130, 132 (where the rondeau is said to be performed *longo tractu* like the *grand chant*), and 162 (where the *Gloria* is said to be sung 'slowly and from perfect longs in the manner of a *grand chant*'). These passages correspond to Seay's translation, *Concerning Music*, 16, 17, and 39–40. It seems difficult to avoid the conclusion that Grocheio is referring to a style of performance comparable to that advocated for plainchant in the early layer of the *Discantus positio vulgaris*, where it is said that 'all notes of . . . plainchant are long and beyond measure, because they contain the quantity of three time units' (Sanders, 'Consonance

such as the setting of *Alleluya: Letabitur iustus in domino* containing the clausula matrix for this motet. As far as we may discern, *rondets* and *refrains* in a light courtly style were virtually the only monophonic forms with which contemporary listeners could compare the shorter motets (of which there are many) in terms of duration, and, as we shall see, many motet texts in the vernacular vociferously invite comparison with such light courtly pieces. The scope of trouvère songs and the larger conductus would have given thirteenth-century listeners a conception of what constituted a substantial musical utterance not so very different from that of their twentieth-century counterparts, and it may not be an anachronistic reaction to smile—as modern audiences may sometimes be seen to do—when a brief motet comes to an abrupt close.

We may be in danger of missing something simple: *A grant joie/IU[stus]*, like many other motets, is a form of *parody*. As I have suggested, its text deals most unexpectedly with some conventions of the pastourelle genre, and its music, derived from a liturgical composition but here given decidedly secular words, is a parody in the simple sense that it displays the quality of 'turnabout' which Bakhtin describes as an essential element in the spirit of medieval festivity:[18]

All the symbols of the carnival idiom are filled with this . . . gay relativity of prevailing truths and authorities. We find here a characteristic logic, the peculiar logic of the inside out . . . of the 'turnabout', of a continual shifting from top to bottom, from front to rear, of numerous parodies and travesties, humiliations, profanations, comic crownings and uncrownings.

There could scarcely be a keener illustration of such festive 'turnabout' than the work of one clausula composer who set the melody of the *Dominus* tenor in reverse and labelled it *Nusmido*.[19]

Bakhtin's concept of the 'carnivalesque', presented in *Rabelais and his World* (first published in English in 1968), has proved helpful to scholars in many fields of study.[20] Although highly repetitive, and presented almost entirely without factual documentation, *Rabelais and*

and Rhythm', 266). Compare Knapp, 'Musical Declamation', 406–7, and Dyer, 'A Thirteenth-Century Choirmaster', 92–3. A performance of Perotinus' monophonic conductus *Beata viscera* on a recent recording by the Hilliard Ensemble, in a style more brisk than anything suggested by Grocheio's words, runs to 6'12" (ECM 1385). A recording of the same piece by the Ensemble Gilles Binchois, in a similar style, reaches 5'44" (H/CD 8611).

[18] *Rabelais and his World*, 11.   [19] Sanders, 'The Medieval Motet', 506.
[20] A recent example, cited from the many available, is Ganim, *Chaucerian Theatricality*.

his World succeeds in characterizing a vast area of festive experience
which is all the more important because it has virtually disappeared
from Western industrial society. No doubt that disappearance puts us
in a vulnerable position, since it is easy to misjudge the character of
something whose continuity has been broken and which, in Bakhtin's
discussion, relies upon somewhat nebulous concepts such as 'the
church' and 'carnival laughter' to be conveyed. None the less,
Bakhtin's book conveys the tone of much medieval festivity.[21] The
concept of holiday in the fullest sense is vital to his argument: a feast-
day of the church's year which may also coincide with a fair, marked
not merely by the official celebrations of the liturgy but also by
'unofficial' disguisings, dances (involving mock crownings),[22] shows,
songs, and more besides: all that is carnivalesque. In Bakhtin's interpretation there is a continuity between the carnivalesque spirit and
the tone of later medieval parody:[23]

medieval parodies were not formal literary and negative satires of sacred
texts or of scholarly wisdom; they merely transposed these elements into the
key of gay laughter . . . Everything they touched was transformed into flesh
and matter and at the same time was given a lighter tone.

This is an important passage; to say that a motet such as *A grant
joie/IU[stus]* is a parody is not to say that it is irreligious or subver-
sive, only that it transposes the serious 'into a key of gay laughter' for
the time that the holiday allows. A carnival, with its caroles, masks,
and loaded market-tables, may seem remote from the milieu of the
motet as we instinctively imagine it, but that is partly because academic research has a tendency to 'officialize' its subject. We do well
to remember Johannes de Grocheio's observation that motets were
performed to 'adorn' the holiday celebrations of the *litterati* (a word
to which we shall return), and this remark involves him in a systematic allusion to his earlier discussion of the rondeau:[24]

[21] This makes Bakhtin's analysis particularly effective when he turns to phenomena (such as
the Dance of Death) which have not been considered in this light before. See *Rabelais and his
World*, 50–1.
[22] 'Mock crownings' of various kinds appear to have been of some importance in choreogra-
phies for caroles.
[23] *Rabelais and his World*, 83.
[24] Rohloff, *Die Quellenhandschriften*, 132 and 144, corresponding to *Concerning Music*, trans.
Seay, 17 and 26.

Rondeau

Et huiusmodi cantilena [rotundellus] versus occidentem, puta in Normannia, solet DECANTARI a puellis et iuvenibus IN FESTIS et magnis conviviis AD
EORUM DECORATIONEM.

This kind of *cantilena* is customarily sung towards the west—in Normandy,
for example—by girls and young men as an adornment to holiday celebrations and to great banquets.

Motet

Et [motetus] solet IN EORUM FESTIS DECANTARI AD EORUM DECORATIONEM,
quemadmodum cantilena, quae dicitur rotundellus, in festis vulgarium
laicorum.

It is the custom for the motet to be sung in their holiday celebrations to
adorn them, just as the *cantilena* which is called *rotundellus* [is customarily
sung] in the holiday celebrations of the laity.

It is revealing that Grocheio compares the social function of the
motet to that of a light and 'unlearned' form that was sung in the festivities of the laity. This takes us one step closer towards the carnivalesque, broadening the base of the motet's ethos and materials, for it
seems plausible that these lay celebrations would have included the
kinds of festivity described by Bakhtin as taking place on days of
liturgical feasts: 'a boundless world of humorous forms and manifestations . . .'.[25]

II

The manner in which Grocheio brings the motet into parallel with
the rondeau defines the tone of many vernacular motets a little further. *A grant joie*/*IU[stus]* is clearly a kind of pastourelle, an essentially light genre that inclines to Pierre Bec's *registre popularisant*.[26]
So are many other two-part pieces in the earliest layers of vernacular
motet composition. This provides another reason for distinguishing
some early motet poetry from the lyrics of the contemporary trouvères, for hardly any named trouvères of substance wrote pastourelles
much before *c*.1240–50.[27] The composers of the early motets, in other
words, show a fondness for texts of a light courtly nature that do not
seem to reflect the contemporary trouvères' taste (in so far as that

[25] *Rabelais and his World*, 4.   [26] Bec, *La lyrique française au moyen âge, passim*.
[27] For details see Page, *The Owl and the Nightingale*, 241 n. 50.

taste can now be reconstructed from the chansonniers). Once again, a certain festive lightness in the tone of the motet is apparent.

Grocheio's readiness to associate the motet with the rondeau accords with the evidence of the musical sources. No doubt Gennrich's famous work on the Old French rondeaux, virelais, and ballades needs to be revised in the light of what has been learned since he published his research.[28] Be that as it may, he has successfully demonstrated that a certain consanguinity joins the corpus of motet texts to a large body of Old French monophonic song, scraps of which are echoed, quoted, fragmented, and otherwise borrowed throughout the motet corpus. Even the song which Grocheio gives as an example of the rondeau, *Toute sole passerai le vert boscage*, can be reconstructed with tolerable certainty from dismembered quotations (with a slightly different text) in a motet.[29] Many of the monophonic songs which are quoted in motets may have been songs for caroles, the public dances that were a conspicuous feature of festive life in northern France during the thirteenth century and which may have mediated between the marketplace realities of festivity and the more sheltered milieu of the motet. The two-part motet *Tout leis enmi les prez/DO[minus]*, uniquely preserved in the tenth fascicle of *W2*, is of special interest in this regard, for it begins with what is almost certainly a quotation, both in words and music, from a carole (Ex. 7).[30] Gennrich drew upon this motet to reconstruct the music of *C'est la gieus en mi les préz*, (Ex. 8), representing a kind of song that was much used for dancing in the thirteenth century in both courtly and urban contexts.[31] After the initial quotation, the motet proceeds with a loose collection of rhyming phrases, which may indicate that the whole piece is a tissue of quotations from caroles and lyrics of other kinds.

Caroles possessed a considerable appeal for the Parisian clergy and can therefore be associated with that social group whom modern scholars tend to appoint as the primary audience for motets. The *Chartularium Universitatis Parisiensis* incorporates numerous docu-

---

[28] *Rondeaux, Virelais und Balladen.*

[29] Ibid. i. 79–80. As Earp has emphasized ('Lyrics for Reading and Lyrics for Singing', 117 n. 3), 'Gennrich is too free in his musical reconstructions and too dogmatic on the issue of rhythm.' His reconstruction of this rondeau, however, seems to rest upon a tolerably secure foundation.

[30] See further on this subject Page, *The Owl and the Nightingale*, 110–54.

[31] On the carole see Stevens, *Words and Music*, 159–71; Page, *The Owl and the Nightingale*, 110–33; and id., *Voices and Instruments*, 77–84.

Ex. 7. Extract from the two-part motet *Tout leis enmi/DOMINUS*.
Adapted from Tischler, *The Earliest Motets*, no. 199

Ex. 8. The rondet *C'est la gieus en mi les préz*, as reconstructed and
transcribed in Gennrich, *Rondeaux, Virelais und Balladen*, i. 10

ments designed to prevent priests, students, and even masters from
taking part in caroles or allowing them to be performed outside their
doors.[32] As we might expect, the link between carolling and liturgical
feasts is evident in these prohibitions; they reveal that caroles were
danced *in die dominico* (1170–2), *diebus festivis* (1252), *in festis beati
Nicolai et beate Katerine* (1275), and that they were part of *festivitates*
(1276). Motets are rarely mentioned outside the writings of theorists,

---

[32] Denifle and Chatelain (eds.), *Chartularium Universitatis Parisiensis*, 5–6, 230, 532, 540, and
586.

but one exception to this rule suggests a certain parity of tone between secular songs, the carole, and the motet. The Dominican friar Pierre de Palude condemns those who sing 'with vainglorious and wanton pleasure' like those who sing motets, chansons, and caroles (see below, p. 69). The frequency with which Robin and Marion appear in the motet repertoire is another link with the carole, for a sermon preached in Paris by Daniel of Paris in 1274 refers to the citizens going 'to the carole so that they can sing of Marion . . . and of Robin'.[33] A passage in Gautier de Coinci's *Miracles de Nostre Dame*, begun *c.*1218 and probably completed (as far as the narrative part of the work is concerned) in 1231, leaves no doubt about the clergy's fondness for *chans de karoles* during the decades that saw the beginnings of the vernacular motets. Gautier's call to his fellow clerics is[34]

> De Tybregon et d'Emmelot
> Laissons ester les chançonnetes.

in which we instantly recognize two conventional rustic companions of Robin and Marion.

For evidence that the clerics at the University of Paris sometimes attended caroles, and with some zest, we need look no further than the early motet repertoire itself (Ex. 9):

> *Duplum* Roissoles ai, roissoles,
> De dures et de moles!
> Faites sont a biaus moles
> Por ces biaus clers d'escole
> Qui dient les paroles
> A ces puceles foles
> Qi chantant as queroles:
> 'Roissoles ai, roissoles.'

I have pasties, pasties, both hardened and soft! They have been turned out of pretty moulds for the handsome clerks from the schools who speak to the wild girls who sing in the caroles: 'I have pasties, pasties.'

> *Triplum* En ce chant
> Qe je chant
> Faz acorder
> Sanz descorder

---

[33] Paris, Bibliothèque nationale, MS lat. 16481, fo. 52ᵛ: 'tu non cantasti sicut angeli; non eis ibant ad coream propter cantandum de Marion ne de Robecon.'

[34] See Page, *The Owl and the Nightingale*, 118.

Ex. 9. The three-part motet *En ce chant/Roissoles ai/DO[minus]*. Adapted
from Tischler, *The Earliest Motets*, no. 130

55

Ce novel deschant
Ainsi m'envois;
Alons a la dance!
Alons i, car j'i vois.

In this song that I sing I make this new *deschant* and thus I enjoy myself; let us go to the dance! Let us go there, for I am going.

Tenor DO[MINO]

The text of the Duplum, with its constantly iterated melody, incorporates what is surely a street-cry, recalling Bakhtin's eloquent passage on Parisian street-cries which 'represented in themselves a noisy kitchen and a loud, abundantly served banquet; every food and dish had its own rhyme and melody'.[35] It is unlikely to be a coincidence that this motet is followed immediately in *W2* by another which evokes the festive life where drink abounds.[36] Both of the texts quoted above refer to the caroles that were a familiar spectacle in Parisian life and the ideal place to make an approach to young women (referred to in the motet in clear terms: *qui dient les paroles/a ces puceles foles*). Such approaches at the carole are vividly shown in contemporary pictorial sources from Paris.[37] Here, therefore, we have a complex situation in which two short poems evoke the abundance of the city's food (always conspicuous on a holiday when caroles were danced and the market-place was crowded), refer to a salient public festivity associated with music, the carole, and appear together in a motet where the composer refers not only to his own polyphonic ability (*faz acorder . . . ce novel deschant*) but also to his desire to go and see the caroles: *alons a la dance*! In addition we hear a street-cry of the city: *roissoles ai*! Like the better-known *A Paris/On parole/Frese nouvele*,[38] this piece seems to be the work of a composer who has discerned the appropriateness of a crowded, noisy motet texture to give a sound picture of a festive, well-stocked city on a feast-day. This motet embodies all the themes of our discussion to this point.

---

[35] Bakhtin, *Rabelais and his World*, 183.

[36] Fos. 197ᵛ–198ᵛ, *Hare, hare/Balaam goudalier/Balaam*, in Tischler (ed.), *The Earliest Motets*, no. 131.

[37] See the illustration from a Parisian manuscript reproduced in Page, 'The Performance of Ars Antiqua Motets', 147.

[38] Tischler (ed.), *The Montpellier Codex*, motet 319.

III

A document of outstanding interest in this context is the discussion of the 'masters of organum' in Robert of Courson's *Summa*, compiled between 1208 and 1212/13.[39] Courson was a papal legate and a Master of Theology in the University of Paris; his *Summa* is concerned, among other things, to define the contexts in which legitimate earnings could be derived from the mass of new trades and callings produced by the urban expansion of the twelfth and thirteenth centuries. Having discussed jobbing scribes who lend their services to usurers at fairs (*in nundinis*), Courson considers the doings of the 'masters of organum' (*opere magistrorum organicorum*) and his criticism of these individuals is that they perform 'minstrelish and effeminate' things before 'young and ignorant persons' (*iuvenibus et rudibus*):[40]

Si queras de operis minorum, puta de scriptoribus in nundinis qui locant operas suas et scripturas feneratoribus cambiatoribus, dico ut supra quod tenentur ad restitutionem omnium eorum que a feneratoribus receperunt. Similiter dicimus quod illicite sunt opere magistrorum organicorum qui scurrilia et effeminata proponunt iuvenibus et rudibus ad effeminandos animos ipsorum, tamen locare possent operas suas in licitis cantibus in quibus servitur ecclesiis. Si autem prelatus lascivus lasciviis talibus cantatoribus det beneficia ut huiusmodi scurrilia et lascivia audiat in ecclesia sua, credo quod lepram symonie incurrit. Si tamen in aliqua sollemnitate pro consuetudine terre decantent aliqui in organis, dummodo scurriles notule non admisceantur, tolerari possunt.

If you ask about the labours of small traders, such as the scribes at fairs who hire themselves and their writings to money-changing usurers, I say, as I said above, that they should be charged to return all of the things they have got from usurers. In the same way we say that the services of masters of organum who set minstrelish and effeminate things before young and ignorant persons, in order to weaken their minds, are not licit; however, they can sell their services with respect to licit chants insofar as they are of use in churches. If, however, a wanton prelate gives benefices to such wanton singers in order that this kind of minstrelish and wanton music may be heard in his church, I believe that he becomes contaminated with the disease of simony. If, however, some sing any organa on a feast-day according to the

---

[39] For a facsimile of the relevant passage of the text from the Bruges manuscript of Courson's treatise, and a discussion of some of the broader issues raised by the *Summa*, see Page, *The Owl and the Nightingale*, 145–54 and Frontispiece.

[40] Text and translation from Page, *The Owl and the Nightingale*, 145–6.

liturgical customs of the region, they may be tolerated if they avoid minstrel-ish little notes.

These remarks date from a time when the vernacular motet was a new development; they do not specifically refer to Parisian conditions, but there was no city which Courson, as a Parisian Master of Theology, knew better, and none in which he had greater legislative authority. His comments may therefore offer a contemporary perspective on the motet reaching back to its earliest layers.

There is clearly much scope for discussion about the meaning of Courson's terms (especially *notule*, to which we shall return), but it can be confidently stated that these masters of organum were singers of polyphony; the words *cantatores* and *magistrorum organicorum* do not welcome any other interpretation. What kind of repertoire could they have been performing for an audience construed by Courson as one of 'young and ignorant persons' in the period 1208–12/13, and which possessed sufficient continuity with liturgical organum for Courson to attribute something (admittedly ill-defined) to both repertories, that is to say *scurrilia/scurriles notule*?

One answer may be that the masters of organum were performing French two-part motets, newly formed from the clausulae they performed when receiving 'official' employment, of the kind to be found so abundantly in the early layers of the vernacular motet. Courson's reference to the way the masters sing 'to the young' recalls Johannes de Grocheio's comparison between the social function (and the pre-vailing tone?) of the motet and the rondeau, the latter sung by the young (*iuvenibus*) in their holiday celebrations.[41] In Grocheio's scheme of things, to associate any musical form with the young is to indicate its essentially light and festive character.[42] Courson's reference to *iuvenibus* may have a similar contextualizing force.

Courson's use of a term with a diminutive (*notula*) in association with the masters of organum may be significant in this context. It answers to the Old French word *notelete* which glosses it in the Mont-pellier glossary.[43] When Johannes de Grocheio uses song-names

---

[41] Rohloff, *Die Quellenhandschriften*, 132, corresponding to *Concerning Music*, trans. Seay, 17.

[42] This point is argued in Page, *Voices and Instruments*, 196–201.

[43] Cited in Godefroy, *Dictionnaire*, s.v. *notelete*. It is striking, in view of Courson's use of the term *notula*, that there seems to have been a 13th-c. Latin term *motula*, apparently used of the motet; the form appears in the celebrated visitation records of Odon Rigaud for Jan. 1261, in a context that recalls Courson's language in other respects: 'Item in festo Sancti Iohannis,

formed with a diminutive it is usually to indicate a lower-style registration, as in *rotundellus* (the rondeau),[44] and the distinction between what Pierre Bec has called the *registre aristocratisant* and the *registre popularisant* in Old French lyric seems to be embodied in Grocheio's two categories of *cantus* and *cantilena*, the latter denoting the lighter forms and distinguished by the diminutive morpheme *-il(l)-*.[45] Courson's *notula* may indicate a brisk, festive tone for what the masters of organum were performing in a secular context.

Surely the most significant term in this complex of words, however, is *motetus*. It has often been observed that *motetus* is a Latinization of Old French *mot*, 'word', and refers to the addition of vernacular poetry to textless clausulae or to clausulae that had already been troped for liturgical use with Latin texts.[46] However, this is not strictly true, for *motetus* is not a Latinization of *mot* but rather of *motet*, which can be analysed as Old French *mot* + diminutive suffix. (The Latin equivalent *motellus* will have arisen naturally when clerics replaced the vernacular diminutive suffix with one native to Latin, namely *-ellus*.) Viewed in these terms the word *motetus* gains in significance. It is of vernacular origin, suggesting (as Sanders and others have emphasized) that the first layer of clausulae troped in Latin were not thought to constitute a distinct new form; the motet was clearly named after its vernacular manifestations. Equally important, but perhaps less well recognized, is that the term *motet* preserves a contemporary perception of the tone of the new form dating from the time when it was first recognized as distinct from the conductus and named. It appears to have been a perception that assimilated the new species to the lighter forms of the monophonic vernacular tradition such as the *rondet* (where we find the same diminutive and the same variation of suffixes; compare *motetus/motellus*; *rondet/rondellus*). In Old French, the term *motet* is widely used to denote the short snatches of poetry and music, some of them possibly fragments of songs and caroles, which are often cited in contemporary poems both lyrical and narrative, and which comprise the phenomenon of the

Stephani et Innocentium, nimia iocositate et scurrilibus cantibus utebantur, utpote farsis, conductis, motulis' (Aubry, *La Musique et les musiciens*, 25).

[44] Rohloff, *Die Quellenhandschriften*, 132, corresponding to *Concerning Music*, trans. Seay, 17.

[45] Page, *Voices and Instruments*, 196–201.

[46] On the term 'motet' see Birkner, 'Motetus und Motette', and Hofmann, 'Zur Entstehungs- und Frühgeschichte des Terminus Motette'.

refrain.[47] For English-speaking scholars, at least, a better term for these *refrains* would be 'mottos', for this word not only implies the brevity, quotability, and intermittently sententious quality of the *refrains*, it is also etymologically cognate with *motet*, a contemporary term for them. Hofmann has shown that a *motet* in Old French could be a snatch of song about a *mal mariée*:

> Et por ceu aloit dixant
> Cest motet par anradie:
> *Ne ma bates mie,*
> *Maleuroz maris,*
> *Vos ne m'aveis pas norrie!*

It could also refer to something as light and ephemeral as an 'instrumental' refrain in the manner of the pastourelle:[49]

> Celle qui par anvoixeure
> Aloit chantant cest motet:
> *Robin tureleure*
> *Robinet!*

In the light of this evidence we begin to appreciate more of the context which prompts Grocheio to compare the function of the motet to a light and popular form, the *rotundellus* or rondeau. At the same time, the tone and nuances of Courson's term *notula*, comprising *nota* plus a diminutive, now become a little clearer. The conclusion seems unavoidable that the motet derived its name from the tendency of its vernacular poetry to borrow, echo, or otherwise employ the light courtly forms of rondet and refrain-motto.

IV

Let us look more closely at the social position and context of the masters of organum mentioned by Robert Courson. I have briefly discussed this matter elsewhere,[50] but it is possible to take the inves-

---

[47] The standard bibliography (which does not treat the musical aspect of the *refrain*) is van den Boogaard, *Rondeaux et refrains*; the only guide to the musical material is still Gennrich, *Rondeaux, Virelais und Balladen*. See also Butterfield, 'Interpolated Lyric'; Doss-Quinby, *Les Refrains*; Earp, 'Lyrics for Reading and Lyrics for Singing'; Everist, 'The Rondeau Motet'; Page, *The Owl and the Nightingale*, 110–33; id., *Voices and Instruments*, 77–84; and Stevens, *Words and Music*, 171–8 and 465–76.

[48] 'Zur Entstehungs- und Frühgeschichte des Terminus Motette', 143.   [49] Ibid.

[50] *The Owl and the Nightingale*, 144–54.

tigation a little further here by giving fuller consideration to the circumstances of Courson's reference to these *magistri organici.*

The passage from his *Summa* quoted above begins with a reference to the commercial activities of 'minor traders' (*de operibus minorum*), and continues with a directive against scribes who hire their services at fairs by producing documents for bankers who charge interest and who are therefore usurers. In common with most of his contemporaries among the theologians, Courson disapproves of usury and in this instance he cannot endure to see it forwarded by the use of literacy. In his reference to these scribes we recognize the notaries who worked for the money-changers and bankers (usually the same persons) at the seasonal fairs, including the famous Parisian fair of Lendit. The services of money-changing bankers were much in demand at these fairs for a great variety of coinage was used in them; France produced many regional currencies and so did the countries whose merchants travelled to the markets. For the bankers, the volume of business was sufficient to warrant the employment of scribes keeping records of the day's transactions, issuing notes of credit, and maintaining a longer term business archive.

After these scribes, Courson considers the masters of organum in the passage quoted and translated above. Next, he turns his attention in a suprising direction:[51]

De cyrurgicis dicimus quod non habent locare operas suas in incidendis calculosis aut herniosis nisi ubi vehementer credunt se debere curare illos, nam si alias tracti cupiditate incidunt eos et occidunt, homicide fiunt.

Concerning surgeons, we say that they are not to hire their services in cutting for stones and for hernias unless they vehemently believe that they must cure them, for they commit homicide if they make incisions for some other reason, motivated by a desire for money, and the patient dies.

We are accustomed to think of surgery as a specialized (and institutionalized) skill, one that deals with human beings when they are intensely vulnerable in every sense of the word. It therefore comes as a shock to find that Courson places surgeons here among the practitioners of minor and almost casual occupations. However, when the matter is regarded in historical terms, it becomes obvious that it is we who are taking an anomalous view of surgery and not Courson. The

---

[51] I cite the text from Bruges, Stedelijke Openbare Bibliotheek, MS 247, fo. 46ʳ, reproduced in facsimile in Page, *The Owl and the Nightingale*, Frontispiece.

lines quoted above are witness to a tradition of medical practice that once existed throughout Europe and Asia in a highly dangerous form: the performance of lithotomy (the removal of stones from the kidney or from the bladder) by surgeons who were often itinerant and quite distinct from the contemporary class of trained physicians. According to two recent historians of surgery, no chapter in the history of the craft 'is so replete with intrigue, perfidy and dishonest dealings' as the history of lithotomy.[52] For reasons that are not entirely clear, stones in the kidney and bladder were very common in the Middle Ages, and until the eighteenth century there were travelling empirics all over Europe who specialized in operations to remove them. In the medieval period these operations were almost exclusively left to itinerant surgeons because the trained physicians did not concern themselves with the 'manual' art of surgery. Furthermore, they were forbidden to practise it if they were in clerical orders on the grounds that 'the Church has a horror of shedding blood'. No doubt many physicians were glad to leave lithotomy to the empirics, for it could be a bloody and traumatic business (as it remained until the twentieth century) with a high risk of infection leading to death. It is this danger of mortality which concerns Robert of Courson in the passage quoted above, and it is clear from another section of his *Summa* that he regarded the issue of a surgeon's responsibility for deaths precipitated by surgery as a matter of importance to confessors who might encounter surgeons who had effectively slain their patients.[53]

Although very different in the nature of their trades, the lithotomists and jobbing scribes who 'frame' the masters of organum in Courson's *Summa* provide a kind of social context for the masters. I have emphasized elsewhere that Courson deals with the masters because they earn money from their activities in a freelance manner that sometimes leads to malpractice.[54] In voicing this concern, Courson reveals his opinion of the masters of organum. It is perhaps a surprising one. Modern scholars hold the works of Leoninus, Perotinus, and the 'Notre-Dame school' in high esteem, but in the early decades of the thirteenth century Courson, an ecclesiastic of high rank who knew Paris and its university well, places the doings of *organiste* very

[52] Wangenstein and Wangenstein, *The Rise of Surgery*, 67.

[53] For an edition of the relevant passage of the *Summa* see Kennedy, 'Robert Courson on Penance', 322.

[54] *The Owl and the Nightingale*, 144–54.

low in the scale of human activities, both in terms of their moral consequence and their importance.

The scribes who precede the masters of organum in Courson's *Summa* worked *in nundinis*, where *nundinum* is the usual Latin equivalent of Old French *foire*, or 'fair'.[55] As for the surgeons, Courson does not say where (or how) they practised. Some of them, we may imagine, were at least partially resident in towns and cities, and their Parisian descendants may perhaps be found among the barber-surgeons of that city, first mentioned in a document of 1301 as *cirurgien barbier*.[56] It seems likely, however, that some of the itinerant lithotomists of Courson's time worked at the seasonal fairs, advertising their services there and arranging operations for some future time. Some of them may even have operated on the spot (the modern reader's revulsion at such a hypothesis has no bearing on its plausibility). There have been itinerant lithotomists in India, moving from market to market, since ancient times; according to Haeger, they may still be encountered.[57] (It is almost impossible to document such activities in medieval Europe because itinerant empirics have left virtually no written records and generally had no institutional affiliation of any kind.)

We therefore find the masters of organum in Courson's *Summa* placed between scribes who definitely worked at fairs and surgeons who may well have done so on occasions. A question naturally arises. Is this section of Courson's treatise devoted to the activities of some small traders associated—however loosely or sporadically—with the fairs? Clearly, we must tread carefully; the evidence is tenuous and cannot be drawn out much further. However, if the prospect of freelance performers of polyphony, both sacred and secular, taking a booth at one or more of the great seasonal fairs seems almost alarmingly implausible today, that may be no bad thing if it reminds us how far our historical imagination may have to travel if we are to understand the full social conditions in which organum and the early motets could be performed and transmitted. It is possible to dwell in a learned paradise of documents, variant readings in chant manuscripts, and the other materials deriving from clerical 'high' culture, forgetting all the while that medieval mechanisms for transmitting

---

[55] See the documents cited in Bourquelot, *Études sur les foires de Champagne*, i. 16.
[56] For the text see Depping, *Réglemens sur les arts*, 419.
[57] *The Illustrated History of Surgery*, 32.

ideas and other intangible resources sometimes worked in ways that the modern bookish mind may never envisage. Being forgetful in this way can lead us to favour a model of 'high' clerical culture that is supposedly Latinate, bookish, and formal, contrasted with a 'low' culture that is supposedly vernacular, non-literate, and carnivalesque. (The distinction between 'official' and 'unofficial' is a different matter.) This opposition is not seriously weakened by passing references in scholarly literature to the excesses of the Feast of Fools, for example, to the evidence for clerical dancing on feast-days, nor even to the richly suggestive notion of an ecclesiastical 'feast' underlying the Christian liturgy. Much of the twelfth- and thirteenth-century evidence that can be brought against it (the information pertaining to caroles of all kinds, for example) has long been a minority interest in comparison with the high-culture productions of the clerical establishment and may always remain so. One aim of this chapter has been to blur this distinction between 'high' and 'low', for the early motet was sometimes both.

3

Johannes de Grocheio, the Litterati, *and Verbal* Subtilitas *in the Ars Antiqua Motet*

I

In the previous chapter I suggested that the base for the materials of the Ars antiqua motet was a broad one, and I now wish to propose that it may have been matched by a breadth in the constituency of the audience for these pieces. The audience for medieval secular music has received little attention,[1] perhaps because it is an issue where musicology dissolves into social and cultural history. As far as the Ars antiqua motet is concerned, the consensus is that these pieces were performed for 'an intellectual élite',[2] but what manner of person— what manner of *mind*—does that phrase evoke in a thirteenth- or fourteenth-century context? Since the Enlightenment, 'intellectual' activity has been associated with the exercise of rational and analytic intelligence in the pursuit of predominantly secular interests, but the writings of those whom Le Goff has called 'les intellectuels du moyen âge'[3] do not always reveal such priorities and rarely pursue such interests. The works of the schoolmen, for example, may be highly analytical (in the sense that they break their material down with divisions and subdivisions), but the *questiones* which they contain are replete with deductions that rely upon faith, not upon reason, to carry conviction. In the 1270s the English theologian Richard of Middleton composes a lecture at Paris to counter a belief that certain grasses and chants can put demons to flight, but he does not question the omnipresence of a personalized supernatural evil, nor does he reject the idea that certain natural materials might have the power to avert

---

[1] Compare Pesce, 'The Significance of Text in Thirteenth-Century Latin Motets', 105–7, who raises the question of the audience for Ars antiqua motets.

[2] See above, 43.

[3] Le Goff, *Les Intellectuels au moyen âge*; on the legitimacy of speaking of 'intellectuals' in a medieval context, see Brocchieri, 'The Intellectual', 181.

the evil eye; his argument, meticulously presented, is that devils do their work with the ultimate permission of God and that no charm can influence His will as made manifest in a demon.[4] Richard brings the analytic and the irrational together in a way that makes the study of medieval thinking so fascinating. It is common knowledge that medieval treatises on practical *artes* such as medicine contain many assertions that could have been falsified by experiment (indeed by experience) but apparently never were, for all their logical organization and their evocation of lofty traditions of teaching.[5]

If the modern reader sometimes feels disorientated when reading such writings it is partly because a great deal of medieval learning maintains an equilibrium between contemplative and inquisitive thought—between the longing of the spirit and the restlessness of the mind. The balance was disturbed by the thinkers of the Enlightenment (to name no others) and has never been fully restored. A thirteenth-century author such as Humbert of Romans can employ at least four terms to distinguish various aspects of clerical 'learning', namely *sensus, intellectus, sapientia*, and *scientia*,[6] and in doing so he exploits a richness of vocabulary inspired by the complex experience of mind and spirit advancing together through study and reflection. It is far from certain that the *scientia, sapientia, sensus*, and *intellectus* of a studious medieval cleric guaranteed the kinds of attainment that a modern musicologist will instinctively wish to associate with the 'intellectual élite' that has been associated with motets: a well-informed interest in music and poetry, let us say, a measure of critical acumen, and perhaps a highbrow (but not an exclusively sober) taste.

To return to our initial question: may the audience for medieval motets be described as an 'élite'? We might first enquire whether the term 'audience' is an appropriate one in this context,[7] for any uncertainty about who medieval people were (in the fullest sense of those words) must also be an uncertainty about the social configurations

---

[4] See Page, *The Owl and the Nightingale*, 159–60.

[5] See e.g. the texts assembled in Lawn, *The Prose Salernitan Questions*, and Siraisi, *Medieval and Early Renaissance Medicine*, 78–114. Siraisi gives a stimulating account of the relationship between theory, authority, and experiment in an area of learning which has many parallels with music, and which is particularly arresting because the intensely practical purpose of medical study was never questioned during the Middle Ages and the consequences of working with poor information or merely bookish theories could be literally fatal.

[6] *Sermones Beati Umberti Burgundi*, i. 56.

[7] For a discussion of some evidence of *c*.1400 relating to this issue, see Page, 'A Treatise on Musicians'.

which they formed. This is not only a medievalist's problem, of course, for a glance at the history of music shows that the word 'audience' is almost useless unless we explain its meaning (as best we can) in terms of people, places, and patterns of attention. The concept of an élite audience, however, is particularly problematic in a medieval context since we have a natural suspicion of any attempt to interpret medieval perceptions of art in terms of such connoisseurship and taste as we associate with the Renaissance and beyond. To ask whether any medieval élite was constituted by the artistic culture of its members is to trip over the question of how 'artistic culture' is to be defined in relation to the Middle Ages.[8] We maintain a sure footing, however, if we recognize that the élites which medieval writers themselves acknowledge are constituted by juridical and legalistic distinctions rather than by anything corresponding to what might now be termed 'cultural' considerations. The *milites* formed an élite by virtue of their juridical status, the *divites* by their power and resources, the *nobiles* by their blood, and the *clerici* (an élite to which we shall return) by their order. An obvious manifestation of something like a cultural élitism is to be found in the distinction between the *courtois* and the *vilain*, a contrast that is common enough in Old French literature,[9] but *courtois* and *courtoisie* principally denote a kind of temporary, festive demeanour that was considered appropriate to the *cortz plenieres* when a magnate was surrounded by his dependants and guests; the term *courtoisie* is undoubtedly élitist, but as it is used in Old French it rarely implies a taste for letters (though it does suggest an appetite for stories),[10] and it implies little admiration for the visual arts beyond a relish for the opulent or exotic.[11] In short, courtesy presents an externalized notion of an individual's culture, equating it with a beautified demeanour, groomed for appearances and for the momentary world of the festive court, convened in full. This is not at all the world of Castiglione's élite courtiers.

This point is worth pursuing because the notion of a cultural élite is perhaps the most influential model that historians have ever devised for the generation and reception of the arts in the West, be

[8] See Alsop, *The Rare Art Traditions, passim.*

[9] Godefroy, *Dictionnaire*, s.v. *courtois* and *vilain*.

[10] On the question of courtesy, letters, and literacy, see Scaglione, *Knights at Court*, 75–8 and 232–2, and Page, 'Music and Chivalric Fiction', 20–1.

[11] Such taste is catered for in many Old and Middle French romances; *Floire et Blancheflour* is a notable example.

they musical, visual, or literary. Musicologists have been much influenced by it, for virtually all the written repertories of medieval music are customarily associated with an élite of one kind or another: troubadour and trouvère songs with the 'courts' of France;[12] the Ars antiqua motet with 'the intellectual élite'; the chansons of Guillaume de Machaut with an élite of royal and princely courts,[13] and so on. It would perhaps be idle to challenge all these interpretations (some of which, I imagine, cannot be challenged), but the general question remains whether it is advisable for modern scholars to speak of medieval audiences for written music with the pleasant mixture of admiration and complacency that comes from evoking them as an 'intellectual élite'. That evocation is certainly consistent with the manner and tone of much twentieth-century scholarship. To give anything scholarly attention is usually to become in some measure its advocate, which explains why modern analyses of medieval works of art rarely conclude that the object of study is *less* sophisticated than might at first be imagined, even though such results would logically be expected now and then if analytic techniques were discovering truths about the works in question. By the same token, it is foreign to the essentially compassionate nature of modern historical scholarship to speak in a minimizing fashion of any medieval activity touching upon matters of taste, not only because such judgements came all too easily to some founding fathers of musical history such as Burney, Ambros, or Adler,[14] but also because centuries of scorn for the Middle Ages have made the medievalist eager to plead the sophistication of what he finds. The judgements about the audience for the medieval motet quoted at the start of. Chapter 2 have the character one would expect, being positive, optimistic, and in one case ('very exclusive social circles') almost hyperbolical.

II

If we are uneasy with such a consistently intellectual and élite audience for the Ars antiqua motet it is partly because of specific charac-

---

[12] See Page, 'Court and City'.

[13] Reaney, *Guillaume de Machaut*, 48–9 (referring to Machaut's mature rondeaux such as *Rose, liz*): 'The rhythmic complexities of this highly melismatic style suggest that such compositions like the motet, were intended primarily for audiences of intellectuals and the elite of the various princely courts.'

[14] See the useful introduction in Mathiassen, *The Style of the Early Motet*, 9–28.

teristics in the repertoire and especially in motet verse. Even at its most austere (and it is rarely very austere), the vernacular poetry of thirteenth-century motets attempts no more than the monophonic chansons enjoyed in the municipal *puis* of the thirteenth century (which are not happily described as forming an 'élite' context). We may be tempted to ask how much learning is required to appreciate the melodiousness of Ex. 4 (see p. 39) in a purely sensual fashion, or to relish poetry such as this:[15]

> Tant fis
> Et tant dis
> Qu'au desus me mis,
> Ma volenté fis
> Tout a mon devis . . .

I spoke and behaved so well that I got on top and did my will exactly as I had planned . . .

A learned taste is not always a sober one, of course, and if some of the patterns uncovered by modern analyses of motets, both words and music, do indeed correspond to any of the *subtilitas* which medieval listeners associated with the form then there was clearly scope for discernment.[16] None the less, it would surely be a mistake to underestimate the immediate appeal possessed by many motets, especially in the first decades of the form's existence when the vernacular motet was an exclusively two-part and monotextual form: almost a polyphonic cantilena.[17] The handful of references to motets which can be found outside the writings of the music theorists confirm that the amorous character of many motet texts dominated the impression that those who disapproved of the genre had been able to form. The Dominican friar Pierre de Palude, for example, condemns those who sing 'with vainglorious and wanton pleasure', like those who sing motets, chansons, and caroles (*vane leticie lascivie . . . in motetis, cantilenis et choreis*),[18] and the existence of Latin, devotional contrafacta of some French motets may sometimes be construed as a contemporary judgement upon the character of the vernacular texts thus replaced.[19]

---

[15] Excerpted and adapted from Tischler, *The Montpellier Codex*, Motet 95 (Motetus).

[16] See e.g. Pesce, 'A Revised View' and 'The Significance of Text in Thirteenth-Century Latin Motets'.

[17] As emphasized by Sanders, 'The Medieval Motet', 533.

[18] Cited in Page, 'The Performance of Ars Antiqua Motets', 147.

[19] Sanders, 'The Medieval Motet', 531, and Pesce, 'A Revised View', 437.

It is time to give fresh attention to the two sources that underly the opinions that we have been examining in general terms: Johannes de Grocheio's *De musica* (*c.*1300) and the *Speculum musice* of Jacques de Liège (*c.*1325). Since the relevant passages in the *Speculum musice* present fewer problems of interpretation than those in Grocheio's treatise, we may consider their evidence first. In the seventh book of the *Speculum musice* Jacques offers something which is extremely rare in medieval treatises on music: a reminiscence concerning some performances that he had attended:[20]

Vidi ergo, in quadam societate, in qua congregati erant, valentes cantores et laici sapientes. Fuerunt ibi cantati moteti moderni et secundum modum modernum, et veteres aliqui. Plus satis placuerunt, etiam laicis, antiqui quam novi, et modus antiquus quam novus . . . Vidi in magna sapientium societate, cum cantarentur moteti secundum modernum modum. Quaesitum fuit quali lingua tales uterentur cantores: hebraea, graeca vel latina . . .

I saw, in a certain gathering in which skilled singers and discerning lay persons were assembled, that modern motets were sung there according to the modern manner, and some old [motets]. The old motets, and the old manner, gave more pleasure—to the lay persons also—than the new . . . I saw in a great gathering of discerning people, when motets were sung according to the modern manner, that it was asked what language the singers were using: Hebrew, Greek, or Latin . . .

Dolores Pesce expresses the prevailing interpretation of this passage when she declares that Jacques de Liège associates the motet with 'connoisseurs' and with the 'intelligentsia'.[21] That seems a fair judgement, but it is worth noting that Jacques has every reason to emphasize—and to exaggerate—the excellence of the performers and the discernment of the listeners assembled on the occasions which he is recalling. His point is that the singers and listeners whose company he shared in those gatherings concurred with his own view of the new motet style as something contrived, irrational, and unappealing; Jacques naturally wishes to establish the credentials of such allies beyond any doubt. It does not follow from what he reports that the singers of motets were always so skilled (*valentes*), nor that the listeners were always so discerning (*sapientes*). None the less, his words have consistently been read as if they described the kind of audience

---

[20] Text from *Speculum musicae*, ed. Bragard, vii. 95.
[21] 'The Significance of Text in Thirteenth-Century Latin Motets', 92 and 105.

that motets habitually received. It might also be suggested that we should be wary of the term 'connoisseurs' in this context, for it does not strike exactly the right note when applied to the musicians and listeners mentioned by Jacques. In current English usage a connoisseur in artistic matters is surely someone who indulges a highly specialized taste in the context of what Alsop has called the 'art traditions' of collectors, dealers, galleries, and other such ancillaries.[22] Jacques's terms are *valentes* ('proficient') for the singers and *sapientes* ('discerning, judicious') for the lay listeners; 'lay connoisseurs' would not be a happy translation of *laici sapientes* since *sapientes* used in this adjectival way suggests a somewhat broader, less fastidious discernment than 'connoisseurs'. 'Discerning laymen' seems better. By the same token, when Jacques speaks a few lines later of *sapientes* being gathered together, the translation 'discerning people' may be preferred.

Let us now turn to the treatise of Johannes de Grocheio. This requires much closer attention, as befits one of the most original—and yet one of the most misunderstood—musical texts of the Middle Ages. It is well known that Grocheio's *De musica*, probably composed *c*.1300, gives an account of the musical forms cultivated in Paris. Unfortunately, very little can be said for certain about the author of this remarkable work. There can be no doubt that he had sampled the musical life of the capital, while his passing references to Aristotelian concepts such as *forma et materia*, and to commentaries upon the *De anima* (among other books) suggest that he had studied in Paris,[23] presumably attending a course of lectures. There is no proof that he proceeded to take a degree, however (for that was not an automatic step), and it may be wise to keep an open mind about the note in the Darmstadt manuscript of the treatise where he is given the title 'magister' and named as a resident teacher in Paris;[24] the scribe may have been guessing on the basis of what he read in the text—much as modern scholars have done—and it is noteworthy that the word *parisius* has been added in a later hand. Recent research suggests that it is possible to pursue Grocheio beyond the walls of Paris, for he may have been a member of the Norman family of De Grouchy (see map)

---

[22] See Alsop, *The Rare Art Traditions, passim.*

[23] For the terms *forma* and *materia* in Grocheio's text see Rohloff, *Die Quellenhandschriften,* 114 *et passim.*

[24] Facsimile in Rohloff, *Die Quellenhandschriften,* 107.

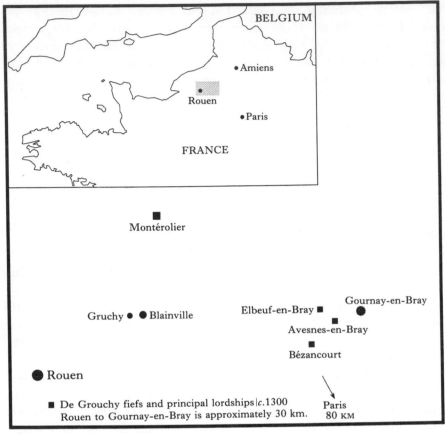

Lands of De Grouchy family

with lands a few days' ride from the capital.[25] There is no competing hypothesis concerning his identity (unless he took his name from the tiny hamlet of Gruchy some 12 km. west of Cherbourg) and a Norman homeland would accord with a passing reference to a Norman musical custom in the treatise;[26] furthermore, Grocheio admits to having discussed certain aspects of his works with one Clement, recently

---

[25] Page, 'Johannes de Grocheio on Secular Music'.
[26] Rohloff, *Die Quellenhandschriften*, 132: 'Et huiusmodi cantilena [sc. rotunda vel rotundellus] versus occidentem, puta in Normannia, solet decantari a puellis et iuvenibus in festis et magnis conviviis ad eorum decorationem.' *Concerning Music*, 17.

identified as a monk of the abbey of Lessay in Normandy.[27] It is possible that Grocheio had some links with this monastic house, a community of more than thirty monks in his lifetime.[28] He may also have been a priest, but it seems impossible to verify the assertion of Mgr Glorieux that he was definitely a priest 'since we possess some sermons by him'.[29]

Table 1. *Johannes de Grocheio's classification of music*

I. *simplex musica vel civilis quam vulgaris musica appellamus. Cantus publicus.*

   VOCAL

   1. Cantus category

      cantus gestualis (the narrative epics, or chansons de geste)

      cantus coronatus/simplex conductus (a 'crowned song'; the High Style trouvère song)

      cantus versualis or *versiculatus* (trouvère songs of less ambition and less seriousness of purpose than the above; possibly including *chansons à refrains* and *chansons avec des refrains*)

   2. Cantilena category

      rotunda vel rotundellus (the rondeau)

      stantipes (the estampie)

      ductia (the carole, sung for dances performed in a ring or chain)

      cantilena entata (songs having *refrain* material 'grafted' into them; compare the vernacular term *motet enté*)

   INSTRUMENTAL performed upon the *viella*

      cantus coronatus

      ductia

      stantipes

---

[27] Page, *The Owl and the Nightingale*, 171–2, and 246 n. 3. The vital piece of evidence is obliterated in Rohloff, *Die Quellenhandschriften*, 130, by his emendation of Grocheio's 'Exaquiensem monachum' (i.e. 'monk of Lessay') to '[exequiarium] monachum', whence Seay's 'Clement, a monk who is an Exequarius' (*Concerning Music*, 15).

[28] See the references to the community of Lessay in the celebrated Register of Odon Rigaud, conveniently accessible in Brown, *The Register of Eudes of Rouen*, 100 (visitation of 1250, 36 monks), 277 (visitation of 1256, 34 monks) and 634 (visitation of 1266, 31 monks).

[29] *La Faculté des arts*, s.v. Jean de Grouchy. No sermons by Johannes de Grocheio are listed in Schneyer, *Repertorium sermonum*.

Table I. *cont.*

II. *musica composita vel regularis vel canonica quam appellant musicam mensuratam*

PER EXPERIENTIAM
  quintus/discantus/organum duplum
CANTUS PRAECISE MENSURATUS
  motetus (habens plura dictamina)
  organum (habens unum dictamen)
    1. *supra cantum ecclesiasticum*
    2. *supra cantum compositum* (conductus)
  hoquetus
III. *tertium genus est quod ex istis duobus efficitur . . . quod ecclesiasticum dicitur*

MATUTINAS, HORAE et MISSA
  Invitatorium
  Venite
  Hymnus
  Deus in adiutorium
  Psalmi evangelistas
  Responsorium nocturnale/Gloria patri
  Versiculus
  Antiphona/neupma
  Introitus
  Psalmus/Gloria patri
  Kyrie eleison
  Gloria in excelsis deo
  Epistola
  Responsorium missae
  Alleluia
  Sequentia
  Evangelium
  Tractus (tempore luctus)
  Credo in unum deum
  Offertorium
  Praefatio
  Sanctus
  Agnus dei
  Communio

Grocheio's classification of the musical forms used in Paris is sum-
marized in Table 1. It has not always been sufficiently recognized that
this classification is one of the major intellectual achievements of
medieval music theory.[30] Grocheio's listing of secular musical forms
may not seem remarkable to anyone who knows the *Leys d'amors*,[31]
for example, nor will his subdivision of polyphonic forms seem especially surprising to those familiar with the treatises of the later thirteenth century. What is remarkable here is the comprehensiveness of
purpose, encompassing monophony, polyphony, and plainsong in a
discussion that is both technical and, in places, quasi-sociological.
The task Grocheio faced was one of exceptional difficulty (there is
true feeling in his understated admission *non est facile musicam
dividere recte*);[32] the intellectual and discursive habits of his day
required him to devise a rigorous scheme of classification for the
musical life of the largest city in Europe at an exceptional time in its
musical history. In the event, his discussion is quite lucid and the
structure shown in Table 1 can be separated from his prose with ease.

Grocheio's discussion has none the less given rise to both confusion
and misunderstanding. In part, this is because his treatise is so ambi-
tious in design that it must be read as a comprehensive interpretation
of the Parisian musical scene. Each passage, and each terminological
usage, has the potential to clarify or to colour the meaning of another.
The *De musica* cannot therefore be treated as a collection of self-
sufficient definitions; it creates its own frame of reference and understanding.

This is a matter of cardinal importance for any attempt to interpret
Grocheio's treatise and it requires illustration. A prime example is
provided by his discussion of the third category of Cantus, the *cantus
versualis* or *versiculatus*. As we may see from the table, Grocheio distinguishes between Cantus and Cantilena, and we miss his meaning
if we fail to recognize that this is a distinction of register: the Cantus register being the more excellent and demanding, the Cantilena
register requiring a little less accomplishment and seriousness of

---

[30] Many authors, however, have done Grocheio the credit of discussing his classification in
some detail. See e.g. De Witt, *A New Perspective*, 122–3 (an excellent discussion); Gallo, *Music
of the Middle Ages*, ii. 10–13; McGee, 'Medieval Dances'; Stevens, *Words and Music*, 429–34;
Stockmann, 'Musica Vulgaris'; Wagenaar–Nolthenius, 'Estampie/Stantipes/Stampita', 399–409.
[31] See the commentary and extracts from the *Leys d'amors* in Page, *Voices and Instruments*,
42–6.
[32] Rohloff, *Die Quellenhandschriften*, 124.

purpose.[33] This registration is a delicate one. It does not provide a means of filing songs into generic categories but evokes certain stylistic *tendencies* within songs and, beyond that, implies varying degrees of formality and diginity for their performance. Van der Werf, who deals somewhat harshly with Grocheio's treatise and misses these points, declares that 'the distinction between cantus and cantilena . . . tumbles down when Grocheo [*sic*] remarks that the cantus versiculatus is called a 'cantilena' by some . . .'.[34] This seems a poor reward for Grocheio's attempt to give a full account of Parisian musical terminology. His meaning is both clear and consistent: since, according to Grocheio, the *cantus versualis* does not possess the excellence of the true High Style trouvère song (which he calls *cantus coronatus*), some people characterize it by a name that suggests a lower registration: i.e. they call it a *cantilena*, probably corresponding to vernacular *chansonette*.

Let us now turn to Grocheio's three musical categories, denoted by Roman numerals in the table. Category III need not detain us long since it is entirely devoted to liturgical plainsong and requires no further discussion here. Category I, however, is a different matter. It embraces music which is monophonic (*simplex*) and which may be either vocal or instrumental; when it carries a text the words are in the vernacular, a conclusion established by the songs which Grocheio cites but also suggested by the term *musica vulgaris*; this might be translated 'vernacular music', where the term 'vernacular' may be understood to bear the sense 'in the native tongue' and also the sense of 'ordinary' as in 'vernacular architecture'. *Musica vulgaris*, in other words, is the generality of music, liked by most people, heard most often, and not requiring the intellectual exertions demanded by Latinity and the craft of polyphonic composition (all of which is encompassed by Category II). Something similar is probably implied by the term *cantus publicus*, which Grocheio uses only once and in a distant corner of his treatise remote from his discussion of these issues.[35]

The term *civilis* requires careful handling. In view of the meanings we have given to *vulgaris* and *publicus*, *civilis* might be assigned the well-attested senses 'ordinary' or 'unassuming' (which do not imply

[33] This registration is discussed and explained in Page, *Voices and Instruments*, 196–201.
[34] *The Chansons of the Troubadours and Trouvères*, 154.
[35] Rohloff, *Die Quellenhandschriften*, 152.

76

'low class').[36] No doubt this is correct. However, Grocheio's avowed aim is to give an account of music as it is necessary for the use and 'social relations' of the citizens (*prout ad usum vel convictum civium*),[37] a choice of words reflecting his concern for the way music ensures peace, prosperity, and good government in the community (*civitas*). What is striking about Grocheio's treatment of this theme, however, is that he only pursues it when his subject is *musica vulgaris*; indeed, he says that the forms of *musica vulgaris*—which include the best trouvère songs, estampies, caroles (*ductie*) and the rest—are 'ordained' because they have the power to mitigate the innate contrarieties of men (*adversitates hominum innatae*).[38] I have argued elsewhere that Grocheio's use of the term 'ordained' (*ordinantur*) recalls other thirteenth-century discussions of what the wise *politicus* should dispose for the government of the people.[39] In Grocheio's treatise, as in other writings which touch upon the ordinances of the *politicus*, this seems an essentially clerical pose. We notice that all the categories of people whose contrarieties can be mitigated by music— kings, nobles, princes of the land, working people, young men and women in festivities—are (or seem to be) lay persons;[40] when it comes to polyphonic forms such as the motet—forms that are supported by an ancillary literature of music theory and by a savant system of musical notation—Grocheio's interest in the power of music to temper human failings seems to vanish. The music that could be most readily composed, and most knowledgeably enjoyed, by a person of clerical education seems to have no contrarieties to cure. If Johannes de Grocheio was indeed a scion of the Norman family of De Grouchy then, as a cleric himself, we may well imagine that he naturally gravitated towards the company of the higher clergy; it would seem that, in his view, they are above this essentially political scheme for *musica civilis*. That term might almost be translated 'the music of those governed by civil law'.

---

[36] *Oxford Latin Dictionary*, s.v. *ciuilis* 7 ('Suitable to a private citizen, unassuming, unpretentious'). In view of Grocheio's belief that *musica civilis* has the power to mitigate the inherent contrarieties of men, it may be that further nuances of the term in his usage would include 'that which is conducive to peaceful cohabitation, civilized'. For a valuable discussion of some of these issues, approaching Grocheio's text from an 'ethnological' perspective, see Stockmann, 'Musica Vulgaris'.

[37] Rohloff, *Die Quellenhandschriften*, 124.   [38] Ibid. 130.

[39] *The Owl and the Nightingale*, 171–3.

[40] For relevant passages in Grocheio's text see Rohloff, *Die Quellenhandschriften*, 130–8, *passim*.

The suggestiveness of that translation is strengthened when we consider the kind of audience that Grocheio envisages for his Category I. This is a matter that leads directly to the final destination of our argument, his account of the motet. Table 1 shows that Grocheio uses a variety of terms to define Category I: *simplex, civilis, vulgaris,* and *publicus.* The adjective *simplex* ('monophonic') is essentially technical, and while a musician such as Grocheio might well judge such *simplex* music to be *civilis* (in the sense of 'ordinary' or 'unassuming') as well as *vulgaris* and *publicus,* we may say that *simplex,* in the sense 'monophonic', is employed in other music treatises,[41] while *civilis, vulgaris,* and *publicus* as a group, embodying Grocheio's distinctive vision of his material, are not.

His use of *civilis, vulgaris,* and *publicus* is complex but neither inconsistent nor evasive. To establish Category I at the point in the treatise where full definitions are in order, all three terms are required, cumulatively defining the content and character of what is, after all, a complex socio-musical phenomenon.[42] None the less, each term can stand alone when, in the body of the treatise, contrasts are drawn between Categories I and II (see Table 1). Thus, where we might expect to find the contrast *mensurabilis/immensurabilis* in any other treatise, Grocheio has the contrastive pairs *civilis/mensuratus*[43] and *publicus/praecise mensuratus.*[44] At the same time, the use of *civilis, vulgaris,* and *publicus* is enriched and extended by the related nouns *cives* and *vulgares,* by occasional formulations such as *vulgares layci,* and by the pervasive influence—to be discussed below—of the legal distinction between *civilis* and *canonica* (see Table 1, Category II, for *musica canonica*). The meaning of each one of these terms is stabilized and underwritten by the initial classification as Grocheio explains it; each usage reactivates the whole scheme while offering some particularization.

Let us consider one particularization: the term *musica vulgaris* (Category I). Who were the *vulgares* who enjoyed it? To pose the question in that form is to turn the adjective *vulgaris* into a general name (the *vulgares*) for those whose tastes and aptitudes are catered for by *musica vulgaris.* This is a legitimate step, for Grocheio himself speaks of the rondeau, one category of *musica vulgaris,* as being

---

[41] See e.g. the treatise of Anonymous 4 in Reckow, *Der Musiktraktat des Anonymus IV,* 46 (referring to Perotinus' monophonic conductus *Beata viscera*), 60, 70, 71, and 82.

[42] Rohloff, *Die Quellenhandschriften,* 124.   [43] Ibid. 152.   [44] Ibid.

enjoyed by the *vulgares laici*;[45] it is also an important step, for the nature of his terms *vulgares* and *vulgares laici* has given rise to misunderstanding in the past. Albert Seay translates them as 'the vulgar' and 'the vulgar laics' respectively.[46] Many scholars have followed him, but John Stevens, Richard Hoppin, and Dolores Pesce have ventured 'the common people'.[47] However, Grocheio's *vulgares* and *vulgares laici* are not just 'the common people'. His category of music called *vulgaris* includes the songs composed for (and in one case composed by) the highest-ranking members of secular society. The *vulgares* include kings and nobles:[48]

[Cantus coronatus] a regibus et nobilibus solet componi et etiam coram regibus et principibus terre decantari . . .

The *cantus coronatus* is customarily composed by kings and nobles and sung in the presence of kings and princes of the land . . .

Grocheio's *musica vulgaris* also includes the instrumental music played before magnates:[49]

Bonus autem artifex in viella omnem cantum et cantilenam et omnem formam musicalem generaliter introducit. Illa tamen quae coram divitibus in festis et ludis fiunt communiter ad tria generaliter reducuntur . . .

A good player generally shapes every cantus and cantilena, and all achieved musical design, upon the viella. The genres which are usually performed before magnates in festivities and sportive gatherings can generally be reduced to three . . .

The music classified as *vulgaris* also includes the songs enjoyed by the young, and the narrative epics that Grocheio prescribes for working citizens and for those of middle station (*civibus laborantibus et mediocribus*).[50] Taken together, these passages produce the following equation:

vulgares = reges, nobiles, principes, divites, cives antiqui, cives laborantes, cives mediocri, iuvenes

Grocheio's *vulgares* and *vulgares laici* therefore cannot be 'the common people' alone, and Albert Seay's translation, 'the vulgar', seems

[45] Ibid. 144.   [46] *Concerning Music*, 26.
[47] Stevens, *Words and Music*, 453; Hoppin, *Medieval Music*, 341; Pesce, 'The Significance of Text in Thirteenth-Century Latin Motets', 92. Compare Stockmann, 'Musica Vulgaris', 6.
[48] Rohloff, *Die Quellenhandschriften*, 130, corresponding to *Concerning Music*, 16.
[49] Ibid. 136, corresponding to *Concerning Music*, 19–20.
[50] Ibid. 130, corresponding to *Concerning Music*, 16.

very wide of the mark, given the current senses of 'vulgar' ('tasteless', 'indelicate'). The conclusion seems inescapable that Grocheio's *vulgares* and *vulgares laici* are the laity considered as a whole.

With that established, let us now briefly examine Grocheio's second category: *Musica composita vel regularis vel canonica quam appellant musicam mensuratam.*

The term *composita*, which might be said to balance *simplex* in the definition of Category I, indicates that the music in question is polyphonic: the art of the polyphonic composer is to 'bring together' (*componere*) separate parts. (Grocheio is quite prepared to use the verb *componere* for the composition of monophonic songs and instrumental pieces,[51] but that does not affect the issue here.) The use of *regularis* in the definition is closely related to this conception of polyphonic composition as a matter that is 'regulated' in a way that monophonic composition is not. This regulation, we may imagine, is to be understood as partly a matter of measure with all that that requires from the composer, performer and scribe in the way of notational expertise and acquaintance with treatises *de musica mensurabili*. Indeed, a principal contrast between Grocheio's categories I and II is that a discussion of notation, and a reference to an ancillary tradition of written music theory, is only necessary in the discussion of Category II. The issue of measurement—and indeed of *precise* measurement—is clearly very important in the establishment of Grocheio's Category II.

What of *canonica*? At first glance this looks like a near synonym of *regularis* (it is dangerous to assume that any of the terms Grocheio uses in these complex definitions are exactly synonymous). A second glance suggests a nuance, however, for Grocheio seems to be drawing a distinction between *musica civilis* and *musica canonica*. Seay translates *musica civilis* as 'civil music' (i.e. the monophonic music of the citizens of Paris) and *musica canonica* as 'music by rule' (i.e. measured polyphony),[52] but 'civil music/music by rule' seems a rather unsatisfactory contrast of concepts. The truth is surely that Grocheio is employing the terms *musica civilis* and *musica canonica* exactly as the lawyers of his day used 'lex civilis' (civil law, governing the laity) and 'lex canonica' (canon law, governing the clergy).

As an observation about verbal play in Grocheio's *De musica*, I do

---

[51] Rohloff, *Die Quellenhandschriften*, 136 ('Componere ductiam et stantipedem . . .').
[52] *Concerning Music*, 12, corresponding to Rohloff, *Die Quellenhandschriften*, 124.

not believe that this point can be denied. However, the opposition *musica civilis/musica canonica* may cut deeper than the surface of the words. We have already seen that 'the music of those governed by civil law' seems to be one apt translation for *musica civilis*, and this accords with the audience for *musica civilis* as Grocheio both describes and illustrates it: the *vulgares laici*, the laity as a whole. A closer look at the forms of *musica canonica* suggests that 'the music of those governed by canon law' may be a telling translation of this term. The forms of *musica canonica* demand a specialized knowledge of notation from those who wish to compose, perform, or copy them; they are reinforced by a literature of treatises, to which Grocheio briefly alludes at several points.[53] These were interests and skills that must have been largely confined to those who had received a preliminary education in grammar and plainchant and who had then built upon it.

Furthermore—and here Grocheio's description of the motet finally comes directly into view—the forms of *musica canonica* are enjoyed by the *litterati*. Grocheio makes this explicit in his remarks about the motet (I use the text of Ernst Rohloff, save that *animadvertunt* in Rohloff's edition has been replaced by *advertunt*, the reading of both manuscripts; this emendation does not affect the sense). I have special reasons for citing the widely used English translation by Albert Seay, to which I shall return:[54]

Cantus autem iste non debet coram vulgaribus propinari, eo quod eius subtilitatem non advertunt nec in eius auditu delectantur sed coram litteratis et illis, qui subtilitates artium sunt quaerentes. Et solet in eorum festis decantari ad eorum decorationem, quemadmodum cantilena, quae dicitur rotundellus, in festis vulgarium laicorum.

This kind of song ought not to be propagated among the vulgar, since they do not understand its subtlety nor do they delight in hearing it, but it should be performed for the learned and for those who seek after the subtleties of the arts. And it is normally performed in their feasts for their beautification, just as the cantilena which is called a rotundellus is performed in the feasts of vulgar laics.

We have already seen that 'the vulgar' and 'the vulgar laics' are not at all satisfactory as translations of Grocheio's *vulgares* and *vulgares*

---

[53] Rohloff, *Die Quellenhandschriften*, 142–4 (a general discussion of mensural notation), 122, 138, and 142 (references to the treatise literature).   [54] Ibid. 144; *Concerning Music*, 26.

laici. I now wish to suggest that '[before] the learned' is equally unsatisfactory as a translation of *coram litteratis* (not to mention translations such as 'men of letters' or 'in very exclusive social circles'). The direction of our argument so far suggests that when Grocheio speaks of the *litterati* he means the clergy as opposed to the laity, explicitly named here as the *vulgares laici*. The use of the Old French adjective *letré* to mean the clergy can be amply substantiated in sources of the twelfth and thirteenth centuries, and the antithesis between *li letré* (the clergy) and *li lai* (the laity) is common and conventionalized in Old French. As early as 1155 Wace speaks of 'Li lai' and 'li lectré',[55] while Baudouin de Condé, a contemporary of Johannes de Grocheio, distinguishes between 'gent laie et letrée'.[56]

This interpretation sheds new light upon Grocheio's remark that motets should be performed 'coram litteratis et illis qui subtilitates artium sunt quaerentes'. Those words may now be translated as follows: '[motets should be performed] before the clergy and before those who seek the refinements in any branch of study'. As this translation is designed to show, the syntax of Grocheio's passage indicates his view that motets should be reserved for the clergy *and* for 'those who seek refinements in any branch of study'—a separate group. These individuals who 'seek refinements' are therefore not clerics of unusual ability and interests (an assumption which has prompted some scholars to pitch the audience for motets very high indeed); they are surely laymen of unusual aptitude, corresponding to the *laici sapientes* who (according to Jacques de Liège) could enjoy pre-Ars nova motets with their clerical associates.[57]

This is not to say, however, that Johannes de Grocheio regards all clerics as fit to enjoy motets; he presumably does not mean that anyone with a tonsure is qualified to appreciate them, for that would include common criminals who had taken a tonsure to escape the jurisdiction of the civil courts, for example.[58] Nor is it to say that he regarded the ideal audience for the motet as being exclusively clerical. He is prepared to concede that one kind of *musica canonica*, the polyphonic conductus, is performed not only before the *litterati* but also before *divites*. In these repects Grocheio's ideal audience for the motet is not quite congruent with the modern concept of a 'learned' or of an 'intellectual élite'. It is not even quite the same as 'men of let-

---

[55] Cited in Tobler-Lommatzsch, *Altfranzösisches Wörterbuch*, s.v. *letré*.   [56] Ibid.
[57] *Speculum musicae*, vii. 95.   [58] Geremek, *The Margins of Society*, 136.

ters' (favoured by Gallo), for the meaning of that phrase varies from age to age: a seventeenth-century writer of theological tracts, an eighteenth-century pamphleteer and novelist, a nineteenth-century classical scholar—these were all 'men of letters' in their day, and the startling differences between them are as apparent as any continuities that bind them. Johannes de Grocheio's *litterati* would certainly have included some very erudite individuals—Masters of Theology, for example—but the term *litterati* does not include such men only (though it does include only men). We can turn to the sermon collection by Humbert of Romans to determine the meaning of *litterati* for a thirteenth-century cleric with a Parisian background, and there it appears that a *litteratus* is any cleric who is pursuing some kind of study with a view to acquiring *scientia*, *intellectus*, *sensus*, or *sapientia*, terms that encompass both more and less than the modern and wholly secularized concept of 'learning'.[59] As suggested above, they convey the various kinds of understanding and material for contemplation which bring a reflective mind to a clearer perception of nature and a deeper conviction of the Christian faith. Members of the lower and higher faculties in the University—the physicians, lawyers, and Masters of Arts—were only one kind of *litteratus*, and not the best kind in Humbert's view since they sold their knowledge by teaching for money.[60] In Humbert's writing the full scope of the term *litteratus* includes parish priests and their curates, secular canons, canons serving a bishop 'as knights serve their castellan', boys and adolescents studying grammar, 'boys in their infancy' learning plainchant, students of logic and philosophy, physicians, students of civil and canon law, and finally (in the supreme position) theologians.[61] That is a very broad constituency, and in the current state of our knowledge it would be unwise to conclude that Grocheio wishes to exclude any of these from his conception of the *litterati* and therefore from the audience for motets.

There is certainly an élitism in Grocheio's view of the audience for motets, but it is the medieval cleric's traditional and conventionalized sense of superiority over the layman (preserved in one Modern English sense of 'layman': one not skilled in any study or craft). It does not have the nuances of class (a post-medieval notion) to be found in Mathiassen's 'very exclusive social circles', and it does not in itself

---

[59] *Sermones beati Umberti Burgundi*, i. 56.   [60] Ibid. 57.   [61] Ibid. 57–70.

imply the literary interests conveyed (at least in common parlance) by Gallo's 'men of letters'. The élitism sensed by Grocheio in speaking of the motet should be perceived in rather different terms: the cleric's sense of distinctive juridical status; his consciousness of advancing mankind's supreme purpose in God while maintaining a powerful influence over temporal powers; pride in the ability to read and write: *clergie*.

III

The assumption that Ars antiqua motets were enjoyed almost exclusively by connoisseurs has inspired musicologists and (more recently) historians of literature to ask how musicians achieved the subtlety (*subtilitas*) admired by Johannes de Grocheio. Fresh researches into particular forms (such as the Latin double motet) have refined our sense of the distinctions that experienced listeners must have drawn between different kinds of motet in the thirteenth century.[62] Studies of the motet traditions known in particular areas (such as Artois) have clarified some of the things which the listeners who shared a 'regional' musical and poetic tradition would have noticed (and no doubt enjoyed) in the pieces they heard.[63] In recent years, as the scope of motet studies has broadened, scholars have traced patterns of verbal sound, repetition and thematic interlace within the texts of motets.[64]

Let us turn to the verse of motets, for there is still no comprehensive study of the motet poetry that was written in great quantity during the thirteenth century. Does that poetry seem to be designed for intellectuals or persons of 'aesthetic sophistication' (Sylvia Huot's phrase) in any exclusive way? Let us establish at once that Tischler and Huot seem to be mistaken when they declare that the texts of thirteenth-century motets 'give a fair cross section of the intellectual trends of the time'.[65] The scholastic method, for example, has left virtually no impression upon the Latin or French motets, even though the pairing of texts in a double motet would have given poets

---

[62] See Pesce, 'A Revised View' and 'The Significance of Text in Thirteenth-Century Latin Motets'.

[63] Everist, 'The Rondeau Motet'. [64] See especially Huot, 'Polyphonic Poetry'.

[65] Tischler, *The Style and Evolution of the Earliest Motets*, i. 203, endorsed by Huot, 'Polyphonic Poetry', 262.

an excellent opportunity for presenting the arguments and authorities pro and contra some particular proposition, perhaps with a *solutio* given in the quadruplum if the motet were a triple composition. If the motet was fostered in the kind of learned (and predominantly university) milieu that has often been evoked by modern scholars,[66] then the failure of the motet repertoire to encompass a musical *questio de quolibet* of this kind is perhaps surprising.[67] In this regard the motet stands somewhat aloof from the 'intellectual trends of the time'. In the same way, motets reveal barely any interest in the 'new' Aristotle —in the *Ethics* and *Politics*, for example, which excited such intense interest during the thirteenth century.[68] To be sure, such things would not necessarily be expected to appear in the vernacular verse of motets, but there are numerous movements in thirteenth-century thought which could have found expression in Old French dupla, tripla, or quadrupla but which rarely (or never) do: changes in the theology of penance,[69] the intensified persecution of Jews and lepers,[70] and changing attitudes to the legitimacy of monetary earnings from various new trades.[71] On the whole, the repertoire of motet verse, both French and Latin, seems more lyrical and recreative than intellectual.

It has been convincingly established that some of the Latin poetry in motets makes skilful and systematic use of repetition and of phonic devices described in manuals of the *ars rithmica*.[72] No doubt such Latin poetry would have been particularly enjoyed by those whose Latin was good, but they need not have been expert, for it is questionable whether the poets who wrote Latin verse for polytextual motets expected that their verses would be fully understood in one performance (or in any number of performances).[73] Of all the musical genres known to the Middle Ages, it is the motet which most candidly acknowledges the importance of verbal sound over verbal sense

---

[66] See e.g. Yudkin, *Music in Medieval Europe*, 357–65.

[67] I know of only one motet that attempts a *questio* structure of this kind, but it is clearly an exceptional work, owing its three Latin texts to a monophonic conductus. See Anderson, *Motets of the Manuscript La Clayette*, no. 3.

[68] Haren, *Medieval Thought*, 145–206.   [69] Page, *The Owl and the Nightingale*, 19 ff.

[70] Moore, *The Formation of a Persecuting Society*, *passim*.

[71] See Page, *The Owl and the Nightingale*, *passim*.

[72] Pesce, 'The Significance of Text in Thirteenth-Century Latin Motets'.

[73] It must be acknowledged that a 'layered' performance of motets (each voice being sung individually, perhaps over the tenor) followed by a 'complete' performance may have taken place in the 13th c., a method which solves the problem of comprehensibility at a stroke.

by placing two or even three texts together, minimizing their intelligibility but maximizing their phonic contrast. Perhaps we should counter the idealist belief of modern scholars that if a text is present in a medieval composition then it was meant to be understood in a fashion that somehow approximates to what a musicologist, armed with dictionaries, concordances, the *Glossa ordinaria*, and more besides can accomplish. Experience suggests that the pleasure derived from hearing the words of a song does not necessarily rest upon a full (or even a moderate) comprehension of their lexical meaning and syntactic relations, let alone of their 'meaning' in any broader sense of the term.[74] Some listeners in the thirteenth century may have enjoyed the sound-patterns of Latin motet poetry without deriving any significant understanding of the sense, much as some modern listeners do today when hearing these motets (or operatic arias, for that matter). This point might be argued on a broad basis, as an observation about the way in which words operate in songs; as far as the motet is concerned, it can scarcely be doubted that many motets were designed to induce an exhilarating impression of words leaving sense behind and beginning to *skirl*.

Let us turn to a fundamental kind of *subtilitas* in the verse of motets: verbal repetition. Here is an example of verbal patterning adduced by Gallo as an illustration of a *subtilitas* which thirteenth-century 'men of letters' would have admired in the poetry of motets:[75]

> *Triplum* EN UN VERGIER M'ENTRAI;
> Chapiau faisant AI TROUVÉE Emmelot.
> Lés li m'assis
> ET S'AMOR LI REQUIS.
> SANS DELAI,
> EL ME RESPONT
>
> *Duplum* EN UN VERGIER M'ENTRAI;
> Dame pleisant I TROUVAI.
> Bele estoit, si l'en amai
> ET S'AMOR LI demandai.
> ELLE RESPONT SANS DELAI

(I follow Gallo in the presentation of these texts, save that (*a*) I have not capitalized 'demandai' in the Duplum for 'requis' in the Triplum,

---

[74] See the many pertinent remarks in Booth, *The Experience of Songs.*
[75] *Music of the Middle Ages*, II, 23.

which belongs to a different order of resemblance than the others noted by Gallo, and (*b*) I have capitalized 'sans delai' in the last line of the Duplum text, which Gallo has unaccountably omitted to mark.) The verbal parallels adduced by Gallo are certainly convincing, but much of the recent research devoted to the subtlety of motets leaves us wondering whether the necessary tests have been done to establish whether such parallels may be adventitious to some degree. Gallo's example certainly stands, and some verbal patternings of this kind are reinforced in the music of motets, giving the musical setting an important role in the adjudication of such cases (Ex. 10). However, when due consideration is given to the vocabulary, phraseology, and syntax of vernacular motet poetry, often remarked upon,[76] would we not expect a measure of fortuitous parallelism to emerge sometimes? Since a test of this kind seems overdue, here is one:[77]

Triplum   Au dous TENS QUE CHANTENT CIL OISEL tant seri
Juer alai
En un PRÉ FLOURI,
Cuillant flouretes trouvai
Un DEMOISEL JOLI,
Qui CHANTOIT souvent

Ex. 10. Extract from the three-part motet *En non Dieu/Quant voi la rose/NOBIS*. Adapted from Anderson, *Compositions of the Bamberg Manuscript*, 112, bars 5–8. Compare Ex. 12

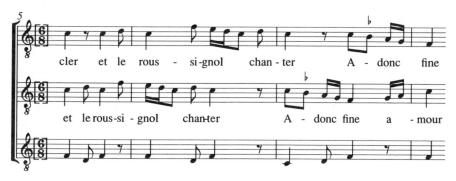

---

[76] See Stakel and Relihan in Tischler, *The Montpellier Codex*, pp. xvi–xix, which includes this astonishing generalization: 'Medieval poetry does tend to seem boringly repetitive to modern readers.'

[77] Texts from Anderson, *Compositions of the Bamberg Manuscript*, no. 18 (Triplum) and no. 10 (Motetus).

Motetus   Au TENS d'esté QUE CIL OISEL
            CHANTENT tuit a haut cri,
            Que verdissent cil PRAËL,
            Et rosier sont FLORI,
            Et cil jone DEMOISEL
            Sunt mignot et JOLI
            Et CHANTENT

These parallels are not as impressive as those in Gallo's example, but they are striking enough, I suggest, to be regarded as comparable in kind, if not in degree. What, therefore, are we to make of the fact that these two texts have been taken from two different and unrelated motets? It is sobering to reflect that some current critical techniques would have led us to regard them as an example (albeit a mild one) of subtlety if they had they been the duplum and motetus of a single motet.[78]

These doubts prompt us to look more closely at another kind of subtlety in motet verse: the device of alluding to tenor cues or texts in the poems of duplum, triplum, or quadruplum. The practice in several recent editions of motet poetry (some of which have provided literary scholars with their research material)[79] is to italicize or underline any words in an upper voice that appear to allude to the tenor cue in this way (thus '*morti*fero' over the tenor MORS, for example).[80] In motets of the earlier Latin (and to some extent of the earlier vernacular) repertoire, this seems a valid practice,[81] for the ability to identify such relationships, and the impulse to ruminate upon them, must have been one of the listening skills that some members of a clerical audience could bring to the performance of a motet. We may also accept that the ears of any experienced listener might pick up 'Hui main' at the beginning of a motet upon HEC DIES, for example,[82] or even '*Tant* grate chievre' above TANQUAM (though I am inclined to doubt it).[83] It is another matter, however, to take an extensive motet poem in the vernacular and italicize one word, 'valour' (appearing in the conventionalized phrase 'sa grant valour'), simply because the Tenor cue is VALARE.[84] Is this kind of subtlety

[78] Compare the techniques employed in B. J. Evans, 'Music, Text and Social Context'.
[79] I refer to Stakel and Relihan in Tischler, *The Montpellier Codex, passim*.
[80] Ibid., no. 35, Quadruplum.
[81] See e.g. ibid., nos. 26 (Quadruplum, Triplum, and Motetus), 36 (Motetus), 189 (Motetus), *et passim*.
[82] Ibid., no. 184.   [83] Ibid., no. 182.   [84] Ibid., no. 168 (Motetus).

to be accepted? Perhaps an isolated instance of 'cuer' should be italicized when it appears above IN CORDE, and if so, why not 'voire-
ment' over VERITATEM, or even 'mon' over MEA?[85] It is difficult
to conceive where such a process might stop, and once again we find
ourselves in doubt about claims of intertextual design in motets on
the level of individual words and phrases.

Several recent studies have concentrated upon the kinds of semantic subtlety that may be discerned in the polytextuality of motets.[86]
As an illustration of the ways in which the poems of motets may be
related, Beverly J. Evans has quoted the following lines from two
poems that comprise a motet in the third fascicle of the Montpellier
Codex:[87]

> *Triplum* Quant repaire la verdor
> Et la prime flourete,
> Que chante par grant baudor
> Au matin l'aloete,
> Par un matin me levai,
> Sospris d'une amourete.
> En un vergier m'entrai
> Por cueillier violete.
> Une pucele avenant,
> Bele et pleisant,
> Juenete,
> Esgardai
> En un requai
> Delés une espinete . . .

Upon the return of the greenness and the early buds, when the lark fills the
morning with joyful song, I got up one morning captured by sweet love. I
entered an orchard to gather violets. I saw there a comely maiden, fair,
pleasing, and young, sitting all alone in a corner beside a thorn-bush . . .

> *Motetus* Flos de spina rumpitur;
> Spina caret
> Flos et aret,
> Sed non moritur.
> Vite florem

---

[85] Ibid., no. 244.

[86] Huot, 'Polyphonic Poetry'; Evans, 'Music, Text and Social Context'; Brownlee,
'Machaut's Motet 15'.

[87] Evans, 'Music, Text and Social Context', 188, corresponding to Stakel and Relihan in
Tischler, *The Montpellier Codex*, no. 44.

> Per amorem
> Flos complectitur,
> Cuius ex solatio
> Sic reficitur
> In vigore proprio,
> Quod non patitur.
> Virgo de Iudea
> Sursum tollitur . . .

The flower is plucked from the thorn; the flower without the thorn withers, but does not die. In love, the flower embraces the flower of life; in this solace it so refreshes itself in its own strength that it does not suffer. The virgin from Judea is lifted up . . .

Evans notes that *flos* appears four times in the opening lines of the Latin (if we include the accusative *florem*), and she then draws attention to *flourete* in the second line of the French. That is perhaps a somewhat contrived point, however, and its value is weakened by a circumstance that she freely acknowledges: *flourete* 'is a word we would expect to encounter in the pastoral setting'.[88] One might add that repetition of the kind 'Flos . . . os . . . os . . . orem' is a common device of syntax and sound in thirteenth-century Latin verse (as Pesce has shown in an excellent study),[89] and it seems unsafe to interpret that repetition as a deliberate interlace—a 'lexical connection'— involving the generically predictable *flourete*. Evans then proceeds with[90]

a second lexical connection . . . evident in the mention of thorns in both texts. The Latin poem opens with the image of the flower plucked from the thorn; the French poem situates the 'amourete' next to a thorn bush [*espinette*].

If this is being offered as a reconstruction of what Grocheio's contemporaries would have judged to be a subtlety in this motet then it may be somewhat misjudged. The appearance of a thorn-bush in the French can be explained in terms of pastourelle conventions;[91] furthermore, the thorn-bush is mere decor in the French and is of no apparent (or no clear) symbolic import, whereas the image of a thorn-

---

[88] Evans, 'Music, Text and Social Context', 189.
[89] Pesce, 'The Significance of Text in Thirteenth-Century Latin Motets'.
[90] Evans, 'Music, Text and Social Context', 189.
[91] Tobler-Lommatzsch, *Altfranzösisches Wörterbuch*, s.v. *espinete*, which quotes three examples of an *espinete* appearing in the context of the pastourelle and related romance narrative.

bush producing a flower is a vital and potent metaphor in the Latin. Is this not an important contrast, and will it not bear directly upon any suggestion that these things are related in a scheme of meaning?

The point that needs to be made plainly, I suggest, is that an enterprising critic, armed with a misconstrued version of Grocheio's remarks about the motet and an audience of 'litterati', can construct a relationship between almost any motet poems if satisfied, for example, with categories as broad as 'sacred/divine love'.[92] This observation requires a specific illustration. Once again, the texts which follow have been taken from two different and unrelated motets. The first is a prolix example of High Style love-rhetoric as it is to be found in motets; the second is a concise Latin hymn to the Virgin:[93]

Motetus	'Hé! bone amourete,
	Plus que riens doucete,
	Praingne vous de moi pité!
	Vostre doucour
	M'a mis en grant doulour
	Et en grieté;
	Nepourquant
	Longuement
	Vous ai servi
	Loiaument
	Si vous pri
	De cuer desirrant,
	Tres savourete, plaisans,
	Tous tens
	Donnés moi
	Un poi
	De confort.'
	Lors m'a soutiment dit
	Si qu'a peinne l'entendi:
	'Aies deport,
	De ces grevances
	En mi est la recovrance.'
	Ce mi fait
	Un poi esperer,
	Mais je n'i puis

---

[92] Compare, for example, Brownlee, 'Machaut's Motet 15'.
[93] Texts and translations from Anderson, *Compositions of the Bamberg Manuscript*, no. 38 (Motetus) and no. 76 (Motetus).

> Oublier
> Les maus qu'el mi fait
> Endurer;
> Pour tant li dis chantant
> Desiralment depriant:
> *'N'ociés pas vostre amant!'*

'Hey, good love, sweeter than all else, take pity on me!' Your sweetness has caused me much sorrow and grief; nevertheless, long have I served you loyally, and I beg of you with an anxious heart, alluring, pleasing creature, always give me a little consolation'. Then she said to me covertly, so that I scarcely heard her: 'Be happy, the cure for these torments lies with me.' This made me somewhat hopeful, but I cannot forget the pains she makes me suffer; for this reason I sing to her beseeching, pleading: *'Do not slay your lover.'*

> *Motetus*   O Maria, beata genitrix,
> Flos honoris materque miseris,
> Tu rosa de spinis nec spinosa,
> Virginum flos, virgo pre ceteris
> Tu vulneris medelam reperis,
> Tu aperis ostia carceris
> Et tuis
> Nos precibus sublevet Dominus
> Ad superna gaudia, pater et filius!

O Mary, blessed mother, flower of honour and mother to those suffering, thou art a rose sprung from a thorn yet without a thorn, flower of virgins, virgin exceeding all others, thou dost find a remedy for wounds; thou dost open the gates of prison, and because of thy prayers, may the Lord, the Father and Son, raise us to supernal joys.

It is not difficult to imagine how the 'intertextuality' of these two poems might be explored if they were part of the same motet. The basic frame of 'earthly/divine love' would provide an interpretative context within which to identify a contrast: love for a secular mistress in the French text; love for the Virgin in the Latin. The next step might be to interpret that contrast as an 'opposition', a term sometimes used as a synonym of 'contrast' in modern critical parlance[94] and favoured because it suggests some deconstructive potential within the text. Next, one might illustrate the 'opposition' between sacred and profane love by arguing that the secular mistress in the

---

[94] As in Brownlee, 'Machaut's Motet 15'.

French poem is almost parodying the intercessive role of the Virgin when she says to her lover: 'Be happy, the cure for these torments lies with me'; in that way she becomes like the Virgin in the Latin poem, 'a remedy for wounds'. Another kind of opposition might be sought in the way the secular lady receives the prayers of the lover, ultimately a plea for sexual compliance (*si vous* PRI *de cuer desirrant*), while the Virgin passes on the devout man's prayers to God (*tuis* PRECIBUS). Just as the French poet's lady is 'sweeter than all else' (*plus que riens doucete*), Mary is a virgin 'exceeding all others' (*pre ceteris*). Might there even be a parodic relationship between the words that begin the two poems: 'He!' and 'O'?

In the current critical climate some literary historians and musicologists would probably endorse this kind of analysis as a way of approaching the combinative *design* of motet poetry. The analysis is therefore both authoritative and meaningless in this case—a worrying state of affairs—because there is no design in the relationship between our two poems; it is entirely fortuitous and reminds us that any set of medieval lyric poems, whether concerned with sacred love or profane love, will display a measure of contrast and agreement in matters of theme and diction. And yet if any interpretative enterprise is to be valid, it is essential that we should be able to distinguish what is probably adventitious from what is probably not—unless we wish to endorse the kind of pluralism in which valid interpretation embraces everything that attention can register and ingenuity can conceive.

IV

Let us establish some bearings. Many of the earlier motets comprise a single, texted line over a plainchant tenor; unless there is some manner of relationship between the text and the tenor cue (as there evidently is in some Latin two-part motets, a relic of their liturgical or paraliturgical function, and as there appears to be in a few French motets),[95] then the question of 'intertextual' relations within the motet does not arise. A large number of motets in the surviving corpus therefore offered the listener an accompanied song comprising a set of rhyming lines, more or less regularized in their syllable count according to the phrase-lengths of the music, and variously overlapping or

---

[95] See Stakel and Relihan in Tischler, *The Montpellier Codex*, nos. 184, 189, *et passim*.

Ex. 11. The two-part motet *Chanter m'estuet/MEA*. Adapted from Tischler, *The Earliest Motets*, no. 166

coinciding with the phrases of the tenor (Ex. 11).[96] To some extent, perhaps, the subtlety of these two-part motets can no longer be savoured; they gratified a new taste for mensuralized song that was developing rapidly in the thirteenth century.[97] The metric and phonic aspects of these motets were probably very conspicuous to thirteenth-century listeners: the sound of the rhymes articulating the poetic lines and the musical phrases simultaneously, for example, and the fluid syllable count of the verse; we remember that Johannes de Grocheio's term for a poem in a motet is a 'distinct set of syllables' (*discretio syllabarum*), a purely formal conception.[98]

It cannot be emphasized too strongly that the poetry used in the great majority of motets is just what we find in Ex. 11: a version (sometimes, indeed, a very scrupulous version) of the courtly and light courtly manner of the trouvères. In recent years, scholarly interest has tended to drift away from such poetry, often regarded as 'trite and drab',[99] and has moved towards the motets whose texts combine different kinds of poetry, mix different registers, or present texts that are somehow interactive, 'intertextual', or dramatic. Motets that have attracted attention include those which combine secular French love-songs with Marian or other religious lyrics in Latin, those which mix different genres and registers (the High Style love-song and the pastourelle, for example), and those whose texts contain contrasting (or 'opposed') presentations of the same or similar themes.[100] It is noteworthy that some of the motets which have been mentioned in recent studies for their dramatic or intertextual qualities belong to the earlier layers of the motet repertoire, being relatively remote in time from Johannes de Grocheio, and that a significant number of them are triple motets appearing in a single fascicle of the old corpus of the Montpellier manuscript (fascicle 2); browsing through that source, one notices the distinctiveness of these dramatic or strikingly intertextual motets within the motet corpus as a whole.

This is not to deny that the principle of contrast operates in the poetry of motets. The poets who wrote for double motets sometimes chose to offset their version of High Style love rhetoric with a poem

---

[96] Compare Sanders, 'The Medieval Motet', 533.
[97] As convincingly argued by Stevens, *Words and Music*, 413–504.
[98] Rohloff, *Die Quellenhandschriften*, 144.
[99] Stakel and Relihan, in Tischler, *The Montpellier Codex*, p. xvi.
[100] See especially Huot, 'Polyphonic Poetry', and Evans, 'Music, Text and Social Context'.

having a lighter tone. Indeed, this contrast is sometimes abrupt (as when a poem in the style of the *grand chant courtois* is twinned with one having elements of the pastourelle, perhaps even with a touch of that genre's intermittent obscenity). However, it has yet to be demonstrated, I suggest, that this contrast has the destabilizing quality that much modern criticism tends to discern and explore:[101]

Triplum	Puisqu'en amer loiaument me sui mis,
	Je chanterai, car talent
	M'en est pris joliement,
	De la bele, qui tant a cler le vis,
	Pour cui amour je soupire souvent,
	Quant je remir son cors gent a devis
	Et sa valour, qui tout mon cuer esprent,
	Que pour li morrai, se de moi pité ne li prent.

Because I have set myself on loving loyally, I will sing. For an agreeable desire has taken hold of me for the fair one who has such a bright face. I sigh often for love of her when I remember the perfect beauty and the worth which have enflamed my entire heart. And for her I'll die, if she does not take pity on me.

Motetus	Quant li jolis tans doit entrer
	Que l'aloete chante cler,
	Adonc m'en alai jouer
	Par delés un vert aunoi.
	Robins i faisoit son dasnoi
	Sans anoi;
	Si grant deduit piech'a n'oi
	Que par son flajoler:
	Le devroit Marote amer.

At the beginning of the joyous season, when the lark sings out clearly, I went out to amuse myself beside a green thatch of alder trees. Robin was there, blissfully lost in his day-dreams. I have not for a long time heard a joy as great as that which came from his flute: Marote should love him.

These two poems present a number of obvious and deliberate contrasts. The Triplum expresses the characteristically hyperbolized sensibility of the *grand chant courtois* and avoids any suggestion of narrative; the Motetus, after a brisk seasonal opening, evokes a light-hearted speaker (*m'en alai jouer*) who hears Robin playing his flute. There may well be a sexual innuendo in the final lines ('I have not for

[101] Stakel and Relihan, in Tischler, *The Montpellier Codex*, no. 336.

a long time heard a joy as great as that which came from his flute: Marote should love him'); how does this relate to the austere rhetoric of the Triplum? It would be easy to over-interpret these contrasts. The two poems present two ways of thinking about the tone of loving: one ardent and conscious of the dignity which strong emotion can confer, the other light and insouciant. As I read them there is variation and contrast, but there is neither conflict nor tension.

In many other motets the contrast between the texts is delicate and assumes a listener who has developed the kind of ear for Old French lyric that many individuals must have possessed in the thirteenth century: the clerics who enjoyed *chans de karoles* and pastourelles as well as songs in a higher style;[102] the middle-class merchants and officials who swelled the numbers of the municipal *puis*. There are indeed subtleties here, for such contrasts require the listener to register whether a poem shows a tendency to thin (and thus lighten) its texture with oaths and asseverations (*hé Dieus . . . biaus sire Dieus . . . se Dieus me gart*); whether it sustains a topos of High Style verse (such as the 'seasonal opening') and if so, with what degree of fidelity to the diction and expansive syntax of the trouvères' grand manner; whether the poet offers serious reflections on the nature of love; whether the lady is respectfully addressed as *dame*; whether the syllable count inclines towards the discipline of the *grand chant courtois*, and so on. Generally, however, the poets who wrote for the French motets set out to produce two love-songs of a similar kind with little variation in tone or diction, and it is in that way, more than any other, that the poems of motets are integrated:[103]

> *Triplum*   Cil s'entremet de folie,
> Qui contre amors veut parler;
> Car honor et cortoisie
> Aprent on d'amer . . .

He enters into foolishness who wishes to speak against love, for one learns honour and courtesy from loving . . .

> *Motetus*   Nus hom ne porroit savoir,
> Que c'est d'amer par amours,
> Car teus se paine en espoir,
> Qu'avoir en puet les douçors . . .

---

[102] On the clerical interest in *chans de karoles* see Stevens, *Words and Music*, 178–86.
[103] Stakel and Relihan, in Tischler, *The Montpellier Codex*, no. 174.

No man could know what it is to love truly, for he suffers in the hope that he can have some of love's sweetness.

There is every reason to expect that Johannes de Grocheio and his contemporaries would have admired poetry of this kind and might well have spoken of it as *subtilis*. It was expected of a trouvère that he should show his wisdom in matters of the heart by making such pronouncements as these in language both elevated and pleasing. These extracts offer that kind of rhetoric with diction of an appropriately high register (*cortoisie, espoir, doucours*) and uncontaminated by the high-front vowel rhymes used in so much of the lighter motet verse (*ami/pri/mari/ami/li* and so on). As a result, *Cil s'entremet de folie* and *Nus hom ne porroit savoir* offer a passable imitation of the trouvères' High Style manner within the constraints of motet idiom where the non-strophic structure of the verse, and the essentially opportunistic nature of the line-lengths, slackens the metrical discipline of the High Style chanson. However, the purpose of pairing these two poems in this motet seems relatively straightforward: it is to double (which is admirable and skilful enough) what is offered by the poetry of two-part, single-text motets such as this (for the music see Ex. 11):[104]

> *Motetus* Chanter m'estuet sans delai
> Pour le tens qui me semont.
> Amors m'ont mis en esmai,
> Qui si m'ont navré parfont,
> Que morir cuit . . .

I must sing without delay on account of the season which urges me to do so. Love has dismayed me; it has wounded me so deeply that I expect to die . . .

> *Tenor* MEA

This kind of verse is so very common in motets that any departures from it are conspicuous. Poems about the corruption of the times, the good life of Paris, or the failings and trials of the religious orders, unusual openings ('The goat will scratch so much . . .'), or highly individual strategies (as when the poem of one motet parodies an official letter)[105] have attracted much attention, and must have caused comment when first heard, but that is precisely because they are relatively rare.

---

[104] Stakel and Relihan, in Tischler, *The Montpellier Codex*, no. 244.
[105] Ibid., no. 334 (Triplum).

V

One manner of appreciating the verbal *subtilitas* of motets may be founded upon the nature of the experience which these pieces offer in performance. For this purpose, recourse to a score of any motet at the very least is vital: the danger of studying the poetry of such pieces in isolation from their music (tempting though that may be to a literary scholar who finds them obligingly printed in that way, complete with translations, in numerous recent editions) is that the essence of the motet experience is thereby missed. The polytextual motet gave composers a chance to relate the simultaneous declamation of two or even three poems with mathematical precision. As far as the poetry is concerned, a principal subtlety of motets may therefore be sought in the *timing* of the texts,[106] this being one of several ways in which the motet explores the idea of duration. In this respect the motet invited a special kind of listening.

Let us momentarily consider a comparison with the polyphonic conductus. A conductus uses only one text; if the listener wishes to understand every element of (at least) its literal sense during performance, then he must construe the Latin, tracing grammatical relationships that will often traverse the boundaries of the poetic lines; like the outlines of a majuscule letter amidst a mass of foliate penwork, these grammatical relationships must be identified within a competing design: the metrical form and the rhyme. That identification will not usually pose an insuperable difficulty to an experienced listener who is also a fluent Latinist aiming for the literal sense in the first instance, but the case is perhaps slightly different when the Latin text is sung to a polyphonic setting in as many as four parts (but generally in two or three). The musical material of such conductus often falls into four-beat phrases, following the accentual rhythm of the poetry, and in performance the music is therefore shaped in a highly assertive fashion which commands the ear's attention but which is often indifferent to the distances between adjective and noun, subject and verb, which the mind must traverse to arrive at the literal meaning. The following stanza from the two-part conductus *Redit etas aurea*, possibly composed for the coronation of Richard I in 1189, will illustrate the point. The text is here laid out according to its

---

[106] I am grateful to Dr Ardis Butterfield of Downing College, Cambridge, for discussing this matter with me.

metrical form and punctuated according to modern conventions; the four-beat musical phrases are separated by incise-marks in both voices of the original notation (represented here by /).[107] The musico-poetic form does not point the sense for the most part, as may be seen from the way it disregards the enjambment at the lines marked with an asterisk. (This enjambment is scrupulously marked by the text scribe):

Pius, potens, humilis,/
Dives et maturus/
* Etate, sed docilis/
Et rerum securus/
* Suarum, preficitur/
* Anglie, daturus/
Rapinis interitum,/   MS: rapinis/interitum/
Clero iuris aditum,/
Locum veritati./

God-fearing, powerful, humble, great, and mature in years yet sweet in tem-per and firm in all his dealings, he is set in command over England, being about to make an end of plunder, a clear path to justice for the clergy, and a place for truth.

The vernacular motet presented a different case. There were no problems in construing the language because the texts were written in the native tongue. The syntax of vernacular motet poetry was usually less elaborate than that of the Latin verse written for conductus; fur-thermore, it was usually related to the phrase-structure of the melodic line. Compare, for example, the musico-poetic structure of the fol-lowing lines with the stanza from *Redit etas aurea* quoted above. Once again the oblique strokes represent the end of a melodic phrase:[108]

Dieus! tant mi plaist a remirer/
Son cors gent et sa face coulouree/
Que je ne la puis oublier nuit ne jour/
Mais sans sejour/
Me convient a li penser/

---

[107] *F*, fos. 318ᵛ–319ʳ. The piece is recorded, using phrasing to respect the enjambment, on *Music for the Lion-Hearted King* (Hyperion, CDA66336), track 7, for which the text given here was prepared using *F* and *W1*, fo. 101ᵛ.

[108] From the Motetus of *Je ne chant pas/Talens m'est pris/APTATUR/OMNES*, edited in Ander-son, *Compositions of the Bamberg Manuscript*, no. 92. The piece is recorded on *The Marriage of Heaven and Hell* (Hyperion CDA66423), track 1.

God! how it pleases me to look upon her fine body and her rich complexion so that I can never forget her night or day but must think of her without respite.

The special challenge issued by a polytextual motet obviously arose, in large measure, from its polytextuality, but that statement (which will surprise nobody) may need a certain amount of qualification. No doubt it would be unwise for any modern scholar to rule, on the basis of modern performance or of intuition, that thirteenth-century listeners cannot have understood two independent and simultaneous texts in a double motet; the proposal that polytextual motets challenged the listener to achieve such a 'double' understanding must therefore be allowed to stand.[109] However, it remains unknown what contemporaries took to be an adequate understanding of polytextual motet poetry. As I have emphasized above, many motets have very similar texts and are so obedient to the conventions of such poetry that a perceived moment of one text and then of another during performance will often be enough to allow the experienced listener to 'place' the verse that he is hearing; it is unknown whether Grocheio's clerics and 'those seeking for refinements in the arts' would generally have pressed understanding any further (although it is possible to imagine how motets with amorous texts could have inspired the discussions about love that appear to have fascinated so many during the later Middle Ages).[110] The existence of triple motets with three simultaneous poems that sometimes deal with different subjects in two languages, French and Latin, proves that the aesthetic of the motet is one which allows verbal communication to decline as metrical, musical, and structural ambitions mount. This was surely not taken to involve a sacrifice of meaning but rather a gain of pleasure that was 'intellectual' in this sense: it produced the exhilaration of *knowing* that a piece contains more than one can ever hope to hear. It might also be maintained, as a general observation, that word-bearing

---

[109] Leech-Wilkinson, 'Ars Antiqua–Ars Nova–Ars Subtilior', 219: '. . . while it is tempting to assume that comprehension was not an ideal for the medieval composer, it seems probable, in view of the motet's status as the most complex of thirteenth- and fourteenth-century musical forms, that striving to follow both texts simultaneously–like following the repetitions of rhythms and phrase-patterns–was part of the intellectual challenge offered by the motet'.

[110] See especially Kelly, 'Medieval Imagination', 20 (discussing the presentation of love in romances and commentaries): 'All these examples and scores of others like them bear witness to the vigor, the variety, and the anguish of thought on courtly love during the four centuries when it was of literary and social concern.'

melody has the power, through its purely musical logic and pattern, to busy the mind in a way that cancels some of the attention and vigilance that is normally brought to language when it is read on the page or heard.[111] If this is true, then words in songs cannot normally possess the same status in terms of meaning as words out of songs.

Viewed in this light, the potential for *subtilitas* in timing two or three poems together is not so much a question of meaning as of musical and verbal pattern. Some of these patterns may require no other explanation than that they are designed to arrest the natural volatility of attention, vital in the performance of a genre which relies upon the listener's willingness to take a close and vigilant interest in the material. When two or three texts are timed together in a motet these patterns are often created by cross-references that require special vigilance from any listener who wishes to discern them. The double motet *En non Dieu/Quant voi la rose/NOBIS* (from which I have already taken an excerpt in Ex. 10) provides a striking example of a simultaneous cross-reference in both music and poetry which demonstrates the motet composers' demand for attention. This motet features a kind of voice exchange in which the Motetus and Triplum end the composition by exchanging the musical and verbal material with which they began (Ex. 12). It is possible that this effect was intended for the delectation of the performers and not of the audience (whose existence, let us remember, is plainly mentioned by Johannes de Grocheio; this is not exclusively performers' music). If, however, such effects were also designed for attentive listeners, then they would have been lost upon any who had not cultivated a musical memory. The same might be said of the motets which introduce passages of musical imitation at a distance; the relative brevity of many motets, when compared, for example, with the strophic conductus, may reflect a realistic assessment of the mind's ability to sustain such attention at the required level.

How do the motet composers time their various texts together? In many cases the techniques involved are simple and intermittently employed, the product of a momentary exertion of creative will towards that kind of coherence and involving no intertextual meaning (or indeed no meaning at all). Among the simplest instances are some

---

[111] Booth, *The Experience of Songs, passim.*

which help to demonstrate the role of an appeal to performance in this context:[112]

> QUI la voudroit lonc tens . . .
> QUI d'amours veut bien joir . . .
> QUI longuement pourroit joir d'amors . . .
> NOSTRUM

On paper, the way in which these three lines begin with the same word may appear to be a subtlety of a fairly low order, and yet this is a technique whose effect in performance can be striking to anyone who has acquired an ear for the characteristic sounds of the motet genre. To synchronize vowels at the beginning of a motet is to make a conspicuous gesture in a polytextual form where, in contrast to a conductus, the listener may hear three different vowels at any moment or even four if the tenor is vocalized. Sometimes, indeed, this synchronization of vowels (which counts for more in the aural effect than the homophony of the consonants) involves the tenor and suggests a vocal performance of the tenor cue:[113]

> MORS a primi patris vicio . . .
> MORS, que stimulo . . .
> MORS, morsu nata venato . . .
> MORS

This example raises questions about vernacular motets such as the following, where any discrepancy between the pronunciation of the first syllable of 'Mulierum' [my] and the vernacular adverb 'mout' [mut] may not weaken the argument that here the tenor cue is also to be sung, producing a synchronization of vowels in all three parts of a double motet:[114]

> MOUT souvent m'ont demandé plusours . . .
> MOUT ai esté en dolour . . .
> MU-lierum

In performance, verbal identity at the beginning of a motet text (leaving the tenor out of the reckoning) almost invariably appears on a

---

[112] Anderson, *Motets of the Manuscript La Clayette*, no. 24. Compare Nathan, 'The Function of Text'.

[113] Anderson, *Motets of the Manuscript La Clayette*, no. 11.

[114] Ibid., no. 34. The piece is recorded on *The Marriage of Heaven and Hell* (Hyperion CDA66423), track 11.

Ex. 12. The three-part motet *En non Dieu/Quant voi la rose/NOBIS*.
Adapted from Anderson, *Compositions of the Bamberg Manuscript*, 112

doi as-sés pe - ner Et cha-pel de flours por - ter   Pour si

et a-mi - e Et ser-vir et hon - our-rer,   Qui   en   joi - e

bele   a - mi - e, Quant voi la rose es - pa - ni - e,

vuelt du - rer;   En non Dieu, que que   nus   die, Au

L'er - be vert et   le   tens cler.

cuer   mi tient li maus   d'a - mer.

perfect consonance; if sung in tune and with a careful match of vowels between the upper voices (which makes precise tuning easier to
achieve), such synchronization can produce a sonority of exceptional
clarity and forthrightness within the sound-spectrum of the motet
because the lowest (and therefore the most conspicuous) harmonics of
the notes in the chord will be in tune, producing a distinctive resonance and an accentuation which is perhaps what this technique of
textual timing is principally designed to achieve.

Other techniques for timing texts in the motet involve simple repetition, sometimes involving as little as a word, sometimes a whole

phrase, and placed in such a way that the effect cannot be fortu-itous:[115]

> *Triplum*   Mout a BIAUTE ce m'est vis / ses CORS est
> *Motetus*   BIAUTE, bonte, et CORS gent de bel atour . . .

In these two voices the repetitions, confined to individual words, appear in a sufficently small space, and in a sufficiently coherent series (the Motetus always enters first) that the attentive ear will not mistake them. They are so brief that an experienced listener will grasp them in phonic terms and intuitively 'read' them as an actualiz-ation of the common poetic tradition upon which both poems draw. Such effects as these may often sound less conspicuous than they appear to the eye in a modern printed text or musical score, and an experience of such moments in performance provides a sense of pro-portion in judging them. They yield only to the most careful aural attention, however bold they may seem to the eye; they do not usually strike a note of wit nor indeed of word-play; they convey the pleasure of pattern—an inner consistency simply for the sake of having design rather than no design. The relationships in the lines quote above have no semantic import apart from the simple emphasis that may arise from repeating words such as *biauté* and *cors* in what is after all love poetry; indeed, there are many instances where such patterns seem to achieve no semantic intensification:[116]

> *Triplum*   QUANT ele m'a en despit/QUIT TANT me fait . . .
> *Motetus*   QUANT qu'a ma dame plera/QUIT TANT a de . . .

A more sustained example of *subtilitas* in the timing of motet texts is revealed by Ex. 13, a compendium of the ways in which a motet poet and composer could repay a listener's concentration. The motet begins with the two texts timed together in a remarkable (but by no means unparalleled) way. They agree in syllable count and (for the most part) rhyme, and are declaimed in a synchronized fashion. They continue in this way until bar 15. Here, as so often in the polytextual motets, it is a *refrain* (or the approach of one) that precipitates a change in the com-positional procedure. The *refrain* enters in the Triplum at bar 18 and the two voices fall out of synchronization. With a masterly touch, the composer does not bring them together immediately, but sets their

---

[115] Anderson, *Motets of the Manuscript La Clayette*, no. 11, bars 8–10.
[116] Ibid., no. 16, bars 6–8.

Ex. 13. The three-part motet *L'autrier/Demenant grant joie/MANERE*. Adapted from Anderson, *Motets of the Manuscript La Clayette*, 6–7. Here transposed down a fifth from the pitch implied by Anderson's transcription

Ex. 13. *cont.*

rhymes in sequence again without making them simultaneous (bars
22–4). By bar 25 the two voices are back together, agreeing in their
rhymes, their syllable count, and in the length of their melodic
phrases. At bar 40 they coalesce with the same word, 'Marot', and
they close sharing the same *words*. Within this remarkably wrought
structure there are numerous fleeting verbal correspondences, all of
which, in a motet possessing this degree of design, have the status of
considered rather than accidental effects:

Triplum	je t'en tieng por sot
Motetus	Qu'en m'en tient por sot
Triplum	souvent regretot
Motetus	Souvent regretot
Triplum	Quant ele ot / La chevrie
Motetus	Econtree la chevrie

These relationships are complemented by a wealth of cross-references
in the music (compare Motetus bars 3, 9, 15, 21, and 33; Triplum bars
18-19; Motetus bars 38–9 and 41–2), enhanced by a striking variety of
texture that moves in and out of note-against-note movement.

This remarkable motet gives some idea of the kinds of detail which thirteenth-century listeners may have regarded as contributing to the subtlety of motets. However, there is one kind of art which it does not attempt: a subtlety of intertextual meaning. The complexity is purely phonic and is not semantic. As I read them, the texts of this motet are designed to be so similar to one another that there is little or no contrast between them.

There is clearly much scope for research in this area, but there is a risk that we may overlook some simple answers to the question of where Grocheio's clerics discerned the subtlety of motets. To enjoy motets in the thirteenth century was surely to develop an ear for them and to indulge a taste for pleasures that are perhaps obvious (and that can be shared by a modern listener): I mean the sense of sheer diversity as the ear catches a moment of one text in the rush of vowel colours and then a moment of another; the impression of lilt as the melodic phrases overlap, so unlike the more regimented declamation of the conductus; the heightened sense of counterpoint as each melodic line is characterized by the sound of its own text; the constant alternation between perfect consonances and pungent dissonances, which even those innocent of theory can learn to relish once taught to do so. To these we might add other pleasures which the modern listener cannot so readily share without sustained exposure to the sound of the music and some knowledge, perhaps, of all thirteenth-century music: a delight in strictly measured melody, for example, or a pleasure in sonorities which are quite exotic in the contexts of thirteenth-century harmony (Ex. 14). To declare that the musicians of Grocheio's lifetime possessed a predominantly aural experience of motets, as we surely may, is not to deny the sophisticated literacy of those musicians, nor is it to suggest that they were indifferent to the visual rhetoric of the manuscript pages from which they sang; it is merely to acknowledge that thirteenth-century musicians heard motets much more often than they examined them, which is exactly the reverse of most modern scholars' experience, and that the *subtilitas* of motets must therefore have lain in large measure with the way the pieces sounded.

Our conclusion about the 'audience' for the Ars antiqua motet flows into what has become a very powerful current in medieval studies. In recent years, scholars in many fields have begun to ask, and with increasing insistence, whether dichotomies such as urban/rural, élite/popular and literate/non-literate, once the mainstay of medieval

Ex. 14. The closing bars of the four-part motet *De la virge/Quant froidure/Agmina milicie/AGMINA* (text omitted). Adapted from Anderson, *Motets of the Manuscript La Clayette*, 30

research, should be allowed to shape our image of the Middle Ages.[117] The motets that circulated in Paris were enjoyed in an urban context, and at no time in the later Middle Ages were towns and cities free from contact with those who spent most of their time in manors, castles, and fields. Many figures in trade and town government moved between urban and rural environments without ceasing. The constitution of an audience for an Ars antiqua motet can never have been simple or 'pure'; in the 1990s, a time when musicologists are increasingly disposed to stress what they suppose to have been the highly élitist quality of the medieval motet, it is worth remembering that, if the arguments of the last two chapters have any validity, then Johannes de Grocheio's 'clergy, and those who care for the refinements of any skill' may have formed a very diversified group indeed.

---

[117] For an outstanding essay in this field see Rubin, 'Religious Culture in Town and Country'.

4

Ars Nova and Algorism

I

IN his *Notitia artis musice* of 1321, Johannes de Muris reveals that measured notation had become a subject of lively interest. Duple mensuration, the new rules for imperfection, and the device of coloration (whereby, in common practice, a coloured note loses one-third of its value) now offered scope for keen enthusiasms and disagreements. These innovations were so significant that Johannes, pondering them at the close of his treatise, found himself reflecting upon the restless and ultimately futile motion of all human thought. 'Opinions and *scientiae revolutiones* race onwards', he declares, 'and come round in a circle . . .'.[1]

That is an intriguing remark. Its general drift is plain but there is a special resonance to the words *scientiae revolutiones*. We notice it because some scholars have related the emergence of the Ars nova to currents in intellectual life that affected other disciplines in the fourteenth century. Max Haas, for example, has associated the momentum of the Ars nova with some abstruse contemporary learning in other fields, including speculative grammar.[2] More recently, Dorit Tanay has suggested that the notational theory of the French Ars nova owes something to speculative thinking in logic, theology, and mathematics, subjects which did experience something of a *scientiae revolutio* in the thirteenth and fourteenth centuries.[3]

In some respects, this is an enticing view. The motets of *Le Roman de Fauvel* suggest that the innovations of the Ars nova were produced, in large measure, by a sheer pressure of musical imagination

---

[1] *Notitia artis musice*, ed. Michels, 107. The full passage runs: 'Currunt enim opiniones et scientiae revolutiones ad circulum revertentes, quamdiu summae placuerit voluntati Eius, qui non necessitatus omnia condidit in hoc mundo et omnia voluntarie segregabit.'

[2] Haas, 'Studien zur mittelalterlichen Musikelehre I'.

[3] Tanay, 'Music in the Age of Ockham'. Compare Werner, 'Mathematical Foundation'.

brought to bear upon the motets of the later Ars antiqua.[4] However, there is also scope for regarding those developments as the result of an intellectual interest in measured notation *per se*. The new music, and the means of recording it, seem to have been fostered in Paris, the centre of theological study and logic; they flourished at a time when exploratory work was being done in mathematics, geometry, and astronomy. What could be more natural than that these intellectual currents flowed in music also, inspiring musicians to redefine the first principles of mensural notation and to extend its resources (Pl. 8)?[5]

Then there are the leading figures of the Ars nova to consider. What is known of them heightens our sense that their art was essentially rational and even 'scientific' in impulse. Johannes de Muris provides a case in point. A recent discovery, an anonymous *Opusculum artis musice* copied in the fifteenth century and apparently the work of an Italian author (Pl. 9), may strengthen the fragile evidence that Johannes composed polyphony, thus enhancing his musical studies, as he is known to have furthered his scientific interests, by experiment:

Musica mensuralis est illa que composita fuit et inventa a pluribus magistris, specialiter a magistro Johanne de Muris et magistro Guillelmo de Mascandio et hoc, ut dictum est, ut nomen dei honorificencius laudetur in cantis, videlicet figuratis, sicut est 'Gloria in excelsis deo' et 'Credo in unum deum', que ad ecclesiarum pertinent cultum. Adhuc musica mensuralis est que inventa fuit ad dilectacionem secularium prout patet in rondellis, in matricalibus et ballatinis.

Measured music is that which was composed and devised by numerous masters, especially by Master Johannes de Muris and Master Guillaume de Machaut, and this, as has been said, so that the name of God may be more honourably praised in vocal music, that is to say in polyphonic [vocal music], as is the case with Gloria in excelsis deo and Credo in unum deum, which pertain to the liturgy of churches. Further, measured music is that which was invented to delight secular persons, as may be seen in rondeaux, madrigals, and ballatas.

---

[4] For the most recent discussion of notational and stylistic developments in the early period of the Ars nova, see *Roman de Fauvel*, ed. Roesner *et al.*, *passim*.

[5] In considering this possibility, however, it is well to remember the remarks of a distinguished historian of science, that 'in the medieval period it was normally external practical demand rather than an internal feeling of intellectual need that led to the development and use of procedures and instruments for obtaining accurate and consistent measurements . . .' (Crombie, *Science, Optics and Music*, 86).

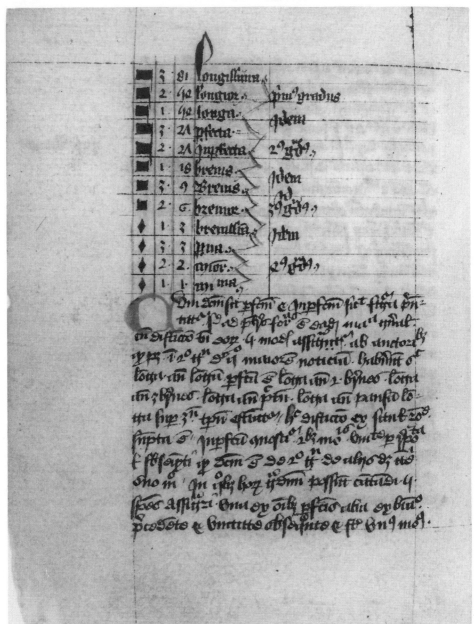

Pl. 8. Table of note-forms and their values, from the *Notitia artis musice* of Johannes de Muris. Cambridge, Trinity College, R.14.26, fo. 113ᵛ. Reproduced by permission

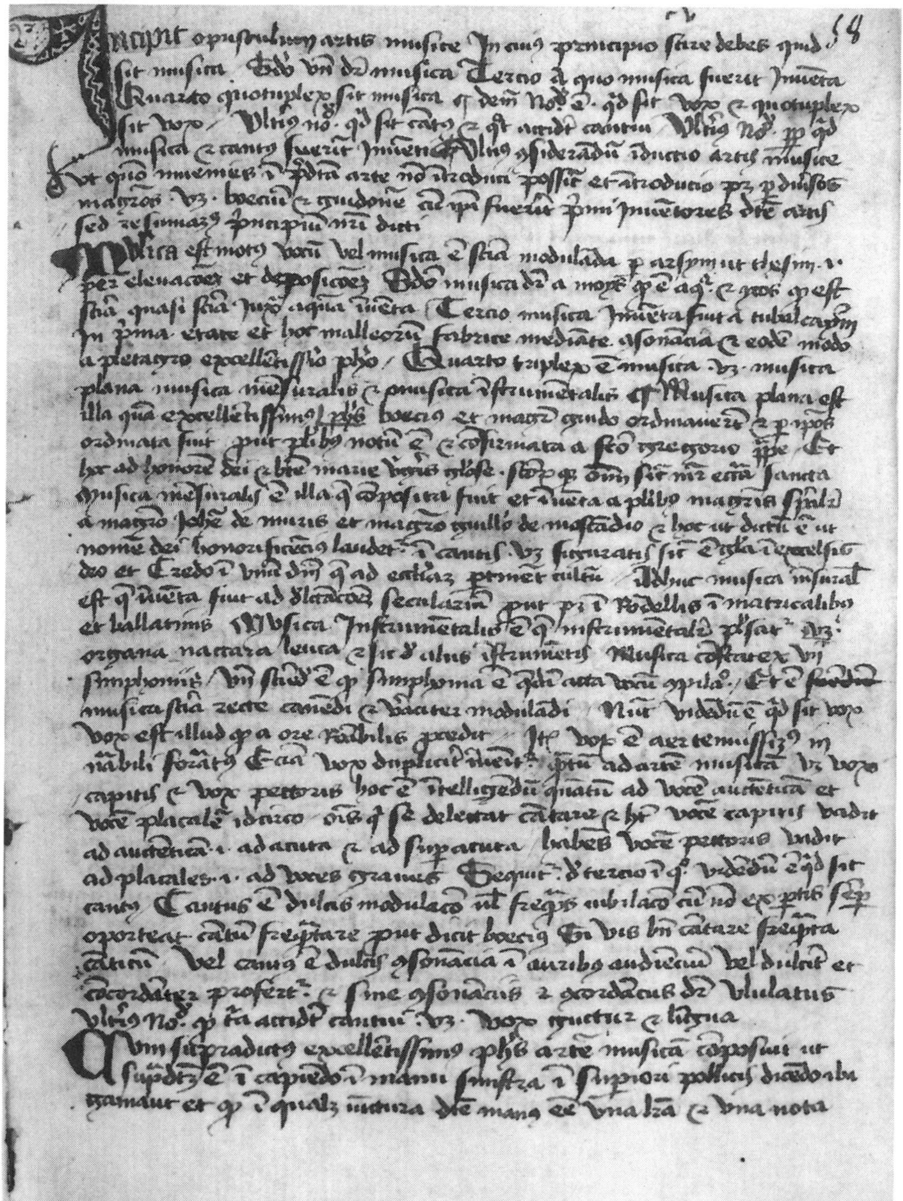

Pl. 9. The opening sections of an anonymous *Opusculum artis musice*. Troyes, Bibliothèque municipale, MS 1877, fo. 58ʳ. The reference to Johannes de Muris and to Guillaume de Machaut appears just above the middle of the folio. Reproduced by permission

The evidence of this passage is not decisive, but if Johannes did compose then we have in him an Ars nova composer who was also a kind of early modern scientist. Indeed, Guy Beaujouan has called him 'un véritable chercheur scientifique'.[6] On 14 May 1333 Johannes was at Évreux to witness a solar eclipse that he predicted for 2 hours and 37 minutes after the passage of the sun over the meridian of Paris.[7] To foresee this eclipse he would have consulted the Alfonsine or Toledan tables, translated from the Arabic by Gerard of Cremona a century earlier;[8] he certainly used an astrolabe, a miraculous manifestation of Islamic cosmography.[9]

I have proposed elsewhere that medieval musicians approached the art of polyphony 'with an enthralled but objective curiosity as a contemporary astronomer might contemplate the workings of his astrolabe',[10] and the lines of interest that could lead a fourteenth-century scholar from astronomy to Ars nova notation and back again are plain. The movement of musical sound through time, like the apparent movement of stars in the celestial sphere, required similar skills from any scholar eager to investigate them, including a fluent numeracy and familiarity with a system of measurement descending to an indivisible, minimum unit. For astronomers this unit was the *atomus*; for musicians, at least in the earlier fourteenth century, it was the *minima*. At first glance, a list of the new notational symbols, arranged according to their value with the aid of arabic numerals (Pl. 8), recalls the appearance of the tables that Johannes may have used to predict the solar eclipse of 14 May 1333.

All this may seem convincing in its way, but this chapter is motivated by a belief that we are in danger of accepting a hyperbolized

---

[6] Beaujouan, *Par raison des nombres*, VII. 30. (This volume of photographically reproduced essays from previous publications by Beaujouan has a discontinuous pagination and is cited in what follows according to (i) the roman numerals assigned to each essay in the reprint and (ii) the relevant page, a legacy from the original printing). It was Beaujouan who, in 1962, discovered the Escorial manuscript of astronomical and astrological material annotated by Johannes de Muris. See L. Gushee, 'New Sources for the Biography of Johannes de Muris'.

[7] Beaujouan, *Par raison des nombres*, VII, *passim*.

[8] Edited in Toomer, 'A Survey of the Toledan Tables'. Beaujouan, *Par raison des nombres*, V, *passim*.

[9] Beaujouan, *Par raison des nombres*, VII. 29 'ita invenimus nos per experientiam altitudinem solis per astrolabium'. The literature on the astrolabe is vast. The outstanding introduction to the instrument itself is North, 'The Astrolabe'. There is much historical material in Beaujouan, *Par raison des nombres*, *passim*.

[10] Page, 'Polyphony before 1400', 79.

image of the Ars nova. Before turning to that theme, however, let us define a position to which most musicologists will readily (and in my view quite rightly) assent. The age of written polyphonic composition in Western Europe, from the organa of the twelfth century to the Ars nova, was one of remarkable progress in scientific knowledge.[11] It is well known that better texts, many of them translated from Arabic, did much to advance what studious clerics knew of astronomy, astrology, geometry, medicine, optics, and mathematics (to name no other subjects). This context of scientific advance gives extra weight to a recent description of the rhythmic modes as a 'discovery'.[12] Our sense that the 'Notre Dame school' stands apart from every previous polyphonic enterprise also rests upon a view of the later twelfth century—especially in Paris—as an age of Aristotelianism. This is the frame of reference for Jeremy Yudkin's chapter on the Ars antiqua, opening with a section on 'Paris: its University and Cathedral'.[13] It is also the context for Tanay's comparative study of fourteenth-century music and mathematics.

What kind of intellectual advance does the notation of French Ars nova music actually represent? It is axiomatic in the history of science that whenever a scale of measurement is extended, then intellectual horizons are also expanding, and the notational symbols shown in Pl. 8 undoubtedly require a greater intellectual effort from anyone who seeks to master them than the symbols of thirteenth-century music. As Seneca remarks, 'anything that is divided into minute grains becomes confused', and it is striking that some of the figures in Pl. 10 appear to be wrong. The concept of a longest note-value which contains the shortest value 81 times, operating within a system that uses duple as well as triple divisions, went far beyond anything envisaged in Franconian notation. This was especially true when such discrepancies of duration were fearlessly exploited between the tenor and the upper voices of Ars nova motets.

Modern editors and transcribers may be somewhat inclined to

---

[11] An outstanding conspectus of work in this huge field of study is now available in Beaujouan, *Par raison des nombres*, with abundant bibliography given there; Lindberg, *The Beginnings of Western Science*; and Crombie, *Science, Optics and Music*.

[12] *The New Grove*, s.v. 'Rhythm'.

[13] *Music in Medieval Europe*, 357–62. For a recent survey of the 'new' Aristotelianism in Paris see Maccagnolo, 'David of Dinant'. Beaujouan, *Par raison des nombres*, V. 519, deals excellently (and succinctly) with some of the conflicts between the 'new' Aristotelianism and Christian doctrine.

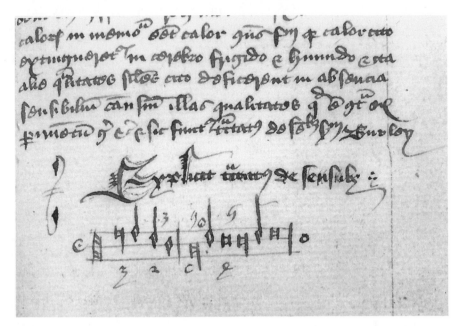

Pl. 10. Note-forms and mensuration signs with arabic numerals indicating values. The actual sequence of note-values relates to a cipher, given elsewhere in the manuscript, spelling the message 'quod Tomson'. Cambridge, Trinity College, R.14.26, fo. 37ʳ. Reproduced by permission

forget that this notation seems both abstruse and puzzling to a beginner who is inevitably trying to conceptualize it in terms of the modern notation used for transcription. To the novice, 'each long equals three bars of 9/8' is a most confusing way of saying that 'each perfect long equals three perfect breves'. It can also be said, however, that French Ars nova notation presented literate minds of the fourteenth century with an unfamiliar challenge. This was the task of becoming completely familiar with symbols that related to a numerical system comprising no less than 81 units and whose members could assume different numerical identities according to whether they were triple (perfect) or duple (imperfect).

No doubt this notation sometimes presented considerable difficulties to men whose education was overwhelmingly 'literary' in the broadest sense of the word, based upon grammar, dialectic, and rhetoric. If we are inclined to underestimate those difficulties today it is because most people in Western society have received a training in basic numeracy: the multiplication tables up to twelve are learnt by every schoolchild rather than by Exchequer clerks alone,[14] and countless technologies rely upon mathematical expertise, both practical and theoretical.

Let us not overestimate those difficulties, however. If we are looking for sources of the Ars nova impulse in contemporary thought and intellectual life, then one of the things we seek is an enhancement of the prevailing arithmetical mentality. This is not the same as a renewal of interest in the abstract or practical powers of number; an enhanced arithmeticism need not encompass any renewed interest in numerical matters at all. It must, however, include some sign that more and more clerics possessed the means to make and to notate fluent arithmetical calculations and to conceptualize the processes involved. In this chapter I shall tentatively suggest that we find such a sign in the later thirteenth century: the spread of an arithmetic using arabic numerals and a decimal system and a sign for zero. This is what fourteenth-century scholars called *algorism*. It seems to erupt into music theory at exactly the right time and place—in Paris *c*.1300—and was fully consolidated there by the 1320s.

II

Dorit Tanay's dissertation of 1989, Music in the Age of Ockham: The Interrelations Between Music, Mathematics and Philosophy in the Fourteenth Century', is a learned attempt to clarify the intellectual dimension of the Ars nova in France. Tanay's principal subject is the notational system of fourteenth-century French music and the language which theorists such as Johannes de Muris employ to explain it. 'Music in the Age of Ockham' is an original and demanding work whose ideas are not easily paraphrased; perhaps they should not be

[14] From the 12th c. there is clear evidence in the writings of the music theorist Frutolf that multiplication tables were considered an aid for players of the advanced arithmetical game called Rithmomachia. See the text and tables in Peiper, 'Fortolfi Rhythmimachia', 178–9. This game was closely allied to the underlying mathematics of musical proportion and would seem to have offered some musicians an extra field of activity for their mathematical interests. Beaujouan, *Par raison des nombres*, I. 650, goes so far as to call it a game which prepared its players for the study of music theory. Regular users of the abacus would memorize these multiplication tables, since the abacus was used 'principally for placing and holding, so that the calculator can see where he is and not lose trace of his sum' (Evans, 'A Note on the *Regule Abaci*', 34).

so, except in the detailed study which they deserve and will undoubtedly receive one day. However, it is already apparent that Tanay's argument, and consequently her image of the Ars antiqua and Ars nova, raises certain questions which can be considered at this early stage in the reception of her work.

For Tanay, the later-thirteenth century is overwhelmingly Aristotelian and Thomist. It is 'a turning-point in the intellectual history of Western Europe' that happened 'in the wake of the rise of the universities and the reception of Aristotle'.[15] On the simplest level, Tanay's argument is that the theorists of the Ars antiqua and the Ars nova often speak of measured notation in a way that betrays their acquaintance with Aristotelian methods of classification and explanation. However, she goes much further and proposes that the *content* of what the theorists say is dominated by Aristotelian principles of thought.[16] This is a vital distinction. Most modern readers of Ars nova theory will accept that French notation of the fourteenth century stands at an intersection of musical imagination and mental ingenuity; they will also accept, I imagine, that by 1300 (and perhaps long before) the subject of mensural notation had acquired the power to fascinate many different kinds of person in many different ways, not all of them bearing upon performance or upon the aesthetic experience of music. In part, this was because measured notation, comprising a set of rationally ordered particulars with a numerical frame of reference, lent itself admirably to the kind of discursive rigour and taxonomic clarity that Aristotle bequeathed to virtually every learned enterprise of the thirteenth and fourteenth centuries. With theorists such as Johannes de Muris, this process of intellectual enrichment (if one chooses to regard it as such) could extend very far, and Tanay's study does much to illuminate it.

It is another matter, however, to propose that the innovations of French Ars nova notation express intellectual interests and even theological beliefs that can be detected in theoretical writings because those interests and beliefs moulded what pre-Ars nova musicians could conceptualize and therefore invent. If I have understood Tanay's chapters correctly, that is what she maintains, and we begin to understand why she leans so heavily upon a 'Thomistic' and 'scientific' fourteenth century whose musical theories 'reflect freedom of

[15] 'Music in the Age of Ockham', 5.   [16] Ibid. 14.

thought, open-mindedness, analytical temperament and, above all, a penchant for carrying each topic of investigation as far as possible'.[17] These are qualities that 'typify scientific thought during the age of Ockham'.[18]

We may agree at once with Tanay that a great deal of mensural theory produced during the thirteenth and fourteenth centuries is permeated by terms and concepts ultimately derived from Aristotle. It would be very surprising indeed if it were not. By the middle of the thirteenth century, a writer who wished to deal with a technical subject in a way that his contemporaries would deem to be rigorous and authoritative was almost required to use some indisputably Aristotelian concepts such as *species* and *genus*, 'subject', 'predicate', 'substance', 'essence', 'proper', and 'accident'. Most of these had been available for many centuries in the Boethian translations of Aristotle; some of them can be traced in plainchant theory as early as *c.*1200:[19]

Habita consideratione tonorum in eo quod omnes proprie terminantur in gravibus per accidens autem in acutis . . .

Having considered how the modes all 'properly' end among the *graves* and 'incidentally' among the *acute* . . .

Quite apart from the usefulness of such terminology to anyone seeking to clarify a technical subject, there was no better way to give an appearance of authority than to cite Aristotle, perhaps with the aid of a florilegium. A great deal of the Aristotelian complexion to be found in the music theorists can be regarded in these terms as either heuristic or superficial (indeed cosmetic). Either way, it usually appears to be a *post factum* addition to what has been independently conceived. There is nothing surprising in that; it was common in the thirteenth century for the didactic methods associated with a subject (the *ars poetica*, for example) to absorb Aristotelian terms and concepts, even though the traditional content of the subject in question had been fixed before the reception of the 'new' Aristotle from 1100. The *ars poetica*, as discussed in the *Parisiana poetria* of Johannes de Garlandia, provides a striking example, for the content of that treatise is a mixture of earlier-medieval and of twelfth-century rhetorical teaching while its manner is often stringently 'Aristotelian'.[20]

It is in this light, I suggest, that we should view the following

---

[17] Ibid. 166.   [18] Ibid.   [19] Page, *The* Summa musice, ll. 1750–1.
[20] Text in *Parisiana Poetria*, ed. Lawler.

passage from the *Introductio musicae secundum magistrum de Garlandia*, quoted and translated by Tanay (here, and in what follows, I quote the Latin texts as Tanay gives them and employ the translations that she provides, even though both might be emended in various respects):[21]

Subjectum in musica est aliquarum vocum seu pausationum coniunctio modo debito ac proprie observato. Predicatum est ipsius musice ars legitima proportionate omnibus suis modis diligenter observatis, cui partem philosophie suponatur ars metrice.

A subject in music is the conjunction of tones or rests in the right and properly observed manner. A predicate is the legitimate art of fitting this music in the right proportion and by observing diligently all the modes; the part of philosophy providing it is the art of Metrics.

There is an Aristotelian colour to this, but while it may be true that the mensural theory of the later thirteenth century could be explained with the aid of Aristotelian terms, this does not mean that those terms were a necessary condition for the invention and development of that mensural theory. Nor does the comparison of melody to the subject of a proposition and rhythm to its predicate seem to take the matter any further.

With a wealth of new evidence to deploy and an unrivalled understanding of its importance, Tanay sometimes overplays her hand. Her discussion shows a tendency to see the evidence of a scholastic mentality in everything she reads;[22] she also discerns the influence of Aristotle and certain medieval thinkers (especially Aquinas and Ockham) to be pervasive in the texts she cites. This is not surprising, for Tanay's discussion gives little sign that she values any other kind of intellectual context for the theorists' writings. An illustration is provided by her discussion of the following passage by Lambertus (admittedly known as 'pseudo-Aristotle'), who is here discussing the perfect long:[23]

Primus modus dicitur, qui tantum componitur perfectis figuris . . . Et hoc patet igitur quod nunquam comprimitur in ligaturis, sed liber excipitur, et solus non patitur unquam a pressuris; regit et non regitur.

---

[21] 'Music in the Age of Ockham', 15.

[22] Ibid. 16, where a theorist who explains something in a rigorous, paratactic fashion is said to be writing 'in [a] typical scholastic manner'.

[23] Ibid. 28.

It is said to be the first mode, for it is composed only of perfect figures . . . And this figure is never combined in a ligature, but always exposed independently, and being alone it never suffers diminution; it rules and is not ruled.

Tanay notes that the phrase *regit et non regitur*, occurring at the end of the Latin extract, recalls the expression *movens non movetur* of Aristotle.[24] So it does, but we should probably think first of this medieval Latin aphorism:[25]

> Regnat, non regitur, qui nihil nisi quod vult faciat
>
> 'He rules, and is not ruled, who only does what he desires'

The meaning (as Tanay suggests) is clearly that the perfect long is the supreme notational form, subject to none.

Let us consider, as a final illustration, the following passage from Lambertus. Tanay is pursuing the theory that Franco and Lambertus derive their understanding of the perfect long 'from the Thomistic doctrine of the analogy of being':[26]

Cum igitur perfecta figura manens in unitate sit fons et origo ipsius scientie et finis, et propterea quod omnis cantus ab eadem procedit, ct in eadem replicatur, et ipsa in numeris consistit temporibus et mensuris, et trinam in se continet equalitatem, videre sequitur quod ipsa prior ceteris esse videtur, eo quod mundi conditor Deus omnia in numero, pondere et mensura constituit, et hoc principale extitit exemplar in animo conditoris.

Since, however, a perfect figure that remains in unity is the fountain and origin of that science as well as its goal, because every melody (cantus) proceeds from it, and is repeated in it, and because [the perfect figure] consists of numbers, times and measures, and contains within itself the equality of three—it follows that, it is prior to all others, because God the founder of the world constituted everything according to number, weight and measure, and this chief example existed in the mind of the creator.

Compare this passage from one of the most famous works of twelfth-century biblical scholarship, the *De arca noe morali* by Hugh of Saint-Victor:[27]

Trecentorum cubitorum longitudo, praesens saeculum designat, quod tribus temporibus decurrit, id est tempore naturalis legis, tempore scriptae legis, tempore gratiae, per quae sancta Ecclesia a principio mundi usque ad finem,

---

[24] Ibid.   [25] Walther, *Lateinische Sprichwörter*, no. 26502.
[26] 'Music in the Age of Ockham', 26.   [27] PL 176, col. 630.

a praesenti vita ad futuram gloriam tendit. Quinquaginta cubitorum latitudo universos fideles significat, qui sub uno capite sunt constituti, id est Christo.

The length of three hundred cubits signifies this present world which hastens forward in three times: the time of natural law, the time of the written law, and the time of grace, through which Holy Church reaches from the beginning of the world to the end, from this present life to future glory. The fifty cubits of breadth represent all the faithful, who are assembled under one leader, that is Christ.

For all their differences of subject-matter, these two extracts display the same fastidious concern, nourished by scripture and scriptural commentary, to elucidate the momentous symbolism of threefold schemes, enhanced by a powerful sense of God as the final unity in whom all numerical speculation can be resolved. Hugh of Saint-Victor's treatise on the ark of Noah is an exceptional text, to be sure, but for the debts of Lambertus' passage we should surely look to a millennium of biblical commentary as much as to the works of Aristotle or of Thomas Aquinas.

III

Let us turn to intellectual concerns of a less strenuous kind: the ideas and the numerate skills required for *computus*. Designed to teach the measurement of time and the establishment of the liturgical year, *computus* issued the only summons to arithmetical thinking that a medieval cleric was sure to encounter in his duties, be they pastoral or contemplative.

The civilization of the Middle Ages instilled a passion for the calendrical. To be satisfied to any degree, this inclination required numeracy and some knowledge of the heavens. A curiosity about exceptional events in the sky, such as an eclipse, was both a natural impulse and a reflex of this fundamental learning; that is why such phenomena are carefully noted in medieval chronicles from the earliest times.[28] To discover how the hours are measured from season to season, to understand the changes of moon and tide, to know when Easter falls—in short, to measure the steps of mankind towards doomsday—that was the goal of much 'scientific' knowledge in the

---

[28] Examples in a chronicle kept by a musician are provided by the *Chronicle* of Hermannus Contractus in Trillmich and Buchner, *Quellen*, entries for 942 and 968.

Middle Ages. On the verge of the Ars nova, Johannes de Grocheio in Paris mentions this study and gives it the traditional name of *compu-tus*,[29] and there are several small works on computistical subjects attributed to Johannes de Muris.[30] It scarcely matters whether they are genuine; it suffices to know that some of his contemporaries and successors thought of him as the kind of man who would be interested in such studies and who would naturally seek to refine them. When we contemplate the figure of Johannes with his eyes fixed upon a solar eclipse in 1333 we are pondering something which was more ancient than it was modern in that year.

We cannot do better than to open the basic medieval textbook of *computus*, the *De temporum ratione* of Bede (d. 735).[31] Today, Bede is principally known as the author of *The Ecclesiastical History of the English People* and therefore as a historian, but in the Middle Ages he was revered above all as *Beda computator*: Bede the author of a treatise on *computus*.[32] His readers were right to be impressed; to turn the pages of the *De temporum ratione* is to be struck by the serenity and diligence that Bede brings to this as to every part of his great project: to support the Roman Church in England with a library of religious learning. It is scarcely an exaggeration to say that Bede's readership for the *De temporum ratione* extended beyond the novices of Jarrow to the entire clerical community of the Middle Ages.

It is significant that there can be no simple translation of the Latin words *De temporum ratione*. The modern notion of time as an infinite sequence reaching into the future, having neither the momentum of narrative nor the guiding hand of providence, is alien to the concept of *tempus* which is measured in Bede's treatise. There is some

[29] Rohloff, *Die Quellenhandschriften*, 150. The passage is quoted and translated below.

[30] Thorndike and Kibre, *Catalogue of Incipits*, cols. 162 ('Auctores calendarii . . .'), 389 ('De regulis computistarum . . .'), 972 ('O quantum gaudium . . .'), 1373 ('Sanctissimo in Christo . . .', sc. 'De correctione kalendarii . . .').

[31] I have used the edition by Jones; the text in PL 90, cols. 293–578 is less reliable, if convenient. Useful introductions to the literature on computus, medieval and modern, include Cordoliani, 'Contribution à la littérature du comput'; Crombie, *Science, Optics and Music*, 86–8 and 130–2; Thorndike, 'Computus'. There is much material of interest in Beaujouan, *Par raison des nombres, passim*, including a striking passage (I. 651) from Thibaud de Langres (12th c.), who compares the use of the Guidonian hand as a musical mnemonic to a system for making computistical calculations using the nineteen articulations of the hand as a mnemonic 'sicut pueri suum gammam solfaizando'.

[32] On this aspect of Bede's reputation see Murray, *Reason and Society*, 146–51, but especially 149–50. Ward, *The Venerable Bede*, is most useful, while Southern, *Medieval Humanism*, 1–8, is outstanding.

common ground between the two concepts, of course, as there is between all the calendrical systems that human ingenuity has devised,[33] for Bede is concerned with the division of the day and night into hours and with the division of the month and year. To measure *tempus* therefore required a knowledge of certain astronomical facts such as the length of the lunar as opposed to the solar year. With these things established, the purpose of Bede's *De temporum ratione* is to teach the calendrical basis of the liturgical feasts with special reference to determining the place of Easter (on the first Sunday following the first full moon after the vernal equinox). The study of *tempus* was wider than that, however, for it was the knowledge of God's handiwork and of His will, a conception of time intensified by the prophets: 'Blessed be the name of God for ever and ever . . . he changeth the times and the seasons' (Dan. 2: 21). The Christian time of the Middle Ages was calculated to begin at a fixed point with the Creation of the World (on a day that computistical studies sought to establish)[34] and to end with the Apocalypse. The beginner in *computus* therefore learnt to perceive some basic facts of astronomy in relation to the sublimity and dread of the Christian scheme of history. It was Christ Himself, for example, who was believed to have set the scale of hours when he asked his disciples: 'Are there not twelve hours in a day' (John, 11: 9), and as biblical references of this kind accumulated, each observation about the phases of sun and moon was endowed with an eschatological urgency. Every detail was surrounded by a nimbus of Scripture that magnified the meaning of the observation without necessarily diminishing any proto-scientific interest that might have clung to it.

As an exceptional illustration of the way such concerns could mature in the mind of a musician, long before the advent of the Ars nova, we may choose Hermannus Contractus (d. 1054), a monk of Reichenau on Lake Constance.[35] Of noble birth, and possessing a

[33] O'Neil, *Time and the Calendars, passim.*

[34] *De temporum ratione*, ed. Jones, 190 (PL 90, col. 317).

[35] There is a rich literature on this remarkable man. The primary source for his life is Berthold's continuation of Hermannus' *Chronicle*. The text of Berthold's 'biography' is printed in MGH, *Scriptores*, v. 267–8. The *Chronicle* is edited in Trillmich and Buchner, *Quellen*, 628–707. Hermannus' treatise on the astrolabe, the first Western manual on the subject, is printed in PL 143, cols. 379–90, and his music treatise is edited and translated by Ellinwood, *Musica Hermanni Contracti*. There is a wealth of information about Hermannus in the following recent studies: Bergmann, 'Der Traktat "De mensura astrolabii" des Hermann von Reichenau'; id., 'Chronographie und Komputistik'; Borst, 'Ein Forschungsbericht'.

mind so acute that it all but overcame his grievous infirmities of body, Hermannus' eminence as a musician was remembered throughout the Middle Ages. It is first celebrated by his pupil Berthold, who praises his skill as a composer.[36] Various chants can be securely attributed to Hermannus and all have been much discussed.[37] Hermannus also compiled a treatise on the modes whose principal purpose, as he explains it, is to help musicians to judge and to compose fine chants:[38]

Oportet autem nos scire, quod omnis musicae rationis ad hoc spectat intentio, ut cantilenae rationabiliter componendae, regulariter iudicandae, decenter modulandae scientia comparetur.

We should know, moreover, that the whole study of music is directed towards this end: that the skills of composing a chant, of judging it and of performing it, all in a rational manner, be brought together.

Hermannus was expert in *computus*. On the simplest level, this expertise pervades his best-known work, the *Chronicle*.[39] Like any chronicle of a medieval religious house, this one measures small steps in the Ages of the World. Hermannus' careful record of regnal and papal years (modelled upon Old Testament chronicles),[40] and his scrupulous notes of celestial events such as eclipses and the appearance of a comet 'visible for fourteen nights', all set his *Chronicle* in the context of *computus*, whose concerns extend from the briefest perceptible instant of time to a year, to an Age, and then beyond.

It is probable that Hermannus not only witnessed the eclipses he describes but also predicted them. Berthold relates that he devised rules based upon his observations (*regulas experientissimas excogitavit*) for the prediction of lunar eclipses,[41] and his surviving writings include the earliest known Western treatise on the astrolabe.[42] The most elaborate statement of Hermannus' interest in *computus*,

---

[36] MGH, *Scriptores*, v. 268.

[37] Most recently and authoritatively by Oesch, *Berno und Hermann*.

[38] Hermannus, *Musica*, ed. and trans. Ellinwood, 47.

[39] Text in Trillmich and Buchner, *Quellen*, 628–707. Hermannus' treatise on *computus* is contained in the Rochester manuscript (possibly from Bamberg, *c*.1000) where one of the two copies of his *De musica* is to be found. For details of this manuscript and an inventory, see Hermannus, *Musica*, trans. Ellinworth, 1–9.

[40] Trillmich and Buchner, *Quellen*, entries for 904, 915, etc.

[41] MGH, *Scriptores*, v. 268. A treatise entitled *Prognostica de defectu solis et lunae* is contained in the Rochester manuscript. See Hermannus, *Musica* trans. Ellinworth, 5.

[42] Text in PL 143, cols. 379–90. See Bergmann, 'Der Traktat "De Mensura astrolabii" des Hermann von Reichenau'; id., 'Chronographie und Komputistik'.

however, is to be found in a letter to a certain Herrandus on a calendrical question, accompanied by a wealth of Roman numerals reaching high sums and containing a respectful reference to 'that most learned priest Bede'.[43] It is here, perhaps, with the obeisance to Bede, that we approach the central concern of all Hermannus' interests: a passion for exactitude wherever it can be achieved in matters that can be seen, by a trained mind, to bear upon mystery:[44]

Denique VII dies et VI horae habent momenta V̄IDCCCCLX. Haec si per CCXXXV menses diviseris, unicuique XXVIIII^{m} momenta contingent, et CXLV remanent . . .

In short, seven days and six hours contain 6,960 moments. If you divide these by 235 months, each of them has 29 moments, and there are 145 moments left over . . .

Hermannus Contractus reveals the antiquity of what may seem to us the 'scientific revolution' of the fourteenth century, embodied in Johannes de Muris, astrolabe in hand, as he contemplates the eclipse of 1333. Like Johannes de Muris several centuries later, Hermannus Contractus observed the stars, predicted eclipses with the aid of tables, studied the astrolabe, and wrote a treatise upon the rational and intellectual bases of music as he understood them. For Hermannus, the central concern whose gravity sustained the orbit of all these interests was *computus*. We may admire his skills as a composer and theorist above all, but Berthold, in speaking of his master, sees things differently. He gives pride of place to his proficiency in *computi ratio*.

IV

A few years before Hermannus Contractus was born, the monk Raoul Glaber had imagined the world to be dressed 'in a white robe of churches'. In the twelfth and thirteenth centuries that garment was adorned beyond anything that either Raoul Glaber or Hermannus Contractus could have anticipated. As new religious orders and foundations began to proliferate, the number of clerics who needed to know something about *computus* increased many-fold. The appearance of vernacular manuals of *computus* soon after 1100 is significant in

---

[43] The text of the letter is printed in Borst, 'Ein Forschungsbericht', 474–7. For references to Bede see 474 and 476.

[44] Ibid. 476.

this respect. It was in the period 1113–19 that Philippe de Thaon compiled an Anglo-Norman treatise on *computus*, the *Comput*. Dedicated to Honfroi de Thaon, chaplain to the royal steward Eudo Dapifer (d. 1120), the *Comput* leaves no doubt about the importance of its subject to clerics at every level of the ecclesiastical hierarchy.[45] In this treatise, Philippe lists the various liturgical books in use ('salters . . . antefiners . . . grahels . . . hymners . . . messels . . . Tropers e leçuners') and asks how clerics can use them if they do not understand *computus*, the key to the liturgical year.[46]

No great arithmetical knowledge is required for an understanding of Philippe's *Comput*, although a passing reference to Turkill, an exchequer clerk and the author of a work on the abacus, suggests that the realm of more advanced and 'official' arithmetic was not sensed to be remote from that of *computus*.[47] Most of the operations in the *Comput* require multiplication (12×30, 5×24, and so on), but we should not underestimate the difficulty which sums of this kind could present to clergy who had not memorized multiplication tables, a relatively advanced aid in the eleventh and twelfth centuries for all save those whose lives brought them into regular contact with practical numerical problems solved with the aid of an abacus.[48] Philippe anticipates that some will belittle the study of *computus* by declaring that they know the calendar of their church by custom, *par us*; his picturesque reply is that 'a man may know how to sing *par us* just as a starling may know how to speak'.[49] This implies that to know anything *par us* alone is to behave like a starling that can speak *par us* without knowing the meaning of what it says. The comparison also implies that to sing *par us* alone is reprehensible—one of several indications in the period 1100–1300 that an ability to read plainchant notation was closely associated with *computus* and that both were regarded as essential clerical skills.

It was mainly during the thirteenth century that the study of *computus* absorbed the technique of algorism: arithmetical calculations with the aid of arabic numerals and a decimal system facilitated by a

---

[45] Text in Short, *Comput*.   [46] Ibid., ll. 39–43.

[47] Ibid., l. 2080; compare also l. 2214. For Turkill, see Murray, *Reason and Society*, 195.

[48] On the various forms and uses of the medieval abacus, and on the differences which distinguish it from the Roman abacus, see Beaujouan, *Par raison des nombres*, IX. 310–12, and Murray, *Reason and Society*, 163–9.

[49] Short, *Comput*, 91–6.

sign for zero.[50] In various forms, arabic numerals had been available to Western scholars for many generations, but it was in the thirteenth century that the use of these 'figures of algorism' (*figure algorismi*) was widely disseminated. They are employed in the most elementary and popular textbook of cosmography in the thirteenth century, Johannes de Sacrobosco's *Sphera* (1230–45)[51] and are the subject of Alexander de Villa Dei's highly influential *Carmen de algorismo*,[52] one of several works written in mnemonic verse *c.*1200 to satisfy a need for new textbooks and much studied in Paris.[53]

The importance of algorism to *computus* is plain on every page of a thirteenth-century treatise on algorism, written in Old French by two *clercs*.[54] As with the *Comput* of Philippe de Thaon, the choice of the vernacular in this algorism reveals the authors' desire to communicate with a wider readership than Latin would allow, and their vivid descriptions of the medieval forms of the numerals ('four is like an *o* with two feet') suggest that many clerics were just beginning to study algorism. What is particularly striking in this text is that the authors' sense of algorism as a tool is dominated by *computus*; they have (or they reveal) no conception that algorism is a flexible device with many technical, bureaucratic, and commercial applications. They care only for *computus*, and no cleric, they flatly declare, can study that subject properly unless he knows algorism, for *computus* is something that 'nul n'atint ne savoir pout/Se il ne seit argorisme' ('that nobody can understand if he does not know algorism').[55] They claim

[50] The spread of Arabic numerals and the art of algorism have been much discussed. The outstanding recent survey in English is Murray, *Reason and Society*, with a good coverage of the earlier literature. Evans, 'From Abacus to Algorism', is also excellent. The subject is treated throughout the series of essays gathered in Beaujouan, *Par raison des nombres*; see especially essays III, V, IX, and XI, the last being a survey of algorism in 13th-c. Paris. As Beaujouan remarks (*Par raison des nombres*, III. 483), it is striking that there is a firm division between treatises on algorism and those on the symbolism of numbers by Geoffrey of Auxerre, Odo of Morimond, and others. Viewed in this light, the new algorism appears a strictly practical and logical technique. This is consistent with the view of arithmetic adopted by writers such as Adelard of Bath, for whom arithmetic is 'a purely theoretical subject which fully exercises the mind' (Drew, 'The *De Eodem et Diverso*', 21). Compare Murray, *Reason and Society*, 204, who argues that medieval scholars shared 'an awareness of [arithmetic's] exceptional logical autonomy . . . and of its call for a specifically intellectual power'.

[51] Text in Thorndike, *The* Sphere *of Sacrobosco*; see esp. 85 and 88.

[52] Text in Halliwell, *Rara Mathematica*, 73–83.

[53] Beaujouan, *Par raison des nombres*, IV. 848. For a music treatise that may have been produced by this drive for new texts, see Alexander de Villa Dei (?), *Carmen de musica cum glossis*, ed. Seay.

[54] Text in Karpinski and Waters, 'A Thirteenth-Century Algorism'.   [55] Ibid., ll. 6–7.

that 'a cleric often suffers shame and fear if he knows nothing of *computus*; if he is ignorant of it he has no right to be a cleric, a deacon, or a priest'.[56] With this remark we begin to sense the importance, indeed the prestige, of computistical knowledge for any men seeking preferment in the Church.

It would make a fascinating study to trace the incursion of arabic numerals into the study of *musica*, a subject often regarded today as having been an essentially numerical preoccupation in the Middle Ages. A preliminary survey suggests that their progress was surprisingly slow. We are surprised because it was the *musici* who helped to keep arithmetical skills alive in the West between the ninth and the twelfth centuries, and many of the operations they studied would have been facilitated by arabic numerals. Many brief treatises are devoted to the measurement of bells, the monochord, the organistrum, and organ pipes, for example, and these texts—at first sight so dull and apparently useless—become luminous with significance when considered in relation to the history of arithmetic in the West. Here is an example, perhaps from *c.*1100 (Pl. 11), concerning the disposition of the tangents of the organistrum:

Quomodo organistrum conponatur
In primis a capite iuxta primum plectrum infra usque ad aliud plectrum quod ponitur post rotulam per duos passus metire et in primo passu pone *c*. Secundus finit. A *c* ad finem metire per III et IIII retro reddit *G*; a *G* ad finem per III et IIII retro pone *D*; a *D* ad finem per III et in primo passu pone *a*; de *a* ad finem per III et IIII retro pone *E*; et ab *E* ad finem per III; in primo passu pone *b*; item a *c* ad finem per II et III retro pone *F*; ab *F* ad finem per IIII; in primo passu pone *b*.

How the organistrum is put together
First, measure from the nut which is next to the first tangent up to the bridge placed after the wheel and divide the distance into two parts; put *c* at the middle point; the half lying beyond *c* will not contain pitches. Now measure from *c* to the end and divide the distance by three; having established this unit count back four units from the bridge beyond the wheel and you will establish *G*; treat *G* as you treated *c* and you will establish *D*; measure from *D* to this nut, divide by three and put *a* one unit beyond *D*; measure from *a* to the nut and divide the distance by three; having established this unit, count back four such units from the nut beyond the wheel and you will establish *E*; measure from *E* to this nut, divide by three and put *b* one unit

[56] Ibid., ll. 8–10.

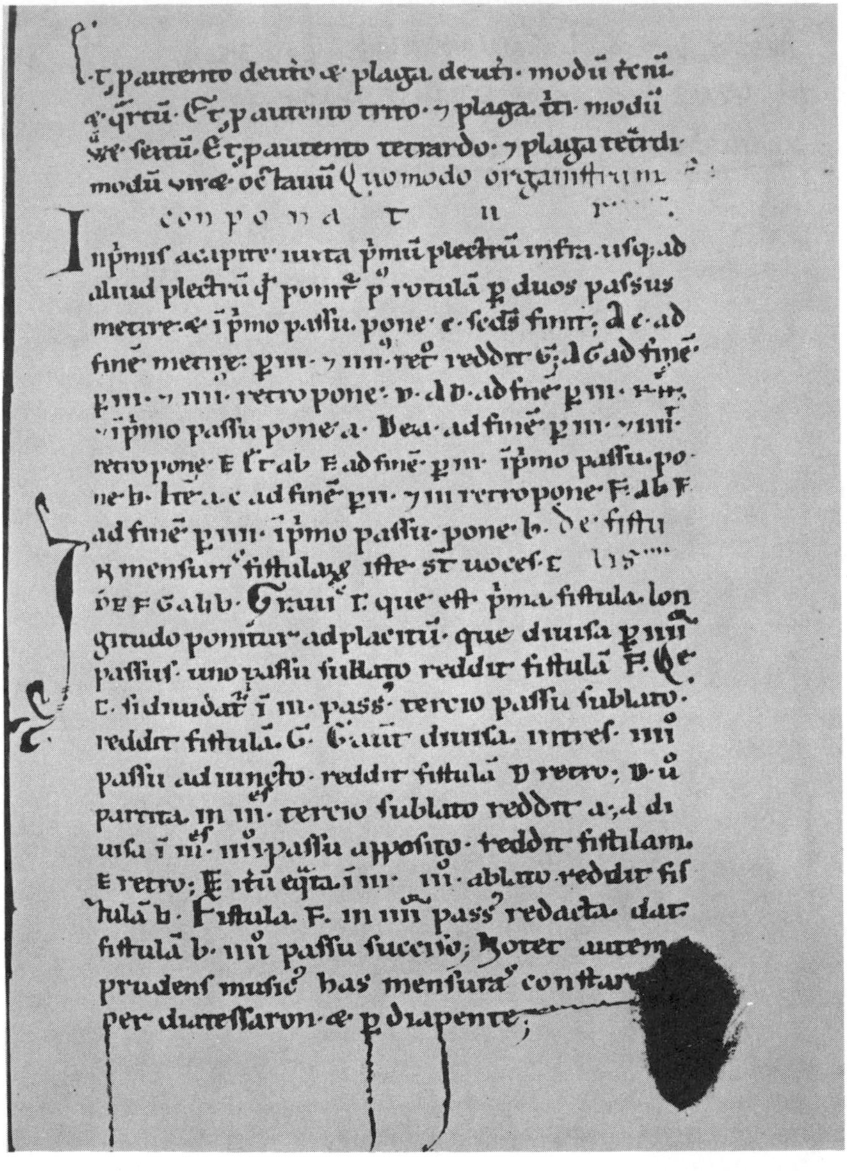

Pl. 11. The treatise *Quomodo organistrum conponatur*. Vienna, Nationalbibliothek, Cpv 2503, fo. 42ʳ. Reproduced by permission

beyond E; again, measure from c to the nut and divide the distance by two; having established this unit, count back three such units and you will establish F; divide the distance from F to the nut by four and put b on the first step.

It is common for treatises of this kind to be highly compressed, but they offer some room for useful mathematical exercises none the less. Once the eye has become accustomed to the ellipses of this one (somewhat eased in the translation) the text proves to be a recipe for a Pythagorean scale involving some strenuous fractions. To establish G from c, for example, is to divide $1/2$ (the ratio for the c) by three and then to multiply the product by four:

$$1/2 \div 3 \times 4 = 2/3$$

To proceed as far as the $b\natural$ is to catapult the fractions up to $128/243$:

$$16/27 \div 3 \times 4 = 64/81 \text{ (to establish } E)$$
$$64/81 \div 3 \times 2 = 128/243 \text{ (to establish } b\natural \text{ from } E)$$

One can imagine the sense of vertigo induced by attempting the last sum with roman numerals:

$$\frac{\text{LXIIII/LXXXI}}{\text{III}} \times \text{II} = \text{CXXVIII/CCXLIII}$$

Even as late as the thirteenth century, the progress of arabic numerals through the pages of music theory is a slow one. A folio from the only complete manuscript of Jerome of Moravia's *Tractatus de musica*, probably copied in Paris c.1300,[57] still uses roman numerals in the texts, in accordance with the prevailing usage of all music theory, both practical and speculative, before the later thirteenth century. It is a different matter with the scribe who marked up the copy, however, for his work reveals a more advanced attitude characteristic of stationers;[58] he uses an arabic numeral to mark the beginning of the second polyphonic treatise in Jerome's compilation, the *De mensurabili musica* of Johannes de Garlandia (Pl. 12).

We turn to the two manuscripts of Johannes de Grocheio's *De musica*, probably composed c.1300, and find that arabic numerals have at last made their way into mensural theory (although the modern edition of his treatise conceals the fact).[59] It is remarkable that when

---

[57] For a recent survey of this important manuscript see Huglo, '*Tractatus de Musica*'.

[58] Compare the remarks in Murray, *Reason and Society,* 172.

[59] Rohloff, *Die Quellenhandschriften,* replaces the arabic numerals of the manuscripts with the Latin names of the appropriate numbers.

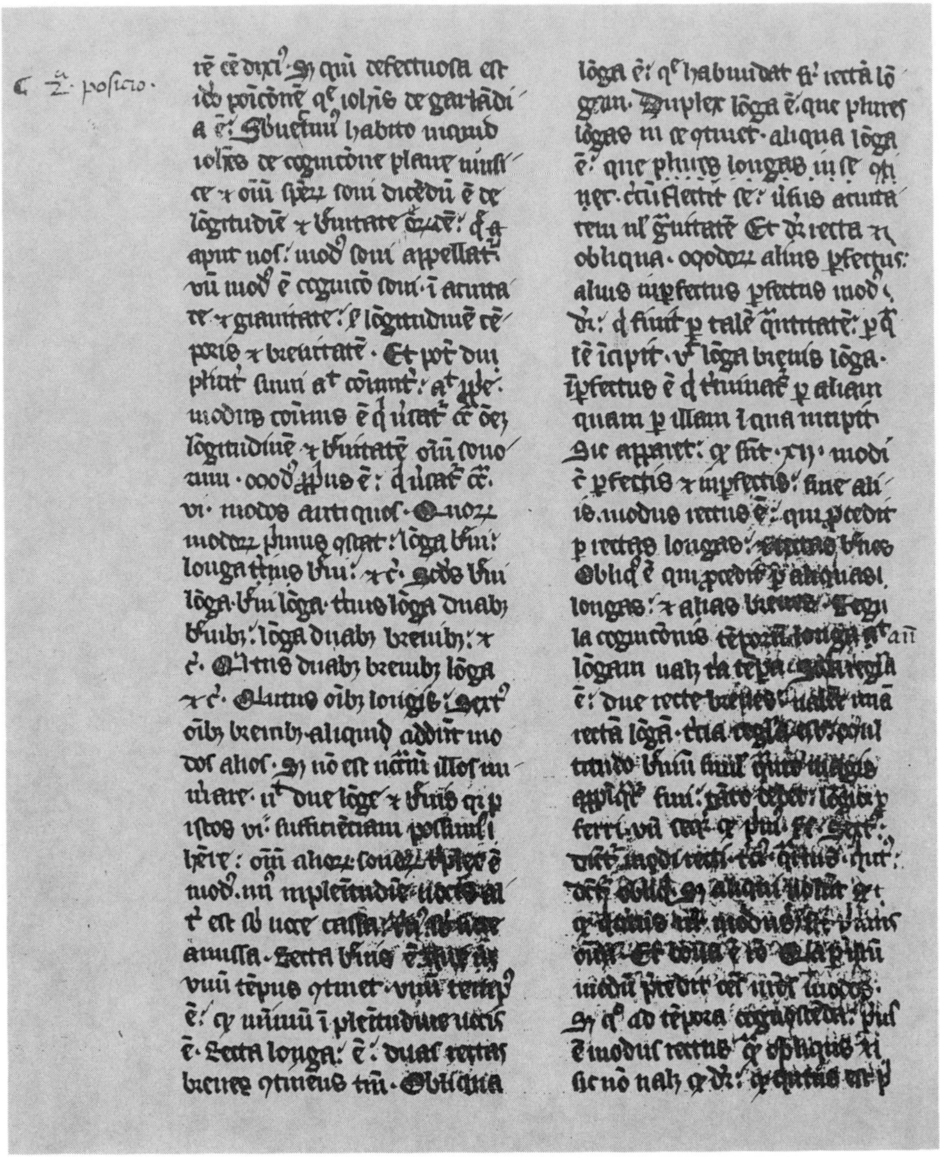

Pl. 12. A page from the *De mensurabili musica* of Johannes de Garlandia as incorporated into the *Tractatus de musica* of Jerome of Moravia. Paris, Bibliothèque nationale, lat. 16663, fo. 66ᵛ

Grocheio discusses material of a 'Boethian' kind (such as the nature of arithmetical proportions) he always uses roman numerals or spells out the numbers in words, but when he turns to mensural notation he uses arabic numerals. Here he is on the discoveries of Pythagoras:[60]

Examinans quinque et ponderans eos invenit unum in dupla proportione ad alterum, sicut sunt XII ad VI.

Here, in contrast, is Grocheio on mensural notation:[61]

musicus ex 3 figuris cantum quemlibet mensuratum [designat]. Per longam enim potest perfectionem vel 2 tempora significare . . .

We have here a contrast of method, and one that reflects contemporary changes in the way arithmetical calculations were made. It is common for medieval treatises on the abacus, or reckoning-board, to use names for numerals or roman numerals; this is the technology of tenth- to twelfth-century calculation.[62] The treatises on algorism, however, use arabic numbers only.[63] Algorism provided a symbol for zero, which did away with the need for the fixed structure of columns characteristic of the abacus, and this new symbol 'enabled the calculator to substitute pen and paper for counters'.[64] This contrast of method in Grocheio's *De musica* suggests that roman numerals and the names of numbers were powerfully associated with the most venerable and elevated concerns of musical theory, as indeed they should have been for any thirteenth-century scholar who had read the *De musica* of Boethius or any plainchant treatise with a section on proportions. The figures of algorism in Grocheio's *De musica*, however, reveal that by the later thirteenth century mensural theory had already begun to absorb algorism. 'XII ad VI' looked like a proper equation for a discussion of theory, but '12 ad 6' suited a practical account of measured notation.

To cross from Grocheio's *De musica* of c.1300 to the *Speculum musice* of Jacques de Liège, probably composed in the years before 1330, is to find that virtually all the speculative and practical concerns of music theory can now be discussed with the aid of algorism:[65]

Si duae multiplices (supple: *proportiones*) *coniungantur, composita ex illis erit multiplex.* Hoc etiam quandoque fit cum superparticularis multiplici

---

[60] Rohloff, *Die Quellenhandschriften*, 112. [61] Ibid. 142.
[62] Evans, 'From Abacus to Algorism', 116. [63] Ibid. [64] Ibid. 115.
[65] *Speculum*, iii. 106.

coniungitur ut hic: 6 3 2, vel hic 12 4 3. Accidit etiam hoc quandoque cum superpartiens sociatur multiplici ut hic: 15 5 3.

The words in italics have been taken from a celebrated thirteenth-century treatise on algorism by the Dominican Jordanus Nemorarius.[66] Jacques clearly exulted in such things, describing how clerics with advanced knowledge of arithmetic could 'sport . . . with proportions . . . and with various and amazing collocations of numbers', displaying their *clarum et profundum . . . ingenium*.[67] However, Jacques's well-known antipathy to certain aspects of the Ars nova demonstrates (if any demonstration were needed) that it was not necessarily an appetite for the intricacies and possibilities of the new notation that led musicians to learn algorism, but rather their participation in an increasingly 'algorisimic' culture. Later musicians seem to have found that arabic numerals offered a concise way of recording the elements of the mensurations (Pl. 10).

It may well have been the study of *computus* that first introduced arabic numerals to many clerics in the thirteenth century. As we have seen, the authors of a French algorism from the 1200s regard these numerals as essential to the proper study of *computus*. Certainly the importance of *computus* did not decline with the proliferation of written liturgical calendars in service-books, not to mention portable calendars for personal use. On the verge of the Ars nova period in Paris we find Johannes de Grocheio proclaiming the importance of computistical studies; he regards them, together with grammar and an ability to read plainsong, as something which every 'man of the church' should attend to:[68]

Et quamquam omnes artes vel scientiae et omnis humana eruditio ad hoc [laudare creatorem] tendat, quantum potest, tres tamen artes ad hoc propinquius ordinantur, puta grammatica, quae scribere cum modo loquendi et proferendi docet, et ars illa, quae temporum distinctionem et eorum computationem tradit, quam computum appellant, quae naturali vel astronomiae subiungatur, et cum his duabus concurrens musica, quae de cantu et modo cantandi discernit. Et istas tres non debet vir ecclesiasticus ignorare.

Even though all arts, all skills, and all human knowledge may incline towards this [the praise of God] as far as is possible, there are three arts which most closely pursue this end. They are grammar, which teaches the

---

[66] On Jordanus see Busard, 'Die Traktate *De Proportionibus* von Jordanus Nemorarius'.
[67] *Speculum*, ii. 163.
[68] Rohloff, *Die Quellenhandschriften*, 150.

manner of writing, of eloquence, and of delivery, and the art which deals with the distinction and computation of time, which is called *computus* and which is placed under the heading of natural [science] or astronomy. Music accords with these two, dealing with chant and the manner of singing. A churchman should not be ignorant of these three.

The spread of arabic numerals, and the dissemination of treatises on algorism, does not signal any 'mathematically directed intellectual curiosity';[69] as Gillian Evans remarks, the new technique seems to give the algorism writers 'no fresh power of insight . . . their grasp of first principles is merely easier'.[70] The adoption of these numerals for computistical studies was not a 'scientific revolution', but if we allow a looser translation of the words *scientiae revolutio* used by Johannes de Muris, we may say that the means of arithmetical thinking certainly took 'a new turn' during the course of the thirteenth century, and it may be no coincidence that the numerical bases of musical notation did the same.

V

Little is known about the day-to-day workings of that notational system. In practice, it must have been supported by a wealth of *social* interchanges. A gifted singer would not be able to learn Ars nova notation as Johannes de Muris knew it in 1321 from the *Notitia artis musice* alone; he would need the help of one who had studied notation and who (for preference) had simultaneously seen its forms and heard its results in performance on numerous occasions. A man of learning with an appetite for the measured notation *per se* would not be able to gain a full picture of what he was studying without some experience of performance. It is possible to imagine many ways in which Ars nova notation was kept alive as a subject of intellectual interest and musical concern by diverse adepts, all aware that the new *ars musica* was an enterprise which required the gifts and interests of many to flourish.

This is the impression that we derive from an important source of information about the social momentum of fourteenth-century polyphony: a treatise on musicians by Arnulf de Saint-Ghislain.[71]

---

[69] Evans, 'From Abacus to Algorism', 123.
[70] Ibid. 122. [71] Text and translation in Page, 'A Treatise on Musicians'.

This unique document may date from *c*.1400, but could be earlier. It evokes a kind of lively gathering (called the 'throng', or *turba*)[72] in which musicians of varied accomplishments assemble to hear polyphonic music. Some of them know little of the art but are eager to learn; some cannot sing but have become so erudite in the theory of music that they teach the art (presumably the intricacies of notation above all) to others more gifted as performers. The implication of Arnulf's treatise is that the art of music is forwarded by the combined efforts and enthusiasms of these different individuals. None is rejected; only presumption and arrogance are scorned.

The innovations of the Ars nova may owe much to this kind of collaborative effort, one in which all serious endeavour associated with the new art by listeners, singers, and 'theorists' (if it makes any sense to enforce these categories) could be pooled and disseminated with small treatises and copies of compositions. More important than these forms of communication, perhaps, were the intangible ones: conversations between enthusiasts and enlivening discussions in the *turba* where musicians gathered for performance. The few references to such gatherings that we possess suggest, more than anything else, that there was much discussion.[73] No doubt these conversations were often dominated by those who, regardless of any practical ability, had made a study of music theory and notation; these are the individuals whom Arnulf de Saint-Ghislain describes, with much admiration, as the musicians 'who keep the glorious treasures of the art and discipline of music in the sanctuaries of their breast, acquired in a praiseworthy fashion by the efficacy of study'.[74] Even if these learned musicians could not sing well (and Arnulf implies that many of them could not), it was none the less their privilege to 'instruct [others] according to rule'.[75] Arnulf remarks upon the 'fertility (*facundia*) of their minds' and declares that 'the theory of musical teaching flows in streams from their breasts';[76] he may be describing one kind of individual that helped to devise the Ars nova notation of France *c*.1300.

It is striking that Dorit Tanay's implied portrait of the Ars nova theorist as a man deeply versed in Aristotelian logic and Thomist theology is not quite in accord with Arnulf's account. His learned musi-

---

[72] Page, 'A Treatise on Musicians', 9–11 (discussion of the term *turba*).
[73] Ibid., considering also the evidence of Jacques de Liège.
[74] Ibid. 19, Latin text, ll. 41–55. [75] Ibid., Latin text, ll. 46–7 ('regulariter edocendo').
[76] Ibid., Latin text, ll. 48–9.

cians are definitely not interested in sophistries that have no direct practical use (*tales non sophisticantur in musica*).[77] Furthermore, Arnulf admires them for their learning but he does not regard them as the controlling aristocracy of musical art, despite what Tanay's evocation of mensural theory as a concern intertwined with Aristotelian and Thomistic speculations might suggest. In Arnulf's scheme of things, the laurels go to expert performers of polyphony who possess an inherent musicality (*naturalis instinctus*) and who 'yield nothing in praiseworthiness to the lark'.[78]

No doubt Arnulf's decision to set such performers apart from the 'theorists' (a term for which he has no equivalent) is a simplification of the truth, but modern experience confirms the general validity of his distinction between gifted performers and 'theorists' who have modest practical skills or who neglect their practical abilities in order to follow musical interests of an intellectual kind. The development of Ars nova notation probably happened at a point where the abilities and interests of these two kinds of musician intersected. They would have shared a belief that, if one wished to be profoundly serious, all numerical relationships, including those of mensural notation, could be explained in relation to Scripture or patristic tradition. These were the primary sources of Christian numerology, and it is no surprise to find such things in the writings of the theorists. They would also have accepted that anything requiring to be learnt by heart—mensural notation included—demands a logical and precise manner with the help of concepts such as 'genus' and 'species' borrowed from Aristotle, a process that could be extended as far as an author wished: from simple explanations, useful to all, to the most speculative ideas, of interest to a few. The existence of some mensural theory with a complex embroidery of ideas drawn from contemporary theology and logic is therefore no surprise either.

Much more suggestive, I propose, is that the only example of musical notation that we may possess in the hand of Johannes de Muris comprises an isorhythmic tenor with the value of each note carefully indicated in Arabic numerals.[79]

---

[77] Ibid., Latin text, l. 52.   [78] Ibid., Latin text, line 59.
[79] For a facsimile, see L. Gushee, 'New Sources for the Biography of Johannes de Muris', pl. 2.

5

Huizinga, The Waning of the Middle Ages, *and the Chanson*

And yet it leaves on the mind a curious impression: a sort of suspicion seizes the reader that if Professor Huizinga is right, most
men who lived in the fourteenth and fifteenth centuries must
have been practically insane.

C. G. Crump

I

THE Mellon chansonnier, a collection of polyphonic songs compiled
in the mid-1470s, has been edited and issued in a luxurious fashion.[1]
The production of such a lavish edition, including an entire volume
of introductory and ancillary matter, presented the two editors,
Howard Garey and Leeman Perkins, with an opportunity to consider
the cultural context of the songs in the manuscript. In his introduction to the poetry, set by composers such as Busnoys, Dufay, and
Ockeghem, Howard Garey declares that the poems open 'a door to
. . . the world so sensitively described by Johan Huizinga in *The
Waning of the Middle Ages*'.[2] Garey is commending what is perhaps
the most famous book ever written about the later Middle Ages in the
North and one that enjoys a 'legendary fame', in the words of Reinhard Strohm.[3] What kind of world is Garey evoking for the songs of
the Mellon chansonnier through the medium of that celebrated book?
With all due deference to the subtlety of Huizinga's thought in *The
Waning of the Middle Ages*, the lasting impression we derive from his
book is that the fifteenth century can be described as one where the
aesthetic longings of aristocratic *courtoisie* have become empty and
stylized, where art has degenerated into escapism in response to the

---

[1] Perkins and Garey, *The Mellon Chansonnier.*   [2] Ibid., ii. 63.
[3] 'The Close of the Middle Ages', 311.

harshness of existence, and where there is no choice but to repeat the outmoded forms of life and thought inherited from the glorious twelfth century, chivalry among them. If Howard Garey and Leeman Perkins set any limits upon their acceptance of Huizinga's vision of this courtly milieu, they do not define them. Indeed, there seem to be no limits for Garey; his declaration that he will 'inspect this world through the poems of the Mellon . . .' does not introduce the kind of critical appraisal that the word 'inspect' might suggest.[4]

Perkins adopts a similar position. In his Introduction to the Music, he emphasizes the importance of *The Waning of the Middle Ages* in any attempt to interpret the aesthetic qualities of the song repertoire. 'Obviously', he remarks, any sound critical and aesthetic assessment of these songs[5]

must be based on historical criteria deriving from an understanding of the social and artistic functions of the created work in its own time and place . . . The courtly society of the fifteenth century that provided the context for the chanson has been discussed repeatedly in considerable detail and is now understood reasonably well.

At this point Perkins cites *The Waning of the Middle Ages* in a foot-note, so implying that the book makes a major contribution to 'an understanding of the social and artistic functions' of the chanson repertoire. It is in this context, I suggest, that we should read Perkins's remarks on the first page of the Commentary volume:[6]

Undeniably, the subject matter [of the secular song forms of the fifteenth century] is largely confined to the highly stylized amorous sentiments of aristocratic courts. In addition the recurrence of certain themes, notably the all-too-cruel suffering of the unrequited lover; the strict adherence to the fixed forms of *ballade, rondeau,* and *virelai*; the conventional turns of phrase; the stereotyped imagery; the excessive reliance upon a basic vocabulary . . . and the acceptance of versification as one of the indispensable skills of the noble and educated classes—all have been derided to some extent by modern critics.

With so many pejorative terms packed into so few lines, this owes a significant debt to the picture of a 'decadent' medieval civilization

---

[4] *The Mellon Chansonnier*, ii. 63.   [5] Ibid. 2.

[6] Ibid. 1. Perkins is surely correct to emphasize that the qualities of 15th-c. songs–'concision, economy of expression, and structural cohesion–have been construed in an unfavorable light by unwarranted comparisons with essentially different categories of musical composition, the contemporary mass and motet'.

given by Johan Huizinga. The whole passage induces a sense of unease. If some modern critics have derided the fifteenth-century belief in versification as one of the 'indispensable skills of the noble and educated classes', then they are so far out of sympathy with a major tradition in Western letters before Romanticism that we wonder what their 'unfavourable' assessment of the chanson repertoire is worth. It is disquieting to sense—as we surely do in reading this passage—that Perkins shares with the critics whom he is paraphrasing a hidden agenda for all 'good' (or at least all truly enlivened) poetry which chanson verse fails to address. Good poetry in this context would appear to be verse that does not offer the modern critic a hyperbolical presentation of aristocratic ideals; it would also appear to be poetry that responds to a new creative impulse with fresh diction and, on occasions, with a fresh form.

These are all anachronistic expectations to bring to the chanson verse of the fifteenth century. The criticisms paraphrased in Perkins's passage could be levelled against the lyrics of many thirteenth-century trouvères,[7] not to mention the chanson verse that was published in such quantities during the sixteenth century. Perkins's comments about the music of the Mellon chansonnier also cause a certain disquiet:[8]

Even the music, though less commonplace than the verse and consequently less vulnerable to similar criticism, has not escaped censure for its lack of formal variety and for the strictures imposed on melodic development by the need for clarity and articulation in presenting the poetry as song . . . [these songs] are musical miniatures . . .

We notice the rather odd (if technically appropriate) choice of the word 'commonplace' to denote the conventionalized character of what was, for the most part, verse of courtly provenance and interest. It is also odd to describe the songs of the Mellon chansonnier as

---

[7] See e.g. the remarks in Dronke, *The Medieval Lyric*, 127: 'From near the close of the [twelfth] century a considerable number of northern French love-songs survive; but while the music is often full of inventiveness and grace . . . the words again and again are those of a bloodless *complainte d'amour* . . . occasionally, though very rarely, in this genre, a trouvère would compose a song in which words as well as melody were individual and alive.' Compare the more sympathetic account in Stevens, *Words and Music*, 13–47. It is worth giving prominence to Dronke's dismissive remarks about the love poetry of the late 12th c. in view of the tendency of scholars in many fields, to be discussed below, to regard the *cortoisie* of the 15th c. as a pale reflection of 12th-c. glories.

[8] *The Mellon Chansonnier*, ii. 1–2.

'musical miniatures', for modern experience suggests that they yield nothing in length to many a Schubert song and may match some shorter Handel arias. It is the last sentence of Perkins's passage, however, that draws attention to itself, for when Perkins refers to the 'strictures imposed on melodic development by the need for clarity and articulation in presenting the poetry as song' he believes himself to be defining a shortcoming of the repertoire, whereas he is only describing an element of its style. What is meant by 'melodic *development*'? Those are hazardous words to employ in a medieval context since it might be argued that the principal aesthetic difficulty that modern musicologists encounter in polyphonic rondeaux, virelais, and ballades is that the music does not develop but works in patterns of (relatively) short-term repetition. We may prefer to believe, however, that Perkins is referring to a certain lack of musical luxuriance in the chanson repertoire arising from the characteristic declamatory patterns of these songs. It is true that many fifteenth-century songs display that characteristic, but why should they be otherwise? What musical standards are the critics of chanson style invoking when they disparage the chanson in these terms?

I have quoted enough from the Mellon edition, I suggest, to illustrate the tendency for musicologists to adopt a view of fifteenth-century court culture that owes much to *The Waning of the Middle Ages* and which appears to express (and to legitimize) a limited enthusiasm for the work of fifteenth-century poets and musicians, whatever the purely academic and thus professional interest these materials may offer. Other, somewhat different, illustrations of Johan Huizinga's influence upon musicology might be drawn from recent works by Wright (1979), Yudkin (1989), Kemp (1990), and Strohm (1985 and 1990), not to mention books and articles by an older generation of scholars such as von Ficker and Bridgman.[9] And yet, anyone

---

[9] For the use made of Huizinga's ideas by Wright, Yudkin, Strohm, and Kemp, see below, and for the earlier generations of scholarship see particularly von Ficker, 'Polyphonic Music', 500 and 505, where Guillaume de Machaut is presented as a 'typical representative' of a 'moribund' culture, and Bridgman, 'The Age of Ockeghem and Josquin', 246. The indirect but powerful influence of *The Waning of the Middle Ages* upon modern performances of medieval music is discussed in Page, 'The English *a cappella* Heresy'. It must be emphasized that musicologists are by no means alone in perpetuating Huizinga's vision of the later Middle Ages some three generations after it was first expressed. For some striking examples drawn from medieval literary studies see Kahrl, 'Chaucer's *Squire's Tale* and the Decline of Chivalry', and Zumthor, 'From Hi(story) to Poem'.

who has ever been disturbed or provoked by *The Waning of the Middle Ages*—for it is both a disturbing and a provocative book—will wish to ask whether musicologists should be so welcoming to Huizinga's vision of a 'declining' Middle Ages.[10] Huizinga's evocation of his period is indeed a sensitive one, as Howard Garey maintains, but our dependence upon it raises questions which encompass our conception of the *formes fixes* and range widely beyond. Do we wish to imagine that Dufay, Busnoys, and Ockeghem lived in the 'continual state of mental crisis' that Huizinga attributed to all people in the Middle Ages?[11] As we examine the masses of Dufay, for example, or the chansons of Busnoys, do we find evidence that 'the mentality of the declining Middle Ages often . . . [displays] an incredible superficiality and feebleness . . .'?[12] Above all, perhaps, are we to regard the courtly songs of the fifteenth century as having provided, in Kemp's words, the 'tonal atmosphere' for a moribund and stultified court culture?

These questions are worth asking, I suggest, because many leading historians of music have cited *The Waning of the Middle Ages* and yet few have engaged with what it says. The strongest challenge that the book has received in musicological literature is perhaps Richard Hoppin's qualified concession that 'the Middle Ages may have "waned" during the fifteenth century, but . . .'.[13] A puzzling situation has therefore arisen. When the studies of musicologists open out to large questions of fifteenth-century court culture they sometimes perceive it in terms of a powerful but highly personal book that is now

[10] The Dutch text of *The Waning of the Middle Ages* (*Herfsttijd der Middeleeuwen*) is available in *Verzamelde Werken*, iii. 3–435, with the original preface to the 1919 edition. The English translation, by F. Hopman, first published in 1924, was produced under Huizinga's direction. I am not qualified to assess the opinion of Weintraub (*Visions of Culture*, 212) that the English translation 'is a very inferior, crippled version of the Dutch original'. For an excellent account of the reception of *The Waning of the Middle Ages*, both in its original Dutch form and in translation, see Hugenholtz, 'The Fame of a Masterwork'.

[11] *The Waning of the Middle Ages*, 226. Compare Guenée, *Between Church and State*, 26–8, who comments on the ubiquity of fear and dread in the society of late-medieval France, but who proceeds to explain this phenomenon in an admirably sensible and historical fashion. Referring to the late Middle Ages as 'such violent times, when the weak as well as women and clerics had much to dread', Guenée comments that fear was regarded as 'the beginning of wisdom', and that it was 'the wise fear of God and the wise fear of the prince, the legitimate fear that every steadfast man might feel, could avow, and might someday use to his advantage–these kinds of fear made fear itself into something other than a violent and reprehensible impulse of the soul. It was an ordinary emotion, a sign of wisdom, proof of sound judgement.'

[12] *The Waning of the Middle Ages*, 225.   [13] Hoppin, *Medieval Music*, 470.

discredited in some important respects.[14] In due course we s
examine some of the objections to Huizinga's ideas that have been
raised by historians of literature and chivalry; for the moment we may
note some theoretical grounds for dissent. There can be few scholars
today who will wish to follow Huizinga in his readiness to regard
'forms of life, thought and art' as expressions of a spirit which 'unites
all the cultural products of an age and makes them homogeneous'.[15]
Nor, perhaps, do many historians working on the fourteenth and
fifteenth centuries now associate their chosen period with 'a prolix
and outworn scholasticism, an outworn, though still influential cult of
chivalry, and a superabundance of images in religious life and
thought', all emanating from a uniting spirit which Huizinga called
'decadent'.[16] Lastly, it is appropriate to emphasize the sheer antiquity
of *The Waning of the Middle Ages*: Anglophone medievalists, in all
disciplines, often cite the book using an imprint date for the English
translation by Hopman, and a recent volume of Chaucer criticism
accordingly dates *The Waning of the Middle Ages* to 1954.[17] However,
the original Dutch edition was published in 1919, a fact which Reinhard Strohm, with a few other musicologists, has been careful to
note.[18]

Although *The Waning of the Middle Ages* says very little about
music, and while many musicological articles devoted to Huizinga's
territory and period manage to function perfectly well, both as musicological and cultural studies, without considering the issues he raises
in any form,[19] the musicologist is none the less well equipped to challenge Huizinga on a major aspect of his interpretation of the later
Middle Ages. I refer to the static formalism that he discerns in the
culture of the fourteenth and fifteenth centuries. The question of
formalism, with all that Huizinga takes it to imply about the decline

---

[14] Many of Huizinga's ideas have been re-examined by historians and literary critics. See, for
example, Aston, 'Huizinga's Harvest: England and *The Waning of the Middle Ages*'; Dronke,
'Arbor Caritatis' (examining Huizinga's view of medieval allegory and symbolism); Ferguson,
The Renaissance in Historical Thought, 373–8; Fleckenstein, 'Johan Huizinga als Kulturhis-
toriker'; Gombrich, *Tributes*, 138–63; Jacob, 'Huizinga and the Autumn of the Middle Ages';
Keen, *Chivalry*, 199, 219, 220, and 237; id., 'Huizinga, Kilgour and the Decline of Chivalry';
Lyon, 'Was Johan Huizinga Interdisciplinary?'; Morgan, 'From a Death to a View'; M. Vale,
War and Chivalry, 1–12 et passim; Weintraub, *Visions of Culture*, 208–46. Vale gives an illumi-
nating survey of Huizinga's formation as a historian.
[15] Vale, *War and Chivalry*, 3.   [16] Ibid.   [17] Ganim, *Chaucerian Theatricality*, 31.
[18] 'The Close of the Middle Ages', 311; Bridgman, 'The Age of Ockeghem and Josquin', 246.
[19] See e.g. Higgins, 'Parisian Nobles'.

of creative energy, bears directly upon our conception of song forms such as the rondeau, virelai, and ballade, and upon the social context of chivalry and *courtoisie* which nurtured them.

It is indeed a context that is offered by *The Waning of the Middle Ages*: a way of giving a broad, cultural meaning to isolated facts or of giving colour to the opening pages of a minutely factual history. I shall illustrate both uses of the book below in an attempt to show that Huizinga's vision of the later Middle Ages has been of little use to musicologists in their fundamental project of coming to terms with medieval music and placing it in an appropriate milieu. This chapter considers three recent books which owe a major debt to *The Waning of the Middle Ages* but use it in markedly different ways: Craig Wright's *Music at the Court of Burgundy* (1979); Reinhard Strohm's *Music in Late Medieval Bruges* (1985); and Jeremy Yudkin's *Music in Medieval Europe* (1989). A separate section will then be devoted to what is by far the most sustained attempt yet made to integrate Huizinga's views with the history of fifteenth-century music, and the only one which manages to close the gap between Huizingaesque generalizations about later medieval culture and precise observations about the songs: four chapters in W. H. Kemp's *Burgundian Court Song in the Time of Binchois* (1990). Kemp's discussion raises important questions about the context of the fifteenth-century chanson, and especially about the nature of chivalric culture, which call for fresh answers now that our understanding of chivalry has moved on since 1919. The time has come to develop a more optimistic assessment of later medieval court culture and the milieu of the chanson.

II

It is not wise to paraphrase *The Waning of the Middle Ages*. David Morgan has rightly said that any 'attempt to summarise [Huizinga's] views must certainly do violence to the nuances of emphasis that he inclined to from time to time',[20] and while something similar might be said of the work of all great historians, there is a special difficulty with *The Waning of the Middle Ages* in this regard. Huizinga (Pl. 13) does not present a linear narrative and does not seek to relate events or to describe the structure of institutions; he makes little use of

---

[20] 'From a Death to a View', 96.

Pl. 13. Johan Huizinga

archival sources and does not pretend to offer a systematic argument. In these respects his book is not factual, and the English translation (which Huizinga helped to supervise) presents the reader with scarcely one documented fact. Huizinga's aim lies elsewhere: he explores the 'soul' of the later Middle Ages through the 'forms of life, art and thought' revealed by chronicles, literary texts, and the visual arts. 'It is essentially an essay on later medieval mentality: on tendencies in thought and behaviour as they expressed themselves *per sensibilia*, in religious ceremony and ritual, in competition, in fine arts and literature . . .'.[21] A noted stylist, Huizinga communicates by striking images, by iteration, and by the use of rhetorical skills.[22]

The fundamental thesis of *The Waning of the Middle Ages* is that the fourteenth and fifteenth centuries in France, Burgundy, and Flanders were not a time of preparation for a new growth of culture but rather one of overripeness and decay. Hence the title of the original Dutch edition, *The Autumnal Season of the Middle Ages* (a metaphor that Huizinga later came to regret).[23] Huizinga became

[21] Jacob, 'Huizinga and the Autumn of the Middle Ages', 144.
[22] See Jansonius, 'De Stijl van Huizinga'.
[23] As pointed out in Gombrich, *Tributes*, 147.

convinced that the aristocratic and learned culture of the later Middle Ages in the North was moribund, spending itself in a proliferation of images, both secular and religious, and therefore unable to dissolve the stylization that characterized both art and life. The aspirations of the nobility, he argued, had become stylized in the code of chivalry which had degenerated from its Golden Age in the twelfth century; it could no longer be reconciled with the nobility's concern for wealth and power and had therefore become empty, a testimony to what can happen in a culture when its 'utilitarian concerns . . . [are] imperfectly integrated with its aesthetic and ethical aspirations . . .'.[24] Tournaments had become a charade by the fifteenth century and were divorced from the needs and realities of war. He found vernacular literature, including the large repertoire of rondeaux, virelais, and ballades, to be stifled by its own conventions, while scholasticism seemed only an absurd pedantry that robbed its practitioners of all sense of proportion. Above all, the circumstances of life were so brutal and painful, even for the nobility, that aristocratic culture was essentially escapist; it was believed to be impossible to change the world because man was inherently sinful, and the only alternative was therefore to retreat into a 'dream': to 'color life with a beautiful appearance'.[25]

This suggestive but profoundly negative view of the later medieval period has been reinforced many times since *The Waning of the Middle Ages* was first published. Cartellieri reaches some similar conclusions in his study *The Court of Burgundy* (1929), and so (with reference to German evidence) does Stadelmann in *Vom Geist des ausgehenden Mittelalters* (1929). Huizinga's view of later medieval chivalry has been endorsed and further illustrated by Kilgour's *The Decline of Chivalry* (1937), Ferguson's *The Indian Summer of English Chivalry* (1960),[26] and Barbara Tuchman's *A Distant Mirror: The Calamitous Fourteenth Century* (1978). To describe the influence of *The Waning of the Middle Ages* itself, however, is to linger upon the first chapter. Entitled 'The Violent Tenor of Life', this remarkable

---

[24] Morgan, 'From a Death to a View', 97.

[25] Weintraub, *Visions of Culture*, 236, translating from *Verzamelde Werken*, iii. 41.

[26] For a critique of some of the views expressed in these works see Ainsworth, *Jean Froissart*, 83; Keen, 'Huizinga, Kilgour and the Decline of Chivalry'; and Vale, *War and Chivalry*, 2, describing the studies by Kilgour and Ferguson as ones in which Huizinga's views are 'unhesitatingly accepted'. For Kilgour's influence upon a recent musicological work see Kemp, *Burgundian Court Song in the Time of Binchois*, 77 n. 14, 88 nn. 89, 92.

piece of writing provides an excellent illustration of the book's great power to impress by an abundance of almost unclassified images rather than by arguments or specific facts. It presents a picture of French and Flemish society in the later fourteenth and fifteenth centuries that is both vivid and dramatic:[27]

To the world when it was half a thousand years younger, the outlines of all things seemed more clearly marked than to us. The contrast between suffering and joy, between adversity and happiness, appeared more striking . . . Calamities and indigence were more afflicting than at present; it was more difficult to guard against them, and to find solace. Illness and health presented a more striking contrast; the cold and the darkness of winter were more real evils. Honours and riches were relished with greater avidity and contrasted more vividly with surrounding misery.

It is important to appreciate the essentially corrective purpose of writing like this. If *The Waning of the Middle Ages* sometimes appears to make some exaggerated claims, and to present a one-sided account of the fourteenth and fifteenth centuries, that may be because Huizinga is offering[28]

correction of prevailing historiographic trends. He reacted in particular to the demand that history meet the rigorous conceptual and logical standards of the natural sciences . . . he turned against the idea that man is primarily a rational creature, moved by utilitarian persuasions . . . Huizinga . . . sought descriptive forms for the 'supra-logical', the playing and dreaming man . . .'.

The Waning of the Middle Ages may therefore appear one-sided because it is a dialogue with voices that are now silent or are no longer heeded—especially those of the historians amongst Huizinga's colleagues who looked askance upon his 'literary' style. There is certainly a powerful rhetoric in the book, and one that was very apparent to those historians of Huizinga's generation who were much concerned with questions of urban economic history and politics— subjects which do not lend themselves to a literary presentation in quite the same way as Huizinga's interest in the 'soul' of an age. In 1920 a Utrecht archivist expressed the views of many when he declared that 'literary laurels are always somewhat dangerous for an historian'.[29] We may hear Huizinga's rhetoric even in the brief passage quoted above from Hopman's English translation of 1924, the

---

[27] *The Waning of the Middle Ages*, 9.   [28] Weintraub, *Visions of Culture*, 212.
[29] Quoted in Hugenholtz, 'The Fame of a Masterwork', 97.

result of an 'adaptation, reduction and consolidation' of the original Dutch edition supervised by Huizinga himself. There is an immediate and compelling declaration of consensus between the author and the reader ('. . . the outlines of all things seemed more clearly marked than to us');[30] there are studied parallelisms of syntax and sense ('the contrast between suffering and joy, between adversity and happiness . . .') where the meaning conveyed lies in the enhancement of the tone; there are insistent pairings of synonyms and antonyms, some of them mildly and some of them potently symbolic.[31]

Taken as a whole, the 'Violent Tenor of Life' chapter in *The Waning of the Middle Ages* is one of the most successful attempts to capture the 'otherness' of the later Middle Ages ever made, and Huizinga embarked upon it to counter the kind of economic and political history which he regarded as helping to make 'the [Middle Ages] more comprehensible and attractive to the modern mind' because it dealt in impersonal issues and rational decisions.[32] Even in the 1970s and 1980s, the literary theorists who have been seeking new and radical approaches to the understanding of the past and the place of texts within it have sometimes been content with Huizinga's portrayal.[33] The same might be said for some historians. Here, for example, is the (whole) medieval period as evoked by the cultural historian Jeffrey

[30] This note of consensus is placed slightly later in the Dutch and its force is perhaps correspondingly reduced (*Verzamelde Werken*, iii. 5: 'Toen de wereld vijf eeuwen jonger was, hadden alle levensgevallen veel scherper uiterlijke vormen dan nu. Tusschen leed en vreugde, tusschen rampen en geluk scheen de afstand grooter *dan voor ons* . . .' [my italics]). It is striking that the English has touches of light rhetorical colour not found in the Dutch; compare, for example, the periphrasis that begins the English sentence 'To the world when it was half a thousand years younger . . .' with the plainer Dutch: 'Toen de wereld vijf eeuwen jonger was . . .'. It is tempting to assume that Huizinga's sense of the literary qualities of his first chapter was sharpened by the passage of time (not to mention by early reviews), and that he chose to intensify it in the English version. On the literary character of *The Waning of the Middle Ages* see Jansonius, 'De Stijl van Huizinga'.

[31] On Huizinga's tendency to interpret the past in terms of antinomies, see Weintraub, *Visions of Culture*, 210.

[32] Hugenholtz, 'The Fame of a Masterwork', 93.

[33] See Burrow, 'The Alterity of Medieval Literature', 388, which discusses the article by Zumthor, 'From Hi(story) to Poem', published in *New Literary History*, a journal devoted to literary theory. Burrow quite rightly comments that 'As a characterization of fifteenth-century Burgundian culture, Zumthor's essay represents no very obvious advance on Huizinga.' It may be readily admitted, however, that literary scholars and historians will be involved in some kind of dialogue with Huizinga's ideas for a long time to come. For a recent example, see Gumbrecht, 'Intertextuality and Autumn'.

Richards in his recent study of minority groups in the Middle Ages, *Sex, Dissidence and Damnation*:[34]

There are continuing and shaping themes in the Middle Ages: the tension between authority and dissent, between communality and individualism, between materialism and spirituality, between eroticism and asceticism: conflict between these opposing forces ebbs and flows, waxes and wanes, sharing that perpetual oscillation between extremes that Johan Huizinga saw as a prime characteristic of medieval life. It was a society capable of sudden and violent outbursts of hysteria and paranoia, violence and enthusiasm, often against a background of demographic crisis or social dislocation, associated frequently with outbreaks of famine and disease.

This is profoundly indebted to the ideas and to the literary style of *The Waning of the Middle Ages*. We hear Huizinga's voice with particular clarity in the antinomies: materialism and spirituality; eroticism and asceticism. Is it wise, however, to place so much emphasis upon these? Kammerbeek and others have argued that this aspect of Huizinga's thought owes much to the writers and essayists who were his contemporaries as a young man. A convincing argument has been made that Dutch artists and intellectuals of the later nineteenth century developed antinomies 'as the framework within which they wanted to pursue their passionate discussions and to reach their tentative conclusions: reason versus passion or mysticism; form versus content; individual versus community, art versus society'.[35] Kammerbeek's essay succeeds in evoking the intellectual background to Huizinga's emergence as a Romantic historian in a certain sense of that term, and there can be no doubt of his tendency to interpret the past in terms of sharp contrasts.[36]

III

'The medieval period was one of extraordinary contrasts.'[37] With those words Jeremy Yudkin opens the survey of 'Life in Medieval Europe' which begins his comprehensive history of medieval music, published in 1989 and the most recent to be attempted. That survey is evidently conceived (whether consciously or not) in imitation of the opening chapter of *The Waning of the Middle Ages*, for it offers an

---

[34] *Sex, Dissidence and Damnation*, 1–2. [35] Kossmann, 'Postscript', 225.
[36] Weintraub, *Visions of Culture*, 210. [37] *Music in Medieval Europe*, 2–3.

emphatic accumulation of generalizations and images, intensified (as in the first sentence of the passage quoted below) by Huizinga's favourite rhetorical device of asyndeton, the omission of conjunctions:[38]

Death was everywhere: in simple diseases, in accidents of nature, in short journeys. It swept wholesale through the land in periodic wars, in natural disasters, or in recurring waves of the relentless plague . . . The physicality of death was a constant preoccupation: paintings, stained-glass windows, and even sculptures contain gruesome depictions of decomposing corpses providing meals for worms.

It is difficult to capture Yudkin's understanding of *The Waning of the Middle Ages*; he praises it for conveying the 'richness and depth' of its period,[39] yet while Huizinga's chapters do indeed convey the luxury of court culture, his theme is not the 'depth' of that civilization but rather what he regarded as its shallowness. Yudkin blurs the focus of Huizinga's pessimistic vision and sees the whole medieval period in those terms. (He distinguishes the First and Second Feudal Ages, but he does so after his intensely generalized opening pages on the horrors of life in medieval Europe.) For good measure, Yudkin adorns his chapter with sensational pictures: a statue whose eyes are devoured by toads; a leprous beggar and a cripple; a horrific instrument for trepanning.

It is neither difficult to appreciate what Yudkin is doing nor in some measure to approve it. During the later Middle Ages (and indeed long after) human beings did not live in consistently nourished and stable communities, nor did they have the freedom from major epidemics that is now enjoyed in the industrialized West. None the less, Yudkin's pessimistic vision does little to explain the extraordinary creative energy of Western musicians during the Middle Ages. It is also possible to have reservations about his method; to emphasize the hardships and horrors of medieval existence is a crude way of arousing a reader's historical imagination, and many historians will surely wish to respond that a great deal of later civilization might be evoked in similar terms. We think of seventeenth-century England as it emerges from the notebooks of John Aubrey, for example, a miasma of filth, plague, lawlessness, horrific public executions, and traumatizing surgery; such was the world of Halley, Marvell, and

---

[38] *Music in Medieval Europe*, 2–3.   [39] Ibid. 17.

Bacon. It is characteristic of Huizinga's thought to minimize such comparisons between the Middle Ages and the sixteenth or seventeenth century, comparisons that are vital if we are to redraw his picture of the later Middle Ages. As Jacob has observed:[40]

The later Middle Ages might indeed mingle cruelty with kindness, but were they any worse than the century depicted by the satirical Hogarth . . . ? The image of death is ubiquitous [in the fifteenth century] but is it any more prevailing than in the later Tudor period . . . ?

There is a different kind of debt to Huizinga in Craig Wright's *Music at the Court of Burgundy 1364–1419: A Documentary History*, for this is a book whose subject and chosen period allow a directed and purposeful use of *The Waning of the Middle Ages*. Wright's book is not, and does not attempt to be, a cultural history; it gathers facts and relates them to administrative and institutional concerns: the needs of the ducal chapel, for example, or the provision of minstrels for court entertainment. The cultural resonances of these concerns are mostly obvious and well established. When Wright inclines towards a general interpretation of musical life within the wider context of Burgundian court culture, his views are almost entirely derived from Huizinga. At one point, for example, he declares that 'tradition, or stylized form, pervaded every aspect of late-mediaeval life, from the intricacy of the poetic "formes fixes" to the impracticality of the armored cavalry charge'.[41] Those remarks are pure Huizinga with their emphasis upon the stylization of life in art and their confidence that chivalric military techniques were obsolete by *c*.1400. Wright also owes something to Huizinga in his willingness to believe that late medieval people were capable of sustained irrational behaviour; would any reasonable man continually send expensively armed and trained knights into combat if it was *impractical* to do so? Wright's assessment simply does not match the fifteenth-century evidence: the chronicler and Burgundian veteran Jean Wavrin, for example, refers to the 'fearful efforts of cavalry',[42] but one can readily excuse Wright for not taking such evidence into account. As Malcolm Vale has observed, historians (not to speak of musicologists) 'have been curiously unaware of the importance of changes which were

---

[40] 'Huizinga and the Autumn of the Middle Ages', 148.
[41] *Music at the Court of Burgundy*, 11.
[42] Quoted in Vale, *War and Chivalry*, 114.

taking place in the techniques of fighting with the lance and, consequently, in the use of cavalry during the fourteenth and fifteenth centuries'.[43]

This is one kind of objection to Huizinga's vision: that it overlooks or misinterprets medieval evidence. Another is that it neglects the parallels between court culture in the later Middle Ages and the courtliness of earlier and later periods. Here is Wright once more:[44]

Sobriquets, anagrams, riddle canons, and the 'mannered' notation were all part of the musical scene of the late fourteenth century, in the same way that blazons, mottoes and symbolic and emblematic devices pervaded the secular courts and knightly orders of the period; the more mediaeval man tried quixotically to recapture the essence and meaning of the archaic code of chivalry in the late Middle Ages, the more importance he placed on artificial devices, on factitious values, and on contrived forms . . . [Baude] Cordier . . . enjoyed deceptive appearance and fanciful forms, as his well-known chansons in the shape of a heart and a circle canon attest. He was a creator of illusions in an illusory age.

Like Huizinga, Wright sees a proliferation of empty, artificial forms, aspirations, and images in the court culture of Burgundy, and he regards chivalry as an 'archaic code' which 'medieval man' was trying to recapture in the fourteenth and fifteenth centuries. We shall return to this disdainful view of chivalry; for the moment it suffices to observe that *The Waning of the Middle Ages* has led Wright into a strangely unsympathetic and even an unfair assessment of his materials. The famous notations of two Cordier songs which Wright mentions, one on staves that form a heart and another on staves that form a circle,[45] do not reveal a love of 'deceptive appearance' (what is deceptive about them?), and Wright's reference to them as 'illusions' for an 'illusory age' is quite mystifying. We may surely regard them as two magnificent examples of calligraphic expertise. Even if we chose to interpret them—together with the love of sobriquets that Wright mentions—as evidence of a certain frame of mind, there would not be anything distinctive to the later medieval period in that mentality; there is no difficulty in finding other periods of the Middle Ages when courtiers adopted sobriquets and developed a taste for cal-

[43] Quoted in Vale, *War and Chivalry*, 115.   [44] *Music at the Court of Burgundy*, 133–4.
[45] Reproduced in Wright, *Music at the Court of Burgundy*, pl. 7 (the circle canon) and Strohm, 'The Close of the Middle Ages', pl. 78 (the rondeau *Belle, bonne, sage* in the form of a heart).

ligraphic contrivances of an ornate kind. The Carolingian court, where Alcuin called himself Flaccus, and where acrostic poems were composed and copied with extraordinary calligraphic ingenuity, provides an example.[46]

A more intriguing engagement with *The Waning of the Middle Ages* is to be found in Reinhard Strohm's *Music in Late Medieval Bruges*,[47] a book which explores the life of a city in the heartland of Huizinga's territory and his period. In a slightly later study, published in 1990, Strohm refers to the 'legendary fame' of Huizinga's book and describes its main thesis as only 'slightly exaggerated'.[48] *Music in Late Medieval Bruges* opens with a chapter on the 'Townscape—Soundscape' of Bruges, recording in a footnote that the chapter has been 'greatly influenced' by the writings of Huizinga.[49] The concept of an opening chapter filled with evocative images has clearly been developed from *The Waning of the Middle Ages*, and indeed the townscape which Strohm evokes in the first chapter of his book will appeal to all those who love Huizinga's work: the ceremonies, the processions, the intoxicating sound of the great public bells, the loneliness of the uninhabited countryside—all these are present in Strohm's resonant description of Bruges. Here and there we may recognize a point of convergence; for Huizinga's meditation on the *Arnolfini Wedding*, by van Eyck[50]

'Jan van Eyck was here.' Only a moment ago, one might think. The sound of his voice still seems to linger in the silence of this room.

there is this from Strohm on the first page of his book, where historical imagination is working at full stretch behind a generally restrained style:[51]

The moment in which Giovanni Arnolfini raised his right hand to confirm the oath which he was to pronounce . . . was witnessed by the painter Jan van Eyck, who recorded 'Johannes de Eyck fuit hic' ('was here') . . .

There is also something of the Dutch historian's method in Strohm's account of the townscape and soundscape of Bruges, for Huizinga once remarked that the historian must 'conjure up living pictures in the private theatre of the mind';[52] Strohm *imagines* the

[46] Godman, *Poets and Emperors*, 56–9.
[47] See esp. pp. 1–9 and 151 n. 1.
[48] 'The Close of the Middle Ages', 311.
[49] *Music in Late Medieval Bruges*, 151 n. 1.
[50] *The Waning of the Middle Ages*, 247.
[51] *Music in Late Medieval Bruges*, 1.
[52] Quoted in Vale, *War and Chivalry*, 4.

fifteenth-century city and expresses those imaginings, controlled by scholarship, in a language that shares Huizinga's ability to rise to moments of verbal exaltation:[53]

The noises of the market-place, the inns, the workshops, the stock-exchange, the public baths—they have all died, and so have the music and the song of the nightingale in the orchard. And yet, these sounds have shaped the townscape, contributing to its order and disorder. The sound of music is still frozen in the shapes of Bruges.

What makes Strohm's use of Huizinga so intriguing is that he admires *The Waning of the Middle Ages* but does not appear to find much evidence of a 'waning' or an 'expiring' medieval world in his own materials. If Strohm is inviting us to imagine Bruges in terms of Huizinga's ideas, then he is so tactful in issuing that invitation that we may be forgiven for missing its summons. What seems to happen in *Music in Late Medieval Bruges* is that Strohm feels the presence of Huizinga in his first chapter because his aims there can accommodate evocative imagery and an elevated diction; when he moves from the general to the particular, however, and when more traditional musicological techniques and discursive practices become appropriate, then the imposing shade of Huizinga departs. Strohm gives a fine description of Philip the Good's entry into Bruges in 1440 complete with its music, banners, pageants, allegorical tableaux, and mass gestures of submission to the duke (1,300 people walking barefoot and bareheaded in a procession), but he does not view it as a factitious display of exhausted allegories, stylized meanings, and gestures. We may suspect that Strohm's sense of the political and social realities of fifteenth-century Bruges is too sympathetic for him to adopt such an interpretation. Strohm is describing the life of a town which lends itself to a discussion of Huizinga's major themes, including the survival of a supposedly 'archaic' chivalry in a realm increasingly dominated in the North by the urban and mercantile towns of Flanders; however, he finds a vital and integrated culture in the city that excites his admiration. The bells of his Bruges are not the ominous instruments of *The Waning of the Middle Ages* tolling through the course of some brutal judicial duel; they are rather the elements in 'a magnificient hierarchy of sound-signals'.[54] Strohm finds the role of music in the processions of Bruges to be 'marvellous' for the way it

---

[53] *Music in Late Medieval Bruges*, 2.   [54] Ibid. 3.

'helped order time and space within urban life'.[55] Taken as a whole, Strohm's book provides a keen illustration of Wallace Ferguson's observation that the power of *The Waning of the Middle Ages* derives 'less from the explicit statement of [Huizinga's] thesis than from the total impression left by a book filled with evocative imagery'.[56]

IV

The most sustained attempt to integrate Huizinga's views and the history of fifteenth-century music is made by Walter H. Kemp in *Burgundian Court Song in the Time of Binchois* (1990). With this book we come at last to precise reflections upon a musical repertory, for the core of Kemp's discussion is provided by the sixty-two polyphonic chansons in *EscA* (El Escorial, Biblioteca del Monasterio, Cod. V.III.24), a Burgundian corpus of the period 1430–55 which includes pieces by Binchois (although only one is attributed to him in that source).[57] Kemp offers nearly fifty pages on the place of these chansons in the court culture of Burgundy, and in doing so he attempts to recover the full meaning of a major repertoire of songs (Pl. 14; Ex. 15).

Kemp links the evidence of Burgundian chronicles, literary texts, art, chivalry, legends, and taste together in a way that is so strongly associated with Huizinga that Jacob has called it 'Huizinga's method'.[58] The chansons of *EscA* lie so close to the heart of Huizinga's interest in play and aesthetic forms of life, and he himself pays so little attention to music, that one can readily feel the lines of force which draw Kemp towards *The Waning of the Middle Ages*; there is so much for him to amplify and illustrate. For proof of the

[55] Ibid. 4.   [56] *The Renaissance in Historical Thought*, 374.

[57] The anonymous chansons are edited in Kemp, *Anonymous Pieces*. On this manuscript see Kemp, *Burgundian Court Song*, and Slavin, 'Questions of Authenticity'.

[58] 'Huizinga and the Autumn of the Middle Ages', 144: 'Huizinga used his literary and artistic texts to enucleate the mental habits and assumptions of the fourteenth and fifteenth centuries. We are doing it today only with a less conscious sense of the peculiar character of a cultural period; none the less we are following Huizinga's method, linking medieval legend, art, chivalry and taste . . .'. For the use of *The Waning of the Middle Ages* in Kemp's book see *Burgundian Court Song in the Time of Binchois*, 75 n. 4, 76 n. 8, 79 nn. 29 and 34, 80 nn. 42 and 43, 87 n. 84, 102 n. 56, 108 n. 5, 109 n. 10, 110 n. 14, and 113 n. 31 (this last with some bibliography listing studies where Huizinga's conception of a 'waning' medieval spirit is discussed). Perhaps the purest use of Huizinga ever to be found in musicological writing is here, p. 113, when Kemp declares that '. . . the Burgundian song-makers themselves were practitioners of Death, "servants of an expiring mode of thought"'. Needless to say, Kemp's quotation is from *The Waning of the Middle Ages*.

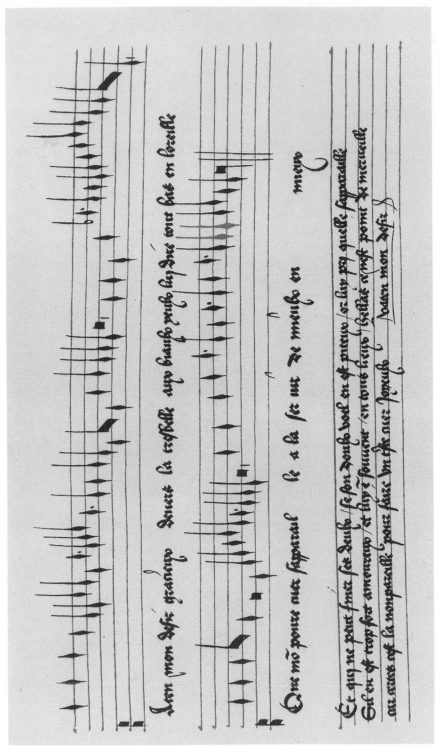

Pl. 14. The Superius part of the anonymous rondeau *Va t'en, mon desir gracieux*. El Escorial, Biblioteca del Monas-terio, V.III.24, fo. 60ᵛ. Reproduced by permission

Ex. 15. The rondeau *Va t'en, mon desir gracieux* (refrain text only).
Adapted from Kemp, *Anonymous Pieces*, 45

attraction, we need look no further than Kemp's assertion that 'Philip the Good, the third Burgundian duke, fashioned a court culture in a dream . . .'.[59] This seems a rather odd choice of words until we recall that the concept of dream is central to Huizinga's view of the declining Middle Ages; it represents one manner of escape that he discerned in cultures where the conditions of life were too distressing or too brutal to face: 'if earthly reality is so hopelessly miserable . . . let us colour life with a beautiful appearance, let us live away in the dreamland of bright fancy, let us temper reality with the ecstasies of the ideal'.[60]

Kemp's debt to Huizinga prompts him to the kind of unsympathetic judgement that we encountered in Wright's study. A striking example is provided by his comment upon a passage in the manual of poetic art by Eustache Deschamps, *Art de dictier*. Deschamps, discussing the liberal arts, remarks that music is the 'medicine' of the arts because it gives relaxation to those who have become exhausted in their studies of other subjects in the trivium and quadrivium.[61] That seems a perfectly natural and indeed humane point for Deschamps to make, and one that accords with the long literary tradition of praise for the medicinal and recreative powers of music. It is all the more surprising, therefore, to find Kemp describing Deschamps, in a somewhat cynical fashion, as a man 'conscious of the grosser realities of his "courtly" setting' and who was therefore prepared to regard music as 'a sanitizing agent'.[62]

What kind of aesthetic and stylistic judgements does Kemp pass upon the *EscA* chansons in the shadow of *The Waning of the Middle Ages*? It cannot be emphasized too strongly that Kemp's evidence for a Huizingaesque reading of the chanson is based almost exclusively upon the poetry of the songs. There is a clear distinction in his book (acknowledged by a division into two parts) between the first five chapters, which discuss the music of the *EscA* chansons in an almost exclusively analytic or technical fashion but say very little about the

---

[59] *Burgundian Court Song*, 67.

[60] Weintraub, *Visions of Culture*, 236, translating from *Verzamelde Werken*, iii. 41.

[61] For text and translation of the relevant extract see Page, 'Machaut's "Pupil"', 488–9: 'Music is the final, and the medicinal science of the seven arts; for when the heart and spirit of those applied to the other arts treated above are wearied and vexed with their labours, Music, by the sweetness of her science and the melodiousness of her voice, sings them her delectable and pleasant melodies . . .'

[62] *Burgundian Court Song*, 87–8.

poetry, and the last four chapters, which discuss the poems of the chansons in terms of chivalry and court culture but say very little about the music. In his analyses of the music Kemp remarks, as one well might, upon the relatively traditional and conservative nature of the harmonic sonorities used in the *EscA* chansons (conservative, that is, relative to the practices of later fourteenth-century French composers), but if he regards the melodies, textures and sonorities of these chansons as a sonic projection of a waning creative energy in later medieval culture, or of a 'Valois chivalric charade', he does not say so (or cannot find a way of saying so). With the poetry it is another matter. It is in Part II of his book, entitled 'The *Chanson* in Burgundian Court Culture' and mostly devoted to the poems of the chansons and their social or literary context, that Kemp turns to Huizinga. It is certainly true, for example, that the songs of *EscA*, and indeed of many other fifteenth-century sources, refer to personifications that will for ever be associated with *Le Roman de la Rose*. There is Bel Acueil, for example:[63]

> Mais Bel Acueil la grand meslée
> Desfit, et y vient au secours.

and Dangier:[64]

> Dangier m'a bien d'un hault osté . . .

At one point Kemp refers to the way fifteenth-century court culture 'perpetuated' these allegorical characters, but a few pages later he takes some of the *EscA* poets to task because their use of allegorical personages does *not* perpetuate the imagery and context of those figures as they appear in *Le Roman de la Rose*. It seems that the fifteenth-century writers cannot win: if they follow Guillaume de Lorris or Jean de Meung then they are to be regarded as derivative poets; if they change anything relating to the personifications as they find them in *Le Roman de la Rose* they are then said to reveal 'the reduction to empty husks suffered by these once-meaningful literary creatures'.[65]

Kemp's willingness to read the poems of *EscA* in terms of a declining, decadent medieval tradition is epitomized in his commentary

---

[63] Ibid. 94.   [64] Ibid. 91.   [65] Ibid. 94.

upon several passages, including this one from the rondeau *Puis que Fortune m'est si dure*:[66]

> c'est trop fort
> Quant soudanement me desnie.

Kemp observes that in this song, as in several others in *EscA*, Fortune 'is deprived even of her wheel' because it is not mentioned. He makes this judgement in relation to what he calls 'the medieval system', apparently a stock of literary and iconographic traditions so stable, in his view, that it can be used to measure the decline of medieval artistic traditions. This seems a very strange critical practice. When did this decline begin in the case of Fortune? Are we to push it back as far as the mid-fourteenth century in France, for example, when Guillaume de Machaut fails to mention Fortune's wheel when he invokes her in his ballade *De toutes flours*? And if the image of Fortune's wheel waned with the Middle Ages, why do we find it (with the nuances of rhetoric and archaism that had always accompanied such references to Fortune) in Boileau and Voltaire, not to speak of Goldsmith and Tennyson?

More significant than these details, perhaps, is Kemp's apparent lack of interest in the rhetorical and phonic aspects of the *EscA* poetry which are likely to have been of some (perhaps of most) importance to contemporaries. Consider, for example, the following rondeau refrain from *EscA*:

> Lune tresbelle, clere lune,
> Qui servez d'un esmay en May:
> A quoy proufite, cest esmay
> L'autre dez fois trop plus que l'une?

This text seems to catch Kemp's imagination, for he devotes several striking and convincing paragraphs to 'literary moon-magic', citing Theocritus, Walafrid Strabo, Chaucer, Lydgate, Christine de Pisan, and humanist manuals of iconography in the process. He is even prepared, perhaps for the first time in his book, to acknowledge a depth of reflection in the *EscA* poetry as he describes the moon of the *EscA* rondeau as 'the boundary of our sublunary world of contingence and mutable fortune'.[67] This is all admirable, but it is surprising that he has no praise for the calculated rhetoric of *Lune tresbelle, clere lune*.

---

[66] *Burgundian Court Song*, 96. [67] Ibid. 101.

The first line is a chiasmus, intensified by asyndeton (*Lune . . . lune*). The musical setting observes this chiasmus with a melodic line of admirable clarity and balance, phrasing naturally at the mid-point of the chiasmus in bar 3 and closing it with a flourish between bars 6 and 10 (Ex. 16). This melody is set over two lower parts which have all the discretion so characteristic of this repertoire. The second line of the poem places two virtual homophones in a prominent position (*esmay en May*), matched by a musical prominence in bar 13, where the cantus rises to its peak for *esmay*, and bars 14–15, where '*May*' is flourished. (These effects are achieved somewhat at the expense of melodic grace.) The stanza ends with an ingenious homonymic rhyme (*lune . . . l'une*) that is all the more conspicuous for having been preceded by another, and which turns the rhymes of the poem into another, greater chiasmus (*Lune . . . en May . . . esmay . . . l'une*). We may be confident that these are among the effects which a fifteenth-century poet would have assumed to be part of the *rhétorique* of his poem, and they deserve close attention in any attempt to perceive the polyphonic chanson in historical terms.

Perhaps the most surprising omission in Kemp's discussion of the Burgundian chanson is any consideration of the rondeau form in which the songs of *EscA* are chiefly cast. This is a significant omission, I suggest, for it is on the grounds of (supposedly) stylized form that the musicologist is particularly well equipped to take issue with Huizinga. Let us consider a rondeau by Guillaume de Machaut, the poet who, more than any other, set the fashion for the *formes fixes* of the fourteenth and fifteenth centuries:[68]

Rose, liz, printemps, verdure,	A
Fleur, baume et tres douce odour,	
Belle, passes en doucour.	B
Et tous les biens de Nature	a
Avez, dont je vous aour	
Rose, liz, printemps, verdure,	A
Fleur, baume et tres douce odour;	
Et quant toute creature	a
Seurmonte vostre valour,	
Bien puis dire, et par honnour:	b

[68] For the text with its musical setting see *The Works of Guillaume de Machaut*, ed. Schrade, rondeau 10.

Ex. 16. The rondeau *Lune tresbelle, clere lune* (refrain text only). Adapted from Kemp, *Anonymous Pieces*, 15–16

Rose, liz, printemps, verdure,   *A*
Fleur, baume et tres douce odour
 Belle, passes en doucour.   *B*

In this layout *A* and *B* represent the two musical segments of the rondeau when they appear with refrain text (italicized above), while *a* and *b* represent the same two segments when they appear without refrain text. The form may therefore be represented as:

$$AB \quad a \quad A \quad ab \quad AB$$

This form has been defined and described many times, often expertly (by David Fallows, for example),[69] but I do not believe that appropriate emphasis has been given to what might be called the 'dynamic' which it reveals in performance. The source of this dynamic is that a rondeau begins with a *proposal*:

$$AB \quad . \quad\quad . \quad\quad .. \quad\quad ..$$

and ends with a *confirmation* of what has been proposed:

$$.. \quad\quad . \quad\quad . \quad\quad .. \quad\quad AB$$

The term 'proposal' may be judged appropriate, for in any performance of a rondeau the ear senses that the first *AB* is being offered for inspection as the material from which the piece is to be assembled; it is part of this process of inspection that, during the performance of the first *AB*, the discerning ear searches in the text and in the music's cadential patterns for the division between the *A* and the *B*, since that is the crucial point for understanding the form as it manifests itself in any particular song. It is a moment that is always found with satisfaction, and it becomes a significant point of style in the rondeaux of the early fifteenth century to insert a highly formalized musical phrase—almost a tag—at the start of the *A* section, which, in performance, has the effect of marking the progress of the form (Ex. 17).

The term 'confirmation' is also an appropriate one in this context, I suggest, since the final *AB* of a rondeau is more than a mere repetition; if it were that alone then it would be dull in performance and purely formal in conception. To be sure, the final *AB* is the most challenging part of a rondeau for a performer, since there is always a

---

[69] Fallows, 'Polyphonic Song'; see also the excellent survey by Earp, 'Lyrics for Reading and Lyrics for Singing'.

Ex. 17. The rondeau *Je voel servir* (refrain text only) by Gilet Velut.
Adapted from Reaney, *Early Fifteenth-Century Music*, ii. 118

danger that it will appear to be an essentially formal gesture with no inner, musical motivation. None the less, in a well-performed rondeau the final *AB* simply has to happen.

Why so? There is another aspect to the dynamic of a rondeau which might be called the *examination*. In this section the *A* and *a* music is subjected to the test of two continuous repetitions (*aAa*) which it must pass if it is to merit the confirmation. The effect of a misplaced or over-emphatic gesture is rapidly magnified as the rondeau moves through its *aAa* phase. An example of a piece which fails the test is *Las que me demanderoye* by the early fifteenth-century composer François Lebertoul and preserved only in Oxford, Canonici misc. 213 (Ex. 18). The opening gesture in the first and second measures, where the Tenor moves above the Cantus and reaches its melodic peak for the whole piece, is too assertive for an *aAa* repetition where it will be heard three times in a row; a more careful composer like Gilet Velut uses such ostentatious crossing of parts to mark the opening of the *B/b* section where a conspicuous gesture sits well, the ear's appetite for such an effect having been prepared by the unvaried *aAa* material that preceded it (Ex. 17). The way Lebertoul's Cantus rises to its peak in measure 11, coupled with a hemiola rhythm in the Tenor and Contratenor which adds further emphasis to the moment, is perhaps too strong a figure for the close of an *A* or an *a* section and palls upon the third consecutive hearing.

Within what I have been calling the 'examination' there is a subtle process of change. The first *AB*, once proposed, undergoes a series of reincarnations, so to speak; some are more lowly than others, but at the end of the piece the cycle has been completed and the refrain is fully alive once more in both words and music: *AB*. This process is easy to describe. After the first *AB* there is a relatively lowly incarnation of the refrain which has only part of the refrain music, the text having changed:

> *AB* *a* . .. ..

Next—and this is a cunning touch, because it is not yet the middle of the piece, but near it—the refrain is reborn with both words and music, but is not complete and it must therefore continue with the cycle of change:

> *AB* *a* *A* .. ..

Ex. 18. The rondeau *Las que me demanderoye* (refrain text only), by
Lebertoul. Adapted from Reaney, *Early Fifteenth-Century Music*, ii. 42

The next stage brings a different kind of existence for the refrain—the closest yet to its full self—as its music returns complete but the refrain text vanishes entirely:

$$AB \quad a \quad A \quad ab \quad ..$$

Finally, the cycle is complete and the refrain returns in full with both its words and music:

$$AB \quad a \quad A \quad ab \quad AB$$

I have chosen somewhat impressionistic language ('incarnation' . . . 'new life') because something of that kind is necessary to convey how, in performance, the deep structure of the rondeau form is concerned with *being* the refrain and *coming to be* the refrain. Viewed in these terms, the rondeau can be seen as a marvellously well-judged form, and we may understand why it should have taken French composers more than a century to exhaust its artistic possibilities.

V

Chivalry, the complex ethic of excellence in arms and demeanour which dominates the romances and chronicles of the fifteenth century, is a key issue in the study of Huizinga's influence. Kemp rightly acknowledges the importance of *chevalerie* in his noteworthy chapter entitled 'Chivalric Humanism and the *Chanson*'. As we have seen, Huizinga's view of fifteenth-century court culture as an escapist dream implies not just escapism but also a powerful idealism ('let us temper reality with the ecstasies of the ideal'), and chivalry was the focus of much aristocratic idealism and aesthetic appetite in the later Middle Ages. Kemp emphasizes that polyphonic songs were often performed at ceremonies with a strongly chivalric tone; 'the *chanson*', he comments, 'was functional in those *extravagances* of what Huizinga called "applied literature": the banquets and shows, when Alexander, Jason and Gideon took on the physiognomy of the courts of Philip and Charles the Bold' (my italics; note the pervasive censoriousness of Kemp's diction here as in other places).[70] Kemp calls this later medieval ethic of warriorhood 'Chivalric Humanism', a borrowed term which is not, perhaps, an entirely happy one; 'humanism' has too many meanings to be useful here without qualification (and

---

[70] *Burgundian Court Song*, 80.

Kemp offers none), and its use in this context seems daring to the point of being provocative. As for the adjective 'chivalric', it is 'tonal rather than precise in its implications'.[71] Kemp is therefore wise to leave this 'Chivalric Humanism' undefined, but it is plain that he regards it as 'a dream' and 'a charade'. In his judgement it is escapist: 'a sensuous inducement to escape from the grossness and violence of reality'.[72]

The problem with this view of Burgundian court culture in general, and of fifteenth-century knighthood in particular, is that it has been so extensively modified by recent work on chivalry that it now appears out of date. Kemp describes Burgundian chivalry as 'a preservation of a memory',[73] as if such nostalgia were somehow characteristic of knightly culture under the Burgundian dukes. In recent years, however, many scholars have argued that chivalric culture was nostalgic at all times in the Middle Ages.[74] Chivalry, like the Christian religion, took its models of excellence and virtue from the remote past. The desire to model a 'fallen' present upon a great past (where Hector, Julius Caesar, Roland, King Arthur, and others existed in a gallery of timeless excellence) was no stronger in the fifteenth century than it had been in the twelfth, although it may sometimes have possessed a different tone;[75] to present the chivalric culture of Burgundy as a 'conscious medieval*ism*'—presumably implying a deliberate attempt to recreate the supposed Golden Age of chivalry in the twelfth century—is unwise, therefore, though it directly accords with Huizinga's views. Something similar might be said of the decision to call the aristocratic courtesy of Burgundy 'the charade of past tense *courtoisie*'. That phrase would have surprised Binchois or Dufay, and it is another manifestation of the long-standing tendency amongst historians and literary scholars to regard the court culture of the

---

[71] Keen, *Chivalry*, 2.   [72] *Burgundian Court Song*, 114.   [73] Ibid. 76.

[74] See the revisionist essays in Benson and Leyerle, *Chivalric Literature*.

[75] Ibid., pp. vii–viii: 'A number of scholars have contributed to current understanding of the extensive body of late medieval chivalric literature, notably the great social historian, Johan Huizinga, in his influential study, *The Waning of the Middle Ages*, and R. L. Kilgour in his book that appeared ten years after Huizinga's, *The Decline of Chivalry as Shown in the French Literature of the Late Middle Ages*. To these might now be added Barbara W. Tuchman's new biography of Enguerrand de Coucy VII, *A Distant Mirror: The Calamitous 14th Century*. All three of these works present late medieval chivalric society as being in a state of decline. The essays in this volume are counter to that prevailing attitude. The point of celebrating Arthur's Round Table was not to lament a decline from the glories of old, but to create an ideal exemplar as a guide for the future.'

twelfth century (the time when that culture first receives sustained expression in the vernacular) as somehow pristine and authentic, a view which almost always, as here, involves a disparagement of the fifteenth century.[76]

These issues gather around the tournament. Chronicles and literary sources leave no doubt that the festivities which accompanied jousts and tourneys were often adorned by the performance of chansons, both in royal or ducal residences and in the halls of prosperous towns such as Bruges.[77] The mid-century romance of *Cleriadus et Meliadice*, for example, seems entirely in accord with the evidence of chronicles when it describes the performance of a polyphonic song at a court festivity after a *pas d'armes* (Pl. 15):[78]

Quant ilz eubrent longuement dansé aux menestrez ilz danserent aux chanchons. Sy commencha Cleriadus que Meliadice auoit faicte. Vng escuier de sa compaignie luy tenoit la teneur, et pensez qu'il estoit bon a oyr, car il chantoit le mieulx que on auoit jamais ouy. Et quant il [l']eubt fait il [la] bailla par escript en la main de Melyadice.

When the company had danced a good while to the minstrels they began to dance to songs. So Cleriadus began to sing what Meliadice had written. A squire from his retinue sang the tenor part for him and you may believe that it was good to hear, for [Cleriadus] sang better than anyone had ever heard before. When he had finished he put a written copy of the song into the hands of Meliadice.

This is fiction, of course, but the *pas d'armes* described in *Cleriadus et Meliadice* seems very close to the *pas d'armes* of reality: 'a later medieval *Gesamtkunstwerk* binding together the arts of war and peace, and employing allegory, poetry, ceremonial and music to achieve its dramatic effect'.[79] Like the *pas d'armes* of contemporary France and Burgundy, the one in *Cleriadus et Meliadice* has a title, 'La Joyeuse Maison', and as in some contemporary practice the protagonist (Cleriadus) adopts a special heraldry for the event, becoming *le chevalier vert* and jousting at 'La Joyeuse Maison' with all comers. At this point in the narrative the knights and ladies are celebrating in

[76] See Vale, *War and Chivalry, passim*.

[77] Compare Strohm, *Music in Late Medieval Bruges*, 83–4: 'Everyone was under the spell of chivalry . . . Flemish songs and French rondeaux were probably recited at the banquets following the tournaments before a large audience.' Strohm's discussion of these issues is outstanding.

[78] Text and translation from Page, 'The Performance of Songs', 447.

[79] Vale, *War and Chivalry*, 68; see also Annunziata, 'The *Pas d'Armes*'.

a hall after the martial events—exactly the context which manuals of tournament practice sometimes specify as an appropriate one for the performance of chansons during chivalric meetings and assemblies.[80] Another sign of the convergence of romance and reality in this passage is that the author of *Cleriadus et Meliadice* gives the verbal text of the polyphonic chanson which is performed in the extract quoted above and it is one so closely related to a song in *EscA* that some kind of interrelationship cannot be doubted (cf. Ex. 15). A comparison of the rondeau refrains will make the resemblance clear:

EscA 61

VA T'EN MON DESIR gracieux,
DEVERS la tres belle aux biaulx yeux,
LUI DIRE TOUT BAS EN L'OREILLE
Que MON povre CUER S'APARAILLE
A la servir de mieulx en mieulx.

Cleriadus et Meliadice

ALEZ VOUS EN MON DESIR amoureux
DEVERS celluy pour quy souuent je veille
LUY DIRE TOUT BAS EN L'OREILLE
Qu'aultre de luy je n'ayme si m'et Dieux . . .
Qu'a bien aymer MON COEUR SY APPAREILLE

The ethos of the polyphonic chansons enjoyed at the Burgundian court would appear to have been profoundly coloured by the tone of chivalric festivity in general and of the tournament in particular, a point acknowledged by Kemp when he quite rightly describes the chansons of *EscA* as having provided the musical element in the

[80] See, for example, the regulations in the tournament treatise of René of Anjou (*Traité*, ed. Pognon, 58): 'Le soir après souper toutes dames et damoiselles et tous les tournoyants se réuniront en la sale ou se feront les danses comme le soir précédent . . .'. Chronicles confirm that the music for these occasions, when festivities were adorned by dancing, was often provided by minstrels playing both *haut* and *bas* instruments, but was also sometimes supplemented with what are usually called either chansons or caroles, a combination also found in the description of royal and noble weddings or indeed important entertainments (*esbatemens*) of any kind: 'en une belle grande salle . . . furent dansses de pluiseurs instrumens, et aussi de chançons' (Morand (ed.), *Chronique de Jean le Févre*, ii. 157). This is exactly the kind of entertainment which is lavishly decribed in *Cleriadus et Meliadice* (Page, 'The Performance of Songs', *passim*). As the alternation of the terms caroles/chansons in the chronicles suggests, the songs were often performed for dancing; *Cleriadus et Meliadice*, however, provides valuable evidence that the songs performed at the prize-giving after jousts (and no doubt on other, comparable occasions) were sometimes polyphonic chansons. It remains unknown whether these chansons were also used for dancing on some occasions, as *Cleriadus et Meliadice* suggests.

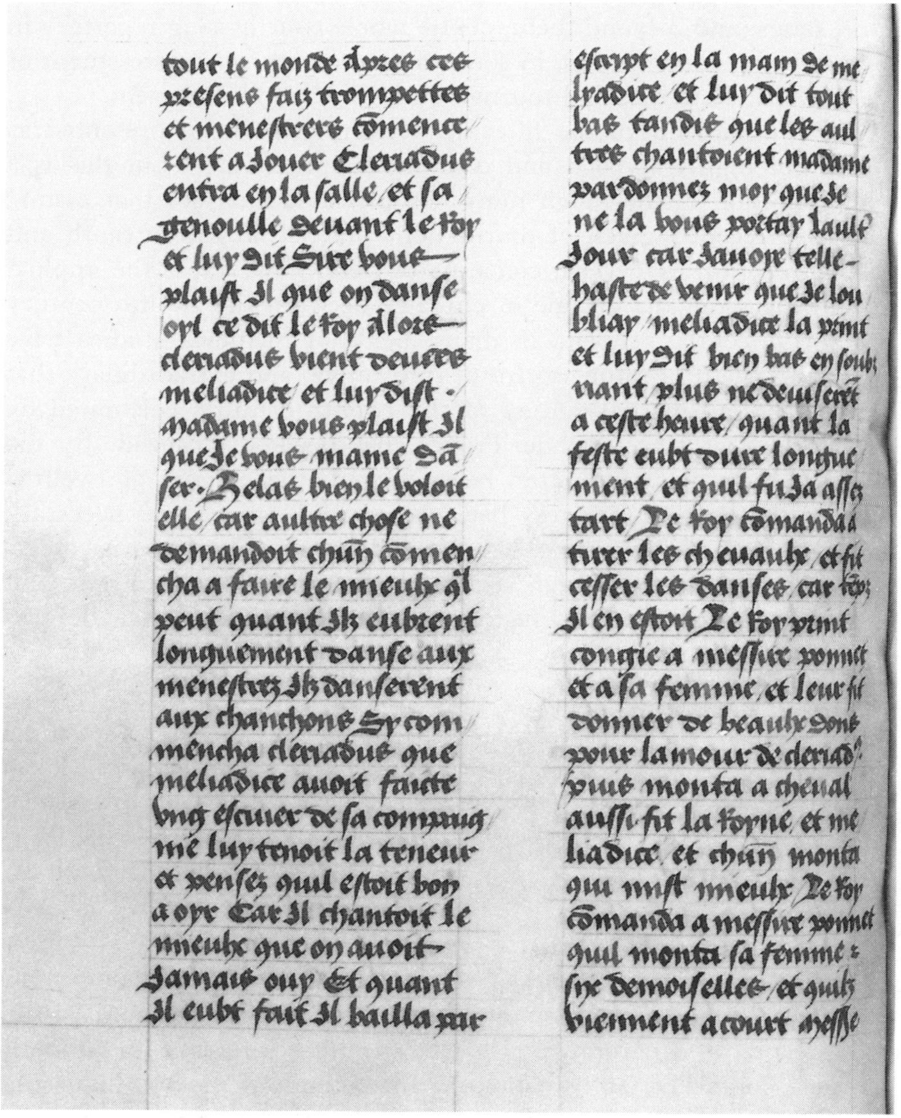

Pl. 15. A passage from the fifteenth-century prose romance *Cleriadus et Meliadice*, describing the performance of a rondeau whose text bears many points of resemblance to *Va t'en mon desir gracieux* from the Escorial chansonnier. See Pl. 14 and Ex. 15. The description begins just past the middle of the left-hand column. London, British Library, Royal 20 C. ii, fo. 70ᵛ. French, third quarter of the fifteenth century. Reproduced by permission

'tonal atmosphere' of Chivalric Humanism.[81] Any assessment of the *EscA* songs (and, beyond them, of the whole courtly song repertory in the fifteenth century) rests, in some measure, upon our assessment of the chivalric festivities and tournaments which enfolded them.

The tournaments of the fifteenth century have been presented as 'futile but highly stylized and ornamental pageants',[82] but this is a poor reflection of the much more sophisticated analyses that historians have recently given of tournament practice in the fifteenth and sixteenth centuries.[83] What concerns us here, however, is the implied judgement about the decline of chivalry between the twelfth century and the fifteenth. Scholars in many fields of medieval studies have found the twelfth century so fresh, innovative, and extraordinary that the courtly and martial culture of the twelfth century, celebrated by writers such as Chrestien de Troyes, has become idealized. By the fifteenth century, it has often been argued, the colours of twelfth-century chivalry and courtesy had become dull, and it was necessary to gild them with hyperbole, luxury, and excess. This view is associated with Huizinga, although it is by no means exclusive to him, and it is still being explored by historians who acknowledge their debt to his work:[84]

Now [in the fourteenth and fifteenth centuries] Orders of knights existed only to serve the courtly pageantry of the lords, the Burgundian Order of the Golden Fleece, for example, [or] the English Order of the Garter . . . These playful fraternities were no longer an essential part of life; they developed quickly into our modern orders, which are nothing more than factories turning out badges of honour. The 'chevalier' became the 'cavalier', the 'squire' became the 'page' on smooth parquet floors . . . The dances turned to ballets, the tournament to a masquerade ball . . .

These are judicious remarks, for they capture some of the ways in which knighthood changed in an increasingly mercantile, bureacratic, and prosperous environment; Borst's cunning reference to 'smooth parquet floors' certainly conveys the ethos of many luxurious fifteenth-century illuminations showing a banquet or dance in hall,

---

[81] *Burgundian Court Song*, 72.

[82] Ibid. 81, quoting N. Denholm-Young, 'The Tournament in the Thirteenth Century', in R. W. Hunt *et al.*, *Studies in Medieval History Presented to F. M. Powicke* (Oxford, 1948), 241.

[83] See the various essays in Anglo (ed.), *Chivalry in the Renaissance*, especially Jackson, 'Tournaments', 90. See also Strong, *Art and Power*, with bibliography given there.

[84] Borst, *Medieval Worlds*, 162–3.

musicians in attendance.[85] However, the major claims of this passage, first published (in German) in 1988, have almost all been overtaken by recent research, some of it a decade old. Juliet Vale has shown that the English chivalric Order of the Garter cannot be adequately described as a 'playful fraternity' serving only a need for pageantry. Analysing a wealth of literary and documentary evidence, she shows that the institution of the Order was directly implicated in the political and military needs of Edward III in his prosecution of his French wars.[86] As for the increasingly elaborate (and expensive) festivities that accompanied tournaments, Borst's evocation of a healthy, twelfth-century tournament gradually declining into silken dalliance in the fifteenth is much indebted to Huizinga. As Malcolm Vale explains:[87]

Huizinga's conclusion that the tournament's character as 'a contest of force and courage had been almost obliterated by its romantic purport' in the later Middle Ages, has been generally accepted. In its later medieval form, we are told, the tournament had become a 'hollow pastime', part of a code of chivalry which was 'a ridiculous anachronism, a piece of factitious making-up'.

In recent years, historians and literary scholars have assembled a different picture of later medieval chivalry:[88]

[Tournaments in the twelfth century] were crude and bloody affairs, forbidden by the Church and sternly suppressed by any central authority powerful enough to enforce its ban. Though older historians, beginning with Léon Gautier, believed that chivalry flowered in the eleventh and twelfth centuries and steadily declined thereafter, the most characteristic form of public expression of chivalric ideals, the tournament, was just beginning in the eleventh and twelfth centuries and thereafter steadily developed, culminating in the fifteenth and even sixteenth centuries . . .

---

[85] For examples see Bowles, *Musikleben*, pll. 27–42.

[86] *Edward III and Chivalry*, *passim*, but esp. 87: 'The Garter . . . needs to be seen as an integral element in this broader political frame rather than as a superficial and unrelated trimming, or a bright idea that happened to inaugurate a new period of harmony between Edward and his knightly subjects. It crystallised a co-operative relationship that had been gradually developing over several years. The order had its immediate origins in the battle of Crécy and Edward's adoption of the Garter device on that campaign, but it was also firmly grounded in the crisis of the 1340s.'

[87] *War and Chivalry*, 64.

[88] Benson, 'The Tournament', 1–2.

Malcolm Vale's outstanding study of chivalry in the later Middle Ages takes a similar view and is worth quoting *in extenso*:[89]

. . . much has been made of the artificiality and unreality of the display which accompanied the later medieval tournament. Unlike their modern successors, fifteenth-century writers were not so convinced of the military uselessness of such chivalric diversions. In 1497, a tournament at Sheen palace offered Henry VII of England's courtiers the opportunity to 'learn the exercise of the deeds of arms' and the king had already proclaimed a tournament there in 1492 to test their military skills before his French campaign of that year . . .

The blood-letting of a heroic age may make some appeal to the imagination, but the wanton squandering of lives in the twelfth-century *tournoi* hardly seems one of the more admirable features of the civilization that Huizinga saw as the supreme medieval achievement . . . In the 1290s, Henri de Laon, in his *Dit des Hyraus*, lamented the fact that knights and squires sought only to win horses from their opponents at tournaments, not to put their endurance to the test. Greed and pride ruled the contest, he alleged, and it was no longer a proof of military capacity. Huizinga might therefore have profitably looked to a period much earlier than the fifteenth century to find evidence for 'decadence' in the code of chivalry.

This revision of Huizinga's conception of chivalry has been effected in various ways. Scholars such as Juliet Vale and Maurice Keen have given far more sympathetic attention to later medieval pronouncements about the military value of the tournament than Huizinga and those under his influence were prepared to do, and Malcolm Vale has drawn the literary and chronicle evidence together with a most enlightening study of the technicalities of fifteenth-century arms and combat. Vale demonstrates quite clearly that, *pace* Craig Wright, the cavalry charge was not an 'impractical' military technique in the fifteenth century: improvements in horse-armour and other technical advances had made the effect of cavalry devastating when used in the right strategic context.[90] Tournaments were a means of keeping the nobility in a state of physical readiness for war and of fostering that spirit of competitive virility that was so important in the chivalric contribution to battle. In the light of this research there seems no good reason to disparage fifteenth-century expressions of the value of chivalric exercise and display. In 1412, for example, shortly after the signing of a treaty between the warring factions of

[89] *War and Chivalry*, 63, 68, and 70.   [90] Ibid. 100–46.

Armagnacs and Burgundians, Christine de Pisan expressed her fervent hope that the French nobility would now present a united front against the English and would always be practised in arms thanks to jousts and tournaments, the cost of these meetings to be met, she envisaged, by a levy on the royal revenues of the *bonnes villes*.[91] The political and practical motivation of Christine's enthusiasm for the joust and tourney cannot be mistaken. Her belief in the military (and indeed patriotic) value of the tournament as a preparation for war, and as a source of honour, was shared by many in the fourteenth and fifteenth centuries; it is plainly expressed in romances and chronicles, and is sometimes embodied in the formal contracts which bound knights to the service of their lords.[92]

Historians of literature have reached comparable conclusions about the continuing strength and importance of chivalric literature: the romances and manuals of war, for example. David Morgan has recently offered a portrait of Burgundian literary culture which has little in common with the heavy and archaizing literary world evoked by Huizinga and others; he refers to 'that well-schooled and articulate Burgundian culture so prolific in the didactic, instructional, exemplary literature of past and present deeds worthy of record because worthy of future emulation'.[93] In an excellent study, Richard Cooper has demonstrated the force and longevity of chivalric literature in France:[94]

Writers like Kilgour and Huizinga tend to dismiss Renaissance chivalry as a decadent and devalued pastiche of its Mediaeval model . . . it can however be demonstrated that, far from waning, interest in things chivalric increased manifold during the Sixteenth century in France.

Cooper then proceeds to demonstrate his claim with a vast bibliography of chivalric material published in France in the 1500s. The appetite for such material was certainly not waning at the close of the Middle Ages.

These changes in the interpretation of later medieval chivalry are epitomized in current scholarship devoted to the *Chronicles* of Jean Froissart, a pivotal figure in the chivalric culture of the later Middle Ages in England, France, and Flanders. As he emerges from the

[91] Ibid. 63.   [92] Ibid. 67.
[93] 'From a Death to a View', 93, with bibliography given there.
[94] *'Nostre histoire renouvelée'*, 175.

pages of *The Waning of the Middle Ages*, Froissart seems a disturbed, weak-minded, almost alien individual, chronicling high deeds of chivalry and low acts of treachery with a naïve delight, and 'without being aware of the contradiction between his general conceptions and the contents of his narrative'.[95] Huizinga finds that he is only capable of giving 'superficial' descriptions of outward circumstances, and that his writing is 'disjointed, empty, without pith or meaning . . . [his] lack of precision is deplorable'.[96] In recent years, however, Froissart has come to appear a very different kind of author, one whose *Chronicles* reveal considerable narrative skill and, when required, a measure of political shrewdness.[97] Peter Ainsworth has praised Froissart's grasp of the situation in London in the later 1380s, including the 'extremely important political role played by the City of London, its Lord Mayor, and aldermen who, especially after 1387, lent regular support to the interests of a John of Gaunt or a Thomas of Gloucester at the expense of those of the king'.[98] Philippe Contamine and others have shown that Froissart writes astutely for a specific audience of aspiring squires seeking examples of the finest chivalrous behaviour[99] and that he has a very clear head for 'occupations, salaries, fortunes, gratuities [and] capital investments'.[100] It has also been emphasized that Froissart embodies a new, rationalistic, and competitive attitude to chivalric accomplishment in which the chivalric class wanted 'officially to record its meritorious activities in terms of an ever more precise gradation of achievement'.[101] As for Froissart's supposed inability to discern the 'contradictions' between the chivalric ethos, which is his principal subject, and the many stories of treachery and cruelty that he has to tell, Ainsworth has helped to clarify that issue with both subtlety and common sense:[102]

Froissart records a whole series of treasonable actions and barbarities, narrates tale after tale of pillaging, ransoms, and petty larceny—whilst apparently failing to discern what we now see as the ostensible contradiction between such accounts and his own declared convictions. But it can be argued that some of the chronicler's convictions were more tacit, taken as read; understood as being part of a discourse that easily found a place for the narration of events justifiable only in terms of the laws of war, alongside the

---

[95] *The Waning of the Middle Ages*, 65–6.
[96] Ibid. 226–7.
[97] See especially Ainsworth, *Jean Froissart*.
[98] Ibid. 97.
[99] Contamine, *La Guerre au Moyen Âge, passim.*
[100] Ainsworth, *Jean Froissart*, 137.
[101] Ibid. 40.
[102] Ibid. 84.

more self-consciously rhetorical paradigms and posturings of traditional chivalry and its more elevated values.

This seems a judicious verdict upon a remarkable author.

VI

History has produced many different ethics of warriorhood: the Greek, the Japanese, the Germanic, the French of the First Feudal Age, the French of the Second Feudal Age, and more besides. In their various ways, all these ethics enflamed a sense of honour and heroism while celebrating the fundamental skills and hardiness of soldiering. The chivalric culture of the later Middle Ages in France and Burgundy brought an ethic of warriorhood to a point of perfection. Chivalry is perhaps to be distinguished from previous cults of warriorhood because it formed an international association which could, at least in theory, control the brutalities of war and lessen the risk of death for those lucky enough to belong to it. When a knight surrendered to another knight he stood a better chance of being taken prisoner and ransomed than if he fell into the hands of archers or gunners. Those men, using long-distance projectile weapons, may be compared with the modern soldier in the sense that an enemy who delayed his offer of surrender until he found himself in very close proximity to them was liable to be killed outright. There is another respect, however, in which chivalry is distinctive as an ethic of warriorhood: it found a place for the erotic. Chivalry did not usually regard *amour des dames* as a ribald pleasure that was incidental (and possibly detrimental) to the proper business of campaigning;[103] for the knight, love was of central importance. His ardour for a lady's esteem was not distinct from his ardour for honour and his sense of pride: his warriorhood was one complex impulse that combined narcissism, erotic energy, a keen sense of honour and a desire to be proved in action.

It cannot be emphasized too strongly that there is no need to turn

---

[103] Some writers of the 15th c., however, pursue a professional and intensely soldierly conception of knighthood in which women and their company are regarded as repugnant to valour and a correspondingly blunt view of sex sometimes prevails. See, for example, *Les Enseignements paternels* (1430–40) by Ghillebert de Lannoy, a counsellor of Philip the Good and a member of the Order of the Golden Fleece (*Œuvres de Ghillebert de Lannoy*, ed. Potvin, 451 and (especially) 464).

to the romances for evidence of this. The importance of *amour des dames* emerges clearly in a manual of chivalry by Geoffroi de Charny, the *Livre de chevalerie* of *c.*1352. Geoffroi was killed at the battle of Poitiers in 1356, having been named *porte-oriflamme* of France by Jean le Bon in 1355. This is what he has to say about the importance of keeping the company of women in a festive context:[104]

li plus beaux gieux et li plus beaux esbatemens, que telles gens qui tel honnour veuelent querre, devroient faire, seroient qu'il ne se doivent point lasser de jouer de jouster, de parler, de dancer et de chanter en compaignie de dames et de damoiseles . . . Car en teles compaignies et telx gieux et esbatemens prennent les bonnes gens d'armes leurs bons commencemens que Regars et Désir, Amour, Pensée et Souvenir, gayeté de cuer et joliveté de corps les met en la voie de l'encommencement à ceulx qui onques n'en auroient eu cognoissance de faire et parfaire les grans biens et honnours dont li bon se sont fais.

The fairest games and the fairest entertainments which should be used by those who wish to seek such honour [of chivalry] will be that they do not for a moment cease the play of the joust, to converse, to dance and to sing in the company of ladies and young women . . . For good men-at-arms make a good beginning in such company, and with such games and entertainments, so that Look and Desire, Love, Thought and Remembrance, gaiety of heart, and fairness of body put them on the path towards those things which they would never have had the knowledge to do and to accomplish: the great excellencies and honours of which good [knights] are made.

This is a knight explaining the festive and chivalric culture that the men of the later Middle Ages devised for themselves. It is that most rare thing in medieval written sources, a statement of something which was felt to be profoundly important but which could be discussed in terms that owed little to classical or biblical example. Geoffroi's passage is indebted to the romances, no doubt, especially in the use of personifications such as Amour and Désir, and in that respect it offers a revealing demonstration of the ways in which romance vocabulary and literary technique could influence a knight's conceptualization of his calling. He affirms that entertainments such as music and dance in the company of women are such an important stimulus to chivalric ambition and honour that they can almost be regarded as a form of education. He explains his reasoning in another passage:[105]

---

[104] Geoffroi de Charney, *Le Livre de chevalerie*, ed. Kervyn de Lettenhove, 480.
[105] Ibid. 486.

Et aussi icelles très-bonnes dames doyvent et sont bien tenues d'amer et honorer ycelles bonnes gens d'armes qui pour desservir d'avoir leur très-bonne amour et leur bon acueil, se mettent en tant de périls de corps, comme li mestiers d'armes désire, quant pour avenir et attaindre à celui hault honnour pour lequel haut honnour ils pensent à desservir d'avoir l'amour de leurs dames.

And also, these excellent ladies must and are indeed bound to love and honour those excellent men-at-arms who, desiring to have their excellent love and their excellent welcome, submit themselves to such physical danger as the profession of arms requires, to come and to reach to that high honour for which they think to deserve to have the love of their ladies.

Geoffroi's talk of the *hault honnour* a lady can grant is neither sly nor coy, even though a lyric tradition reaching back as far as the twelfth century would sanction an erotic reading of such words; he is describing an intense ardour for the praise of the opposite sex—and of one member in particular—that is at the heart of chivalry's essentially narcissistic and exhibitionist version of masculinity.

The history of *Jehan de Saintré*, composed in the first half of the fifteenth century and called a *beau traicté* by its author, Antoine de La Sale, provides a remarkable insight into the ways in which a young page might prosper at court if he had chosen the *mestier de dames servir*. Antoine writes with authority, having served three dukes as a page and subsequently as a squire (which rank he never exceeded) before 1448, when he passed into the service of Louis of Luxembourg, count of Saint-Pol.[106] The work describes the rise of a young *varlet* of good birth, Jehan de Saintré, at the royal court of Jean II, king of France from 1350 to 1364, and lingers upon the capital importance of his accomplishments and demeanour, both of which single him out for notice by the ladies. One of them, named only as *une dame des Belles Cousines de France*, shows him many signs of favour and occasionally gives him presents of money, which Jehan de Saintré spends in ways that are as meticulously detailed in the romance as in any account-book of the period:[107]

pourpoint de damas bien cramoisy	vj escus
deux paires de chausses	ij escus
deux paires de fins draps linges	i escu

---

[106] Antoine de La Sale, *Jehan de Saintré*, ed. Misrahi and Knudson, p. ix.
[107] Compiled from ibid. 50–7.

One of the values of this text is that it gives some historical substance to the literary convention of 'serving' *les dames* and growing in stature thereby, finally emerging as a *tres vaillant chevalier*. Saintré, as a young page at the court, has a quality of fine bearing (*debonnaireté*) which brings him into the *grace* of the king, and in addition to performing the reasonably well-defined duties expected of a page, many of them connected with serving in the hall, he also 'servoit . . . especialment les dames en tous les plaisirs et services que elles lui commandoient, a son pouoir'.[108] These 'services' include being drawn into the lady's chamber to converse with her and her female attendants, conversations that Antoine de La Sale describes with a keen memory of the terrifying aspect which court decorum could assume in the eyes of a young page little experienced in such matters and fearful of inadvertently giving offence. Very often the conversation in the chamber turns to love, at first taking the form of the most merciless teasing, which sometimes brings the young Saintré to tears.[109] In all his doings, Saintré fulfils what John Stevens has called the eleventh commandment of courtesy, namely 'thou shalt please',[110] and as he receives more gifts of money from his lady patron he becomes the more conspicuous at court for a finery that matches his *debonnaireté*. . . . He is particularly noticed for the excellence of his singing and dancing:[111]

Et au iiij^e jour le roy voult que la royne le feist convier et semondre, et les gentilz hommes de sa compaignie, tous a disner. Et aprés les dansses et chanssons, ou Saintré, qui tresbien chantoit, et aucuns de sa compaignie plurent tresgrandement au roy, a la royne et a tous.

And on the fourth day the king wished that the queen should summon and bring him [Jehan de Saintré] and the gentlemen among his companions to dinner. Afterwards there were dances and songs, in which Saintré, who sang very well, and some of his companions, pleased the king, the queen, and indeed everybody greatly.

Saintré is noticed by the king himself: such was the publicity which the arrangement of a fifteenth-century hall could give to the musical activities of a page or squire dancing or singing while the magnate sat enthroned at one end.[112] It is tempting to suppose that Antoine de La

---

[108] Antoine de La Sale, *Jehan de Saintré*, 2.   [109] Ibid. 7–8.

[110] *Music and Poetry in the Early Tudor Court*, 155.   [111] La Sale, *Jehan de Saintré*, 109.

[112] See the illustrations drawn from 15th-c manuscripts in Bowles, *Musikleben*, pll. 36–8.

Sale may be thinking of polyphonic performance in this reference to singing by Saintré 'and some of his companions', for there is evidence that a few individuals in the company of pages, squires, and other *gentilz hommes* around a king or magnate could sometimes configure into a performing ensemble for polyphonic chansons when required. In the romance of *Cleriadus et Meliadice*, Cleriadus performs the superius of a polyphonic rondeau in the hall while a squire 'de sa compaignie' performs the tenor.[113] In another passage Cleriadus summons one of the pages ('lesquelz estoient tous gentilz hommes') from his retinue and one of his squires to sing a polyphonic song with him.[114] As I have observed elsewhere, these passages are reminiscent of Jean le Robert's eye-witness description of Philip the Good's visit to Cambrai in January 1449, when the duke was entertained during a delay in his departure by two choirboys (probably from the cathedral) who sang a song while 'one of his gentlemen held the tenor'.[115] Taken together, these passages, coloured by the vivid details provided in the history of *Jean de Saintré*, leave little doubt that an ability to 'hold' a tenor or to sing the superius of a polyphonic chanson was a valuable skill for a page or squire with the status of *gentil homme*; in the progress from page to squire to knight that ability could provide a means of gaining attention, of winning the most advantageous presents, and of integrating oneself within the utterly controlling and authoritative culture of court decorum and chivalrous ambition.

The performance of polyphonic chansons during the prize-giving ceremonies after tournaments, suggested by the romance of *Cleriadus et Meliadice*, among other sources, would have intensified the involvement of such songs with what contemporaries regarded as the essential martial vigilance of peace-time chivalric sports and display. Geoffroi de Charny, who upholds the values of a man-at-arms who likes to 'chanter et danser', is one of many fourteenth- and fifteenth-century writers who explicitly acknowledge the connection between warfare and the tournament; in another of his chivalric treatises, the *Livre*, he puts his opinion into verse:[116]

Tous faiz d'armes sont bons et biaux;
Pren le premier que trouveras.
Et bien me semble,

---

[113] See above.   [114] Page, 'The Performance of Songs', 448.
[115] Ibid.   [116] Quoted and translated in Vale, *War and Chivalry*, 65.

Jouster te faut en ta jouvence
Et tournoier pour cognoissance,
Et pour la guerre.

All deeds of arms are fine and good; take the first that you come across. It seems to me that you should joust in your youth and tourney for recognition and for [training in] war.

The narcissism, flirtation, and exhibitionism mentioned above were fanned in the tournament, with its specially constructed stands for spectators, women prominent among them (Pl. 16), and in the prize-giving ceremonies, when the honour of giving the award to the best knight was often entrusted to a woman after *danses et chansons* (Pl. 17).

Leeman Perkins is surely correct to maintain that a reliable analysis of the style and merits of the polyphonic chanson must be a historical one in the sense that it will consider the nature of the society which inspired the songs and used them. The reinterpretations of chivalric culture offered by Malcolm Vale, Juliet Vale, Maurice Keen, L. D. Benson, and others leave no aspect of artistic life in the courtly milieux of the late Middle Ages untouched, and the importance of chivalric culture in understanding the milieu of the chanson has been rightly emphasized by Kemp. Now that historians and literary specialists have done so much to revise Huizinga's view of the 'dream-like' character of late medieval chivalry and courtliness, I suggest that some musicologists may have underestimated the continuing cultural importance and integrity of polyphonic love-songs in the court culture of the later Middle Ages. At a time when war was endemic, and when the duty of every aspiring man-at-arms was to 'soy excerciter et instruire a choses qui touchent la guerre',[117] the lyrics of *EscA* and many other sources deal with love perceived in a way that was believed by many (Geoffroi de Charny included) to be of genuine importance for the cultivation of a sense of martial honour and ambition. Indeed, the involvement of the *EscA* poetry with moral themes of the highest consequence and authority explains, at least in part, the static and repetitive nature of the diction and expression to which those moral themes are entrusted.

Any musicologist who discerns the voice of a waning Middle Ages in the literary themes and musical textures of songs like those in *EscA*

---

[117] Ghillebert de Lannoy, *Œuvres*, 450.

Pl. 16. A tournament encounter. London, British Library, Harley 4432, fo. 150^r. French, fifteenth century. Reproduced by permission

Pl. 17. The presentation of the prize (a jewel with a spray of ostrich feathers) after a tournament. From the tournament treatise of René d'Anjou. Paris, Bibliothèque nationale, fr. 2692, fo. 70ᵛ. French, fifteenth century. Reproduced by permission

may wish to address certain questions before embarking upon either a stylistic analysis or a broad, cultural study.

First, have scholars sometimes used Huizinga's vision of a declining Middle Ages to legitimize their own reluctance to admire musical compositions which work on a relatively small scale *and which do not develop*?[118] No doubt a rash enthusiasm for fifteenth-century songs might make too much of them, just as an unsympathetic taste has, in the past, made too little; however, there can be no true historical understanding of these chansons without a sympathetic ear for what they habitually do—not just a fastidious taste for individual moments or nuances where the poet or composer seems to triumph over the tradition that nourishes him.[119]

Secondly, is the conception of court culture that we have inherited from Huizinga and others distorted by a familiar reflex of historians: their willingness to believe that what they do not possess themselves was possessed in abundance by the men of past ages? Ceremony, luxurious pageantry, a view of manhood that sets great store by action, a tendency to release passionate and irrational impulses whatever the consequence, aesthetic cravings manifest in every part of life—all these things, so Huizingaesque, have passed from the life of industrialized democracies.

Thirdly, does our inherited view of fifteenth-century court culture combine a legitimate fascination and an illegitimate distaste? Arno Borst's vision of a noble, truly martial chivalry in the twelfth century that was, in his judgement, gradually overtaken by pageantry in the fourteenth evinces a scorn that scholars of the twentieth century have been surprisingly quick to feel as they contemplate the materials of late medieval chivalry and courtesy. It is almost as if the scholars themselves, secure in the reflective tranquillity of universities, have appointed themselves the guardians of an ethic of moderation, manliness, and martial efficiency which fifteenth-century chivalry seems to affront.

Finally, and related to the above: how often is the modern scholar's sense of a stylized and 'waning' civilization in the later Middle Ages defined by his or her recoil from the intense luxury and hyperbolized emotion of chivalric culture? The modern academic conscience is often deeply puritanical in its perception of aristocratic luxuriance

---

[118] I am grateful to Elizabeth Randel for discussing this point with me.

[119] Compare Perkins and Garey, *The Mellon Chansonnier*, ii. 2.

and insouciance; one need only examine the critical tradition that has developed around the opening Fitt of *Sir Gawayn and the Green Knight* to be convinced of the strength of that puritanism.[120] Descriptions of lavish court festivities of the kind to be found there— as in many fifteenth-century romances and chronicles—present a wealthy society at play with all sense of political or social responsibility suspended; the prospect may sometimes be subtly disturbing. If chronicles such as those of Froissart, and romances such as *Cleriadus et Meliadice*, defeat modern expectations, it is largely because those texts delight in presenting human beings in a state of moral and material excellence. As Poirion has said: 'idéaliser, c'est chercher le sens, la vérité qui se cache derrière l'ébauche, la médiocrité, l'imperfection des actions humaines'.[121] It is time to consider the ethos, style, and technique of the fifteenth-century chanson as the expression not of some 'fantasy', 'dream', or 'charade', but of a vital and confident culture, many of whose essentials—at least within the realm of chivalric courtliness—were to survive well into the sixteenth century.[122]

---

[120] See Wilson, *The Gawain-Poet*, 116–17.   [121] Cited in Ainsworth, *Jean Froissart*, 84.
[122] See the various essays in Anglo (ed.), *Chivalry in the Renaissance*, and Vale, *War and Chivalry*, 147–74.

Afterword: Towards the Renaissance?

A RECURRENT concern of this book has been to examine the ways in which we constitute the Middle Ages by generalizing about them. Two principal generalizations have emerged, one pertaining to the twelfth and the thirteenth centuries, the other to the fourteenth and the fifteenth centuries.

The first might be called the cathedralist interpretation, for its origins lie with the work of nineteenth-century architectural historians, especially Émile Mâle. Drawing upon the work of his forebears, many of whom associated the Gothic style in architecture and the restoration of Gothic buildings with political and social restoration,[1] Mâle set out to describe what he saw as the symbolic universe of medieval cathedrals. His writings have been enormously influential, flowing into the work of Panofsky, Simson, and others. Mâle's legacy has also contributed to the exegetical school of literary criticism, still a 'great unfinished business of Medieval Studies'.[2] In musicology, the cathedralist view has found a powerful voice in several generations of scholars who have perceived the culture of the Middle Ages as quintessentially rational, constructivist, and Pythagorean.

A second generalization might be called the 'Waning' interpretation. Based upon the powerful image of the twelfth century as 'medieval society in its prime',[3] this interpretation defines the culture of the Middle Ages in the North as luxurious yet overripe, losing itself in a proliferation of stylized forms as ideal and reality diverged. It is associated with Johan Huizinga but has been developed (rarely refined) in numerous subsequent books; it seems to have provided many influential musicologists with their view of the late Middle Ages in France and Burgundy.

These two interpretations have much in common. Huizinga regarded 'the mind of the declining Middle Ages' as one fastidiously

[1] Patterson, *Negotiating the Past*, 30. [2] Ibid. 5.
[3] Contamine, *War in the Middle Ages*, 65–118.

189

concerned with structures and hierarchies; he discerned there a tendency to 'build cathedrals' with all knowledge and thought.[4] His belief in a twelfth-century prime when chivalry was pristine, when scholasticism was incisive, and when literary forms were fresh owed as much to Abbot Suger and the emergence of Gothic architecture as to Abélard or to Chrestien de Troyes. However, the two generalizations that I have distinguished have something more in common than these benign patterns of association: they both conspire to diminish our sense of the humanity of medieval civilization.

This book takes a historicist viewpoint in the sense that it assumes the existence of a 'transhistorical humanness': an appreciable continuity of human thought and feeling from age to age.[5] The chapters have accordingly been spent discarding images of the Middle Ages which seem to be either contrary to the evidence or to be counter-intuitive. Some of the counter-intuitive arguments have taken the form of warnings, issued by scholars in many fields, that we may expect certain things of medieval culture and definitely not expect others. I accept that a principal duty of medieval studies is to define the 'otherness' of the Middle Ages; indeed, that is vital if we are to arrive at any kind of critical practice. However, I suggest that warnings about the 'alterity' of medieval civilization should be treated with respect but also reserve until experience has proved them to be justified. The musicological field is marked by many such warning-signs; we need look no further than Albert Seay's assertion that the primary purpose of sounding music in medieval opinion was 'the concrete demonstration of the fundamental ratios'.[6] So much for the sensuous melodies and the wilfully exotic sonorities of Machaut.

What generalizations about 'the Middle Ages' should be allowed to stand? For musicologists at least, it may be too early to say. There is not enough evidence to hand as yet; not enough compositions have been studied or performed. What has become increasingly clear, however, is that the concept of a Middle Age has often been implicitly championed by Renaissance specialists who need it if they are to sustain their belief in a great reawakening when the sun of Italy penetrated the shutters of the European mind. The consequence of this view, which often makes the Middle Ages appear a time of slumber, is that the full humanity of men and women in the Middle Ages is

---

[4] *The Waning of the Middle Ages*, 217.   [5] Patterson, *Negotiating the Past*, 17.

[6] *Music in the Medieval World*, 21.

diminished once again. We have encountered this in Chapter 1 with Kenneth Clark's *Landscape into Art*, where the medieval artist looks out upon a world 'frozen by the icy winds of doctrine'.[7] We now find it in Burckhardt:[8]

In the Middle Ages both sides of human consciousness—that which was turned within as that which was turned without—lay dreaming or half awake beneath a common veil. The veil was woven of faith, illusion and childish prepossession . . .

Here is the familiar metaphor of the medieval slumber, a time when the sense of individualism—celebrated by Burckhardt as the glory of the Italian Renaissance—was dormant.

Despite the appearance of Colin Morris's *The Discovery of the Individual 1050–1200* and other important studies that have engendered a lively debate,[9] this damaging interpretation of the Middle Ages continues to be repeated, even in works which are supposed to represent the cutting edge of literary history and criticism.[10] In recent musicological writing it is aired in Claude Palisca's *Humanism in Italian Renaissance Musical Thought*, a book which seeks to demonstrate the usefulness of the 'Italian Renaissance' as a concept in musicological research:[11]

Whereas medieval man was conscious of himself only as part of a group, individual personality being veiled in faith, illusion and childish prejudices, Burckhardt observed that in the Italian cities of the Renaissance individuals who had an objective view of themselves and independent spirits emerged.

[7] See above, 8.

[8] *The Civilization of the Renaissance in Italy*, 81. For a recent collection of challenging studies concerning the concept of the Renaissance see 'The Idea of the Renaissance in France', essays in *The Journal of Medieval and Renaissance Studies*, 22 (1992).

[9] Morris, *The Discovery of the Individual 1050–1200*; Benton, 'Consciousness of Self'; Bynum, 'Did the Twelfth Century Discover the Individual?'

[10] See, for example, Belsey, *The Subject of Tragedy*, 33–54, but especially 18 ('In the fifteenth century the representative human being has no unifying essence') and 48 ('The precariously unified protagonist of [the] Renaissance . . . points forwards to a fully-fledged humanism rather than backwards to the Middle Ages . . .'). For an excellent and forceful discussion of this question see Aers, 'A Whisper in the Ear of Early Modernists'. Aers takes issue with various Renaissance specialists (and others) who would locate the emergence of interiority in European literature in the 17th c., and specifically in Shakespeare's *Hamlet*. Compare 186: 'There is no reason to think that languages and experiences of inwardness, of interiority, of divided selves, of splits between outer realities and inner forms of being, were unknown before the seventeenth century, before capitalism, before the "bourgeoisie", before Descartes, before the disciplinary regimes addressed in Foucault's *Discipline and Punish*.'   [11] Palisca, *Humanism*, 3.

Professor Palisca is paraphrasing Burckhardt, so he may not agree with every detail of this formulation; however, if he does not assent to it in every particular then he might have done well to define the limits of his agreement. The theory that self-knowledge was smothered by layers of 'illusion' in the Middle Ages seems ill founded in the light of what is now known about the social and political uses of medieval chivalric pageantry, the aspect of medieval culture that has consistently been spoken of in terms of 'illusion' and which has been presented in that light by Huizinga and his many followers. More alarming, I suggest, is the statement in the above quotation that individual personality was 'veiled in faith' during the medieval period, for that harsh judgement perpetuates Burckhardt's unsympathetic attitude to the spirituality of the Christian Middle Ages. Was the character of St Bernard of Clairvaux, for example, *veiled* by his Christian belief? Not for Dom Jean Leclercq, apparently, who finds in Bernard 'une intense personnalité.[12] What of St Anselm, in whom Southern discerns a mind both 'rapid and penetrating, a bundle of nervous sensibility'?[13] If we are to gauge the scope for individualism in medieval culture from scholars such as Southern on one side, or from Burckhardt on the other, then there is no difficulty in deciding whom we should choose.

II

Every discussion of the Renaissance as a concept in musical history must eventually return to the theorist Johannes Tinctoris. His voluminous writings contain what may be the only fifteenth-century passages of genuinely seminal importance for this issue. In some famous paragraphs of his *Liber de arte contrapuncti*, written in 1477 at Naples, Tinctoris mentions the theoretical writings of the ancients that deal with the concords from which music is made; he has this to say about the music of Antiquity, of the recent past, and of the present:[14]

To these concords, also, the older musicians, such as Plato, Pythagoras, Nicomachus, Aristoxenus, Philolaus, Archytas, Ptolemy and many others, even including Boet[h]ius, most assiduously applied themselves, but how they were accustomed to arrange and put them together is only slightly

---

[12] *St Bernard*, 17.　　　　　　　　　　　　　　[13] *Medieval Humanism*, 9.

[14] Translation from Tinctoris, *The Art of Counterpoint*, trans. Seay, 14–15; text in Tinctoris, *Opera theoretica*, ed. Seay, ii. 12.

understood at our time. And, if I may refer to what I have heard and seen, I have held in my hands at one time or another many old songs of unknown authorship which are called *apocrypha* that are so inept and stupidly composed that they offended our ears rather than pleased them.

In addition, it is a matter of great surprise that there is no composition written over forty years ago which is thought by the learned as worthy of performance. At this very time . . . there flourish, in addition to many singers who perform most beautifully, an infinite number of composers such as Johannes Okeghem, Johannes Regis, Anthonius Busnoys, Firminus Caron and Guillermus Faugues, who glory that they had as teachers in this divine art Johannes Dunstable, Egidius Binchois and Guillermus Dufay, [all] recently passed from life.

I am not about to deny the importance of this remarkable passage; many musicologists will undoubtedly wish to suggest that any discussion of the Renaissance in music must begin with the attitude which Tinctoris reveals here and with the movement in musical composition that he so astutely discerns, reaching back some forty years to the 1430s. I do wish to suggest, however, that Tinctoris's words deserve to be read with a great deal of care. Consider, for example, a recent paraphrase of his remarks:[15]

Tinctoris . . . moves on to discuss musical compositions themselves, the focus of his interest. The musical compositions by the learned ancients, he continues, however great they may have been, have not survived. The 'old' songs that he has seen are inept and ugly. Only in the last forty years has musical knowledge flourished . . . *This brief historical summary of music composition employs a typical Renaissance historical narrative: ancient achievement, followed by a decline, and then a recent renewal.*

This leaves something to be desired. We do not find anything in Tinctoris' text corresponding to Moyer's concessive remark about the musical compositions of the ancients: 'however great they may have been'. Tinctoris does not refer to the ancients' compositions except to say that nothing is known for certain about their use of counterpoint: 'how they were accustomed to arrange and put [concords] together'. Tinctoris is not, therefore, employing what Moyer calls 'a typical Renaissance historical narrative' because, as far as his chosen subject of contrapuntal composition is concerned, he is not invoking what Moyer calls the 'ancient achievement'. As for his account of modern

---

[15] Moyer, *Musica Scientia*, 65. The emphasis is mine.

music, Tinctoris seems to be so far from habitually or complacently thinking in terms of a 'Renaissance narrative' that the poverty (as he sees it) of contrapuntal expertise before the 1430s actually *astonishes* him: 'it is a matter of great surprise'.

At bottom, Tinctoris's passage is a statement of musical taste. He is saying, in effect, that he and his contemporaries are displeased by compositions which do not habitually exploit thirds and sixths as consonant intervals, which do not control dissonance with scrupulous care, which are not fully melodious in at least the superius and tenor, and which (perhaps) do not possess, or show a tendency towards, a contratenor bassus. It is easy to imagine a musician of fourteenth-century France making comparable judgements about the mono-phonic songs and motets of the Ars antiqua. Many passages in the *Speculum musice* of Jacques de Liège suggest that such judgements were indeed being made by *c*.1330.

Like Moyer's book, Professor Palisca's *Humanism in Italian Renaissance Musical Thought* attempts to assuage the doubts that musicologists may have about the concept of an Italian Renaissance but none the less raises those doubts in an acute form. I conclude this book with brief examination of the opening chapter of Palisca's study. Cautiously entitled 'An Italian Renaissance in Music?', the chapter reveals how the enterprise of urging the significance and distinctive-ness of the Italian Renaissance leads to a sustained indifference to earlier achievements while fortifying the view that there must have been a 'Middle Ages' preceding the 'Renaissance'.

The image of the twelfth-century 'prime'

'In the royal courts of the North', Palisca remarks, 'such as those of the dukes of Burgundy, a money economy also grew [comparable to that of Italy], as did learning, vernacular literature, and art', but, as Ferguson remarks, with Palisca's approval, 'they retained the forms of feudal and chivalrous society . . . Literary reflections of these forms had by the fifteenth century lost the vitality that had inspired the feudal literature of the twelfth and thirteenth centuries.'[16]

This is a version of an argument that became very familiar in Chapter 5, and one which recent work on fifteenth-century chivalry and court culture has done much to question.

---

[16] Palisca, *Humanism*, 4, citing W. K. Ferguson, *Renaissance Studies*, 131.

Underestimating 'medieval' scholarship and scientific rationality

Palisca declares that Aristotle's *Politics* was read by 'Renaissance musicians', being a work 'previously unknown except to a very few'.[17] This is puzzling, for it is well known that William of Moerbeke completed a full translation of the *Politics* in the years 1260–70 and that the book was studied intensely thereafter. Its influence upon the thinking of musicians and those interested in musical questions is already evident in the second half of the thirteenth century with the writings of Albertus Magnus and Johannes de Grocheio.[18]

Something similar might be said for Palisca's discussion of various theoretical doctrines supposedly initiated (or transformed) by Humanism. It is bold to suggest that humanistic scholarship and rationalism were the forces which eventually led musicians and theorists to abandon their belief in the music of the spheres. 'If celestial harmony had advocates in the fifteen[th] and sixteenth centuries,' Palisca writes, 'it also had detractors.'[19] But we find a noted *thirteenth-century* detractor among musicians in Johannes de Grocheio. As we saw in Chapter 1, Grocheio is a stern rationalist in these matters. 'Celestial bodies in movement do not make a sound,' he declares, 'although the ancients may have thought otherwise.'[20] He cites the authority of Aristotle for this assertion, just as Tinctoris was to do nearly two hundred years later. Grocheio has no faith in *musica humana* either: 'Nor also is sound innate in the human constitution; who has heard a constitution sounding?'[21]

There is a paradox in the way many scholars, pursuing Renaissance interests, perceive the 'mind' of the Gothic era. They discern in it both an intense rationalism (especially a structural rationalism) but also an intense, pre-scientific credulity, clothed in the imposing forms of the Catholic faith but visible none the less to the discerning observer. However, if we review research on the advance of rationalism between 1100 and 1600 it becomes clear that in this matter—as in

---

[17] Ibid. 12.

[18] See Page, *The Owl and the Nightingale*, 172–3. Moyer, *Musica Scientia*, 67, makes much of Tinctoris' reading of the 'humanistic' Aristotle of the *Politics* and *Poetics*, without considering the pre-15th-c. use of the *Politics*.

[19] Palisca, *Humanism*, 181.

[20] See above, 17.

[21] See above, 17. Compare Moyer, *Musica Scientia*, 64–5 and 102–3, who falls into the same trap as Palisca. After a careful survey of the late-15th-c. 'Italian' theorists (Burtius, Ramos de Pareja, Hothby, Tinctoris, and Gafurio) one of the few decisively 'Renaissance' qualities Moyer finds among them seems to include precisely Grocheio's stance as taken by Tinctoris.

so many—historians vary in their assessment of where the story begins according to the point where their own interests and expertise allow them to take it up. Radding, for example, finds a proto-scientific attitude already in the twelfth century, when 'intellectuals saw fire, rain and lightning where their predecessors saw the miraculous intervention of God or the saints . . .'.[22]

The vigour of the medieval 'theoretical' tradition

No doubt it may be said with justice that a 'music-theoretical madness' seized Italy during the last quarter of the fifteenth century.[23] However, no medievalist will wish to see that feverishness interpreted as a sign of the supposedly vigorous and 'Renaissance' character of musical culture in Italy during that period. The last two decades of the thirteenth century saw the production of major treatises by Franco, Jerome of Moravia, Lambertus, Anonymous 4, and the Sowa anonymous; the period *c*.1280–*c*.1300 therefore represents one of the most productive and intense periods in the history of pre-Baroque theory. Furthermore, virtually all the ancient models which Palisca cites as a source of inspiration to Renaissance theorists—including the technical works by Vitruvius, Quintilian, Galen, Horace, and Vegetius—were read and studied during the medieval period and were therefore nothing new in the Renaissance. Reviewing the wealth of Ars antiqua (or indeed of Ars nova) theory, not to mention the riches of plainchant theory from the eleventh to the thirteenth centuries, it becomes harder to accept Palisca's broad assertion that 'the treatise as a genre receive[d] a spur through humanism'.[24]

Nor can we easily accept it as distinctive of the Italian Renaissance that 'the encouragement of patrons was an important factor in stimulating the production of treatises. Some . . . were directly commis-

---

[22] 'Superstition to Science', 966.

[23] Palisca, *Humanism*, 8. For an account of the major theoretical works compiled (and printed) in Italy during this period see Moyer, *Musica Scientia*, 37–103. She points out that the 'major scholars' of the 16th c. 'consistently dated the beginning of their own discursive tradition to Nicolaus Burtius, Bartolomeo Ramos, and especially Franchino Gaffurio and Giorgio Valla'. This is quite correct, but it is hardly surprising. The works of these authors, to whom we might add Tinctoris, show many lines of cross-influence, all were *printed* (Tinctoris only partially), and some of them, especially the materials by Gaffurio and Tinctoris, are very comprehensive. The prominence of this group in the 16th-c. vision of music theory is only to be expected. Moyer's search for the proto-Renaissance elements in these treatises is, on the whole, remarkably unsuccessful, and often leads her to disparage the authors' achievements (e.g. 50 [on Burtius], 63 [on Hothby], 67 [on Tinctoris]). [24] Palisca, *Humanism*, 9.

sioned by secular and religious leaders.'[25] The term 'patrons' is often one to alarm a medievalist, who does not usually encounter in his materials the kind of free-standing, private 'interest' in learning and the arts that the Renaissance scholar seems to find so often in his. None the less, many medieval treatises, especially those on plainchant theory, were commissioned (in a relaxed sense of the word) by the promptings of ecclesiastical colleagues and, in some cases, by senior churchmen whose word was a command to their juniors in the clerical hierarchy.[26] Such men fostered musical learning in an enquiring and humane manner, which often involved extensive reference to Horace's *Ars poetica*, to name no other book of the ancients;[27] there is always a danger that we may overlook their benign and constructive influence simply because they were medieval churchmen rather than secularized Renaissance scholars. We also remember Franco of Cologne's intriguing reference to the 'magnates' who had entreated him to write the *Ars cantus mensurabilis* (*c.*1280).[28] As we saw in Chapter 3, the kind of mixed lay-clerical audience for the motet, described by Johannes de Grocheio as 'the clergy and those who care for the refinements of any skill', may well have created a context in which writers such as Franco could present themselves as acting upon the entreaty of notable personages, whether lay or ecclesiastical.

Medieval attitudes to composition and the modes

To argue that 'more and more during the Renaissance, practical theory was penetrated by . . . the desire to rationalize practice and

---

[25] Ibid.

[26] See the beautifully poised and rhetorical remarks on this matter in the treatise of John 'of Affligem' (*De Musica*, ed. Smits van Waesberghe, 44–6).

[27] The authors of the *Summa musice* (*c.*1200) make frequent use of Horace's *Ars poetica*, revealing the characteristic medieval view of the study of plainchant as a kind of applied grammar. Other authors cited include Terence, Virgil, and Ovid. See Page (ed. and trans.), *The Summa musice*, *passim*. Moyer, *Musica Scientia*, 43, comments that one section of Burtius' *Musices opusculum* (1487) contains a 'reference to Cicero on the importance of beginning with a clear definition of first principles . . . Burtius' book is one of the earliest works on music to include such a source.' This is an amazing remark, since many medieval plainchant treatises are liberally supplied with snippets from Virgil, Terence, and Horace, to look no further. Later (*Musica Scientia*, 51) Moyer praises Burtius for having enlarged 'the body of classical sources available' by citing Cicero's *Dream of Scipio*. It need hardly be said that Macrobius' commentary upon the *Dream of Scipio*, and the text of Cicero which accompanied it, was one of the most fundamental books of medieval culture. See Lewis, *The Discarded Image*, 60–9.

[28] *Ars cantus mensurabilis*, ed. Reaney and Gilles, 23. Another manuscript tradition reads 'magistrorum'.

make it conform to the precepts of *musica theorica*'[29] is to describe
something that is fundamental to the plainchant treatises of the
Middle Ages. These works often urge the composers of new chants to
follow a strict modal grammar and thus make their practice 'conform
to the precepts of *musica theorica*'. Nor is there anything distinctive to
Renaissance music theory in the proposition that polyphony should
be considered in relation to the modal structures of plainchant; by the
1370s, and perhaps significantly earlier, some French composers and
theorists had begun to consider secular polyphonic forms such as the
rondeau, virelai, and ballade in terms of the plainchant modes.[30]

The question of whether fourteenth-century composers ever
selected a mode or modal affiliation in accordance with a wish to
induce a certain feeling or affection in the listener raises the highly
complex matter of musical expressiveness and the nature of the
ancient sources which prompted Renaissance musicians to consider it
(as we are accustomed to believe) afresh. The view that there was
indeed a seismic change in this matter during the Renaissance, as
evinced particularly in ideas about the relation of words and music,
has been developed in many influential studies.[31] This is not the place
to question it (indeed, perhaps it cannot be questioned), but Palisca's
brief and suggestive treatment of the issue none the less calls for comment.

If we agree that the plainchant modes were 'fascinating to Renaissance musicians not simply because they were a link to a noble
ancient past but also because they were thought to unlock the powers
of music over human feelings and morals',[32] then we may also agree
that they were fascinating to medieval theorists for exactly the same
reasons. It may be granted that the 'Greekness' of the modes was
often more keenly sensed in the fifteenth and sixteenth centuries, and
this did indeed reflect a certain awareness—indeed a certain connoisseurship—of Graeco-Roman civilization. It is also true that many
medieval discussions of the modes are severely purposeful, pursued
within the liturgical frame of reference, and with the density of biblical language, that can hide all signs of intellectual penetration and

[29] Palisca, *Humanism*, 10.
[30] Ellsworth, *The Berkeley Manuscript*, 84–5, esp. 84, ll. 7–9: 'Restat et nunc quidem de cantibus aliis, puta motetis, baladis, et huiusmodi, de quibus tonis sive modis iudicandi fuerint aliqua declarare.'
[31] Most recently in Stevens, *Words and Music*.   [32] Palisca, *Humanism*, 12.

humane learning to eyes accustomed to a Burckhardtian view of 'the mind of the Middle Ages'. None the less, the differing aesthetic properties of the modes were widely discussed by plainchant theorists as early as *c*.1100, when one of the most influential passages on this topic was composed by John 'of Affligem' (a theorist who is the subject of a distinguished essay by Professor Palisca).[33] A century later, the authors of the *Summa musice* use a wide range of vocabulary to describe the wealth of aesthetic response that can be induced by the modes: one may be 'delighted', 'fortified', 'attracted' in a caressing way, 'soothed' or 'moved' according to the mode in question and the nature of one's musical taste.[34] This is well known. What needs to be stressed is that when Palisca finds a conception of musical composition in the sixteenth century that requires a composer to consider what feelings he wishes to induce in his listener and then to choose the mode accordingly,[35] he has found something which can be glimpsed in treatises on chant as early as the twelfth century. The *Summa musice* advises the composer of new chants to consider, before he begins his work, how he will best satisfy the wish of the one who has sought him to compose (the *petens*; throughout the discussion of composition in that treatise, as in John's *De musica* of a century earlier, the concept of a listener who has asked for the work to be made, and to whose judgement and taste it will eventually be referred, is strong, as in some of the Renaissance materials discussed by Palisca).[36] The authors of the *Summa musice* advise the composer to choose a mode that is known to be aesthetically pleasing to him who has 'commissioned' the piece; if that information cannot be had, let the composer marry the mode to the character of the text, choosing relatively low-lying modes, such as the first, if the matter of the text is grave or sad, and relatively high-lying modes, such as the fourth, when the mood is happy or joyous.[37]

That teaching may seem simple enough, even naïve, and there can be no doubt that such pronouncements, intended for the reflective study of monastic minds saturated with the melodies and language of the liturgy, can seem less attractive and incisive to the mind of the modern secularized scholar than the writings of a sixteenth-century humanist. However, I suggest that we should view such teaching as a significant statement of a medieval attitude. Let us hear Palisca once

---

[33] In Babb, *Hucbald, Guido, and John*, 87–100.   [34] Page, *The* Summa musice, 118–19.
[35] Palisca, *Humanism*, 13.   [36] Page, *The* Summa musice, 118–21.   [37] Ibid.

more. 'The idea that music should move the affections, as oratory and rhetoric were intended to do, was a new goal for composers' in the Renaissance.[38] Was it really so new? Around 1300, Johannes de Grocheio believed that trouvère songs in the High Style could move the souls of kings and princes to boldness, bravery, magnanimity, and liberality—a lofty purpose indeed, even for oratory and rhetoric.[39] The idea that music can move the minds and hearts of those who hear it is fundamental to Grocheio's discussion of secular music.

I do not suggest that Professor Palisca is unaware of any of the medieval sources and concepts that I have mentioned here; he assuredly knows them well, and his defence of the idea that there was an Italian Renaissance in music rests upon more than the single, introductory chapter with which we have been engaging. It would appear, however, that he does not regard these medieval antecedents of his Renaissance materials as any barrier to the claim that there was a major new departure in the Western European way of thinking about music in the 'Renaissance'. That is a view I cannot share. The qualities and tones of sixteenth-century humanist reflection upon music theory are certainly different from those which characterize fourteenth-century writings, but the Ars nova treatises are different in their turn from the antecedent literature of the thirteenth century, which is different again from the plainchant theory of the twelfth. In this field we need not only a twelfth-century Renaissance but a thirteenth- and a fourteenth-century one as well. Indeed, the period 1100–1600 in the musical life of the West is so fertile and inventive that it seems all Renaissance from beginning to end.

[38] Palisca, *Humanism*, 15.   [39] Original text in Rohloff, *Die Quellenhandschriften*, 130.

Bibliography

ABRAHAM, P., *Viollet-le-Duc et le rationalisme médiéval* (Paris, 1934).

AERS, D., 'A Whisper in the Ear of Early Modernists; or, Reflections on Literary Critics Writing the "History of the Subject"', in D. Aers (ed.), *Culture and History 1350–1600: Essays on English Communities, Identities and Writing* (New York, 1992), 177–202.

AINSWORTH, P. F., *Jean Froissart and the Fabric of History: Truth, Myth, and Fiction in the* Chroniques (Oxford, 1990).

ALEXANDER DE VILLA DEI(?), *Carmen de musica cum glossis*, ed. A. Seay (Colorado Springs, Colo., 1977).

ALSOP, J., *The Rare Art Traditions* (London, 1982).

ANDERSON, G. A. (ed.), *Compositions of the Bamberg Manuscript* (Corpus mensurabilis musicae, 75; American Institute of Musicology, 1977).

——*Motets of the Manuscript La Clayette* (Corpus mensurabilis musicae, 68; American Institute of Musicology, 1975).

ANGLO, S. (ed.), *Chivalry in the Renaissance* (Woodbridge, 1990).

ANNUNZIATA, A. W., 'The *Pas d'Armes* and its Occurrences in Malory', in Benson and Leyerle (eds.), *Chivalric Literature*, 39–48.

ARLT, W., *et al.* (eds.), *Gattungen der Musik in Einzeldarstellungen: Gedenkschrift Leo Schrade*, i (Berne and Munich, 1973).

ASTON, M., 'Huizinga's Harvest: England and *The Waning of the Middle Ages*', *Medievalia et Humanistica*, NS, 9 (1979), 1–24.

AUBRY, P., *La Musique et les musiciens d'église en Normandie au XIIIe siècle* (Paris, 1906).

BABB, W. (trans.), *Hucbald, Guido, and John on Music* (New Haven, Conn., 1978).

BAKHTIN, M., *Rabelais and his World* (Bloomington, Ind., 1984).

BALTZER, R. A., *et al.* (eds.), *The Union of Words and Music in Medieval Poetry* (Austin, Tex., 1991).

BARNES, C. F., *Villard de Honnecourt: The Artist and his Drawings* (Boston, 1982).

BARRAL I ALTET, X. (ed.), *Artistes, artisans et production artistique au moyen âge*, 3 vols. (Paris, 1986–90).

BAYLESS, M. K., 'Parody in the Middle Ages: The Latin Tradition', Ph.D. diss. (Cambridge, 1991).

BEAUJOUAN, G., *Par raison des nombres: l'art du calcul et les savoirs scientifiques médiévaux* (Aldershot, 1991).

BEC, P., *La Lyrique française au moyen âge*, 2 vols. (Paris, 1977).

BEDE, *Opera de temporibus*, ed. C. W. Jones (Cambridge, Mass., 1943).

BELSEY, C., *The Subject of Tragedy* (London and New York, 1985).

BENSON, L. D., 'The Tournament in the Romances of Chrétien de Troyes and *L'Histoire de Guillaume le Maréchal*', in Benson and Leyerle (eds.), *Chivalric Literature*, 1–24.

——and Leyerle, J. (eds.), *Chivalric Literature* (Kalamazoo, Mich., 1980).

BENTON, J. F., 'Consciousness of Self and Perceptions of Individuality', in R. L. Benson and G. Constable (eds.), *Renaissance and Renewal in the Twelfth Century* (Oxford, 1982).

BERGMANN, W., 'Chronographie und Komputistik bei Hermann von Reichenau', in D. Berg and H.-W. Goetz (eds.), *Historiographia mediaevalis: Festschrift für Franz-Josef Schmale* (Darmstadt, 1988), 103–17.

——*Innovationen im Quadrivium des 10. und 11. Jahrhunderts: Studien zur Einführung von Astrolab and Abakus im lateinischen Mittelalter* (Stuttgart, 1985).

——'Der Traktat "De Mensura astrolabii" des Hermann von Reichenau', *Francia*, 8 (1980), 65–103.

BESSELER, H., *Bourdon und Fauxbourdon* (Leipzig, 1950).

BIRKNER, G., 'Motetus und Motette', *Archiv für Musikwissenschaft*, 18 (1961), 183–94.

BLOOMFIELD, M. W. et al., *Incipits of Latin Works on the Virtues and Vices, 1100–1500 AD* (Cambridge, Mass., 1979).

BOETHIUS, A. M. S., *Fundamentals of Music*, trans. C. M. Bower (New Haven, Conn., 1989).

BOOGAARD, N. VAN DEN, *Rondeaux et refrains du XIIe siècle au début du XIVe* (Paris, 1969).

BOOTH, M. W., *The Experience of Songs* (New Haven, Conn., and London, 1981).

BORST, A., 'Ein Forschungsbericht Hermanns des Lahmen', *Deutsches Archiv für Erforschung des Mittelalters*, 40 (1984), 379–477.

——*Medieval Worlds: Barbarians, Heretics and Artists* (Cambridge, 1991).

BOURIN-DERRUAU, M., *Temps d'équilibres, temps de ruptures: XIIIe siècle* (Nouvelle histoire de la France médiévale, 4; Paris, 1990).

BOURQUELOT, M.F., *Études sur les foires de Champagne*, Mémoires présentés par divers savants à l'Académie des inscriptions et belles lettres, 2nd ser., 2 vols. (Paris, 1865).

BOWLES, E. A., *Musikleben im 15. Jahrhundert* (Leipzig, 1977).

Bibliography

——'The Role of Musical Instruments in Medieval Sacred Drama', *Musical Quarterly*, 45 (1959), 67–84.

BRANNER, R., 'Books: Gothic Architecture', *Journal of the Society of Architectural Historians*, 32 (1973), 327–33.

BRIDGMAN, N., 'The Age of Ockeghem and Josquin', in D. A. Hughes and G. Abraham (eds.), *New Oxford History of Music*, iii (London, 1960), 239–302.

BROCCHIERI, M. F. B., 'The Intellectual', in J. Le Goff (ed.), *The Medieval World* (London, 1990), 181–209.

BRÖCKER, M., *Die Drehleier*, 2 vols. (rev. edn., Bonn, 1977).

BROWN, S. M. (trans.), *The Register of Eudes of Rouen* (New York and London, 1964).

BROWNLEE, K., 'Machaut's Motet 15 and the *Roman de la Rose*', *Early Music History*, 10 (1991), 1–14.

BUCHER, F., 'L'Architecture vernaculaire ou l'empreinte des particularismes locaux', *Dossiers Histoire et Archéologie*, 47 (1980), 66–82.

BURCKHARDT, J., *The Civilization of the Renaissance in Italy*, trans. S. G. C. Middlemore (Oxford, 1944).

BURKE, P., 'History of Events and the Revival of Narrative', in P. Burke (ed.), *New Perspectives on Historical Writing* (Cambridge, 1991), 233–48.

BURNETT, C. (ed.), *Adelard of Bath* (London, 1987).

BURROW, J., 'The Alterity of Medieval Literature', *New Literary History*, 10 (1979), 385–90.

BURROWS, T., 'Unmaking the Middle Ages', *Journal of Medieval History*, 7 (1981), 127–34.

BUSARD, H. L., 'Die Traktate *De Proportionibus* von Jordanus Nemorarius und Campanus', *Centaurus*, 15 (1970), 193–227.

BUTTERFIELD, A. R. T., 'Interpolated Lyric in Medieval Narrative Poetry', Ph.D. diss. (Cambridge, 1988).

BYNUM, C. W., 'Did the Twelfth Century Discover the Individual?', *The Journal of Ecclesiastical History*, 31 (1980), 1–17.

CAHN, W., 'Medieval Landscape and the Encyclopedic Tradition', in Poirion and Regalado (eds.), *Contexts*, 11–24.

CALDWELL, J., *Medieval Music* (London, 1978).

CAMILLE, M., *The Gothic Idol* (Cambridge, 1989).

CARTELLIERI, O., *The Court of Burgundy* (London, 1929).

CHAMBERLAIN, D. S., 'Philosophy of Music in the *Consolatio* of Boethius', *Speculum*, 45 (1970), 80–97.

CLARK, K., *Landscape into Art* (London, 1949).

CONTAMINE, P., *War in the Middle Ages*, trans. M. Jones (Oxford, 1984).

COOPER, R., '*Nostre histoire renouvelée*: The Reception of the Romances of Chivalry in Renaissance France', in Anglo (ed.), *Chivalry*, 175–91.

Bibliography

CORDOLIANI, A., 'Contribution à la littérature du comput ecclésiastique au moyen âge', *Studi medievali*, 3rd ser. 1 (1960), 107–37.

CROMBIE, A. C., *Science, Optics and Music in Medieval and Early Modern Thought* (London and Ronceverte, 1990).

CURTIUS, E. R., *European Literature and the Latin Middle Ages* (London, 1953).

D'AVRAY, D. L., *The Preaching of the Friars: Sermons Diffused from Paris Before 1300* (Oxford, 1985).

DE BRUYNE, E., *Études d'esthétique médiévale*, 3 vols. (Bruges, 1946).

DE LUBAC, H., *Exégèse médiévale: les quatre sens de l'écriture*, 3 vols. (Paris, 1959).

DENIFLE, H., and CHATELAIN, A. (eds.), *Chartularium Universitatis Parisiensis*, 4 vols. (Paris, 1889–97).

DEPPING, G.-B. (ed.), *Réglemens sur les arts et métiers de Paris* (Paris, 1837).

DE WITT, P. A. M., 'A New Perspective on Johannes de Grocheio's Ars Musicae', Ph.D. diss. (University of Michigan, 1973).

DOSS-QUINBY, E., *Les Refrains chez les trouvères du XIIe siècle au début du XIVe* (New York, 1984).

DREW, A., 'The *De Eodem et Diverso*', in Burnett (ed.), *Adelard of Bath*, 17–24.

DRONKE, P., 'Arbor Caritatis', in Heyworth (ed.), *Medieval Studies for J. A. W. Bennett* (Oxford, 1981), 207–53.

——*The Medieval Lyric* (2nd edn., London, 1978).

DUBY, G., *Le Temps des cathédrales* (Paris, 1976).

DYER, J., 'A Thirteenth-Century Choirmaster: The *Scientia Artis Musicae* of Elias Salomon', *Musical Quarterly*, 66 (1980), 83–111.

EARP, L., 'Lyrics for Reading and Lyrics for Singing in Late Medieval France: The Development of the Dance Lyric from Adam de la Halle to Guillaume de Machaut', in Baltzer *et al.* (eds.), *The Union of Words and Music*, 101–31.

ECO, U., *Art and Beauty in the Middle Ages* (New Haven, Conn., and London, 1986).

ELLSWORTH, O. B. (ed. and trans.), *The Berkeley Manuscript* (Lincoln, Nebr., and London, 1984).

EVANS, B. J., 'Music, Text and Social Context: Reexamining Thirteenth-Century Styles', in Poirion and Regalado (eds.), *Contexts*, 183–95.

EVANS, G., 'A Note on the *Regule Abaci*', in Burnett (ed.), *Adelard of Bath*, 33–5.

EVANS, G. R., 'From Abacus to Algorism: Theory and Practice in Medieval Arithmetic', *British Journal for the History of Science*, 10 (1977), 114–31.

——'Schools and Scholars: The Study of the Abacus in English Schools, c.980–c.1150', *English Historical Review*, 94 (1979), 71–89.

Bibliography

EVERIST, M., 'The Rondeau Motet: Paris and Artois in the Thirteenth Century', *Music and Letters*, 69 (1988), 1–22.

FALCK, R., *The Notre Dame Conductus: A Study of the Repertory* (Musicological Studies, 33; Henryville, Ottawa, Binningen, 1981).

FALLOWS, D., 'Polyphonic Song', in Knighton and Fallows (eds.), *Companion to Medieval and Renaissance Music* (London, 1992).

FASSLER, M., 'The Role of the Parisian Sequence in the Evolution of Notre-Dame Polyphony', *Speculum*, 62 (1987), 345–74.

FERGUSON, A. B., *The Indian Summer of English Chivalry* (Durham, NC, 1960).

FERGUSON, W. K., *The Renaissance in Historical Thought: Five Centuries of Interpretation* (Boston, 1948).

——*Renaissance Studies* (New York, 1963).

FICKER, R. VON, 'Polyphonic Music of the Gothic Period', *Musical Quarterly*, 15 (1929), 483–505.

FLECKENSTEIN, J., 'Johan Huizinga als Kulturhistoriker', in L. Grenzmann *et al.* (eds.), *Philologie als Kulturwissenschaft: Festschrift für Karl Stackmann* (Göttingen, 1987), 326–41.

FRANCO OF COLOGNE, *Ars cantus mensurabilis*, ed. G. Reaney and A. Gilles (Corpus scriptorum de musica, 18; American Institute of Musicology, 1974).

FRIEDLÄNDER, M. J., *Essays über die Landschaftsmalerei und andere Bildgattungen* (The Hague, 1947).

FROBENIUS, W., 'Die Motette', in H. Möller and R. Stephan (eds.), *Die Musik des Mittelalters* (Neues Handbuch der Musikwissenschaft, 2; Laaber, 1991), 272–94.

GAGE, J., 'Gothic Glass: Two Aspects of a Dionysian Aesthetic', *Art History*, 5 (1982), 36–58.

GALLO, F. A., *Music of the Middle Ages* II, trans. K. Eales (Cambridge, 1985).

GANIM, J. M., *Chaucerian Theatricality* (Princeton, NJ, 1990).

GENNRICH, F., *Rondeaux, Virelais und Balladen*, 2 vols. (Gesellschaft für romanische Literatur, 43 and 47; Dresden, 1921 and Göttingen, 1927).

GEOFFROI DE CHARNY, *Le Livre de Chevalerie*, ed. M. le baron Kervyn de Lettenhove, in *Œuvres de Froissart*, i, pts. 2–3 (Brussels, 1873), 463–533.

GEREMEK, B., *The Margins of Society in Late Medieval Paris* (Cambridge, 1987).

GHILLEBERT DE LANNOY, *Œuvres*, ed. Ch. Potvin (Louvain, 1878).

GLORIEUX, P., *La Faculté des arts et ses maâtres au XIIIe siècle* (Paris, 1971).

——*La littérature quodlibétique de 1260–1320* (Kain, 1925–35).

GODEFROY, F., *Dictionnaire de l'ancienne langue française*, 10 vols. (Paris, 1881–1902).

Bibliography

GODMAN, P., *Poets and Emperors: Frankish Politics and Carolingian Poetry* (Oxford, 1987).

GOMBRICH, E. H., *Tributes: Interpreters of our Cultural Tradition* (Oxford, 1984).

GROCHEIO, J. DE, *Concerning Music*, trans. A. Seay (2nd edn., Colorado Springs, Colo., 1973).

GUENÉE, B., *Between Church and State: The Lives of Four French Prelates in the Late Middle Ages* (Chicago and London, 1987).

GUIDO OF AREZZO, *Micrologus*, ed. J. Smits van Waesberghe (Corpus scriptorum de musica, 4: American Institue of Musicology, 1955).

GUMBRECHT, H. V., 'Intertextuality and Autumn: Autumn and the Modern Reception of the Middle Ages', in M. S. Brownlee, K. Brownlee, and S. G. Nichols (eds.), *The New Medievalism* (Baltimore and London, 1991), 301–30.

GURLITT, W., *Form in der Musik als Zeitgestaltung* (Wiesbaden, 1955).

GUSHEE, L., 'New Sources for the Biography of Johannes de Muris', *Journal of the American Musicological Society*, 22 (1969), 3–26.

——'Questions of Genre in Medieval Treatises on Music', in Arlt *et al.* (eds.), *Gattungen der Musik*, 365–433.

GUSHEE, M., 'The Polyphonic Music of the Medieval Monastery, Cathedral and University', in McKinnon (ed.), *Antiquity and the Middle Ages*, 143–69.

HAAS, M., 'Studien zur mittelalterlichen Musiklehre I: Eine Übersicht über die Musiklehre im Kontext der Philosophie des 13. und frühen 14. Jahrhunderts', *Forum Musicologicum*, 3 (1982), 323–456.

HAEGER, K., *The Illustrated History of Surgery* (London, 1988).

HALECKI, O., *The Limits and Divisions of European History* (Notre Dame, Ind., 1962).

HALLIWELL, J. O. (ed.), *Rara Mathematica* (London, 1839).

HAREN, M., *Medieval Thought* (London, 1985).

HARRISON, F. LL., and DOBSON, E. (eds.), *Medieval English Songs* (London, 1979).

HERMANNUS CONTRACTUS, *Musica*, ed. and trans. L. Ellinwood (Rochester, NY, 1936).

HIGGINS, P., 'Parisian Nobles, a Scottish Princess, and the Woman's Voice in Late Medieval Song', *Early Music History*, 10 (1991), 145–200.

HOFMANN, K., 'Zur Entstehungs- und Frühgeschichte des Terminus Motette', *Acta musicologica*, 42 (1970), 138–50.

HOLLY, M. A., *Panofsky and the Foundations of Art History* (Ithaca, NY, and London, 1984).

HOPPIN, R., *Medieval Music* (New York, 1978).

——'A Musical Rotulus of the Fourteenth Century', *Revue belge de musicolo-gie*, 9 (1955), 131–42.

HUGENHOLTZ, F. W. N., 'The Fame of a Masterwork', in Koops *et al.* (eds.), *Johan Huizinga*, 91–103.

HUGLO, M., 'La Place du *Tractatus de Musica* dans l'histoire de la théorie musicale du XIIIe siècle—étude codicologique', in C. Meyer, *Jérôme de Moravie: un theoricien de la musique dans le milieu intellectuel parisien du XIIIe siècle* (Paris, 1992), 33–42.

HUIZINGA, J., *Verzamelde werken*, 9 vols. (Haarlem, 1948–53).

——*The Waning of the Middle Ages*, trans. F. Hopman (London, 1924).

HUMBERT OF ROMANS, *Sermones beati Umberti Burgundi*, 2 vols. (Venice, 1603).

HUOT, S., *From Song to Book: The Poetics of Writing in Old French Lyric and Lyrical Narrative Poetry* (Ithaca, NY, and London, 1987).

——'Polyphonic Poetry: The Old French Motet and its Literary Context', *French Forum*, 14 (1989), 261–78.

JACKSON, W. H., 'Tournaments and the German Chivalric *renovatio*: Tournament Discipline and the Myth of Origins', in Anglo (ed.), *Chivalry*, 77–91.

JACOB, E. F., 'Huizinga and the Autumn of the Middle Ages', in *Essays in Later Medieval History* (Manchester, 1968), 141–53.

JACQUES DE LIEGE, *Speculum musicae*, ed. R. Bragard, 7 vols. (Corpus scriptorum de musica, 3; American Institute of Musicology, 1955–73).

JANSONIUS, F., 'De Stijl van Huizinga', in Koops *et al.*, *Johan Huizinga*, 53–72.

JOHN OF AFFLIGHEM, *De musica cum tonario*, ed. J. Smits van Waesberghe (Corpus scriptorum de musica, 1; American Institute of Musicology, 1950).

JOHN OF GARLAND, *The Parisiana Poetria*, ed. and trans. T. Lawler (New Haven, Conn., 1974).

JORDAN, R. M., *Chaucer and the Shape of Creation: The Aesthetic Possibilities of Inorganic Structure* (Cambridge, Mass., 1967).

——*Chaucer's Poetics and the Modern Reader* (London, 1987).

KAHRL, S. J., 'Chaucer's *Squire's Tale* and the Decline of Chivalry', *Chaucer Review*, 7 (1973), 194–209.

KARPINSKI, L. C., and WATERS, E. G. R., 'A Thirteenth-Century Algorism in French Verse', *Isis*, 11 (1928), 45–84.

KELLY, D., *Medieval Imagination* (Madison, Wis., 1978).

KEEN, M., *Chivalry* (New Haven, Conn., and London, 1984).

——'Huizinga, Kilgour and the Decline of Chivalry', *Medievalia et Human-istica*, NS, 8 (1977), 1–20.

KEMP, W. S., *Burgundian Court Song in the Time of Binchois* (Oxford, 1990).

——(ed.) *Anonymous Pieces in the Chansonnier El Escorial, Biblioteca del Monasterio Cod. V.III.24* (Corpus mensurabilis musicae, 77; Neuhausen-Stuttgart, 1980).

KENNEDY, V. L., 'Robert Courson on Penance', *Medieval Studies*, 7 (1945), 291–336.

KIDSON, P., 'Panofsky, Suger and St. Denis', *Journal of the Warburg and Courtauld Institutes*, 50 (1987), 1–17.

——Review of F. Bucher, *Architector* (New York, 1979), *Journal of the Society of Architectural Historians*, 40 (1981), 329–31.

KILGOUR, R. L., *The Decline of Chivalry as Shown in the French Literature of the Late Middle Ages* (Cambridge, Mass., 1937).

KNAPP, J., 'Musical Declamation and Poetic Rhythm in an Early Layer of Notre Dame Conductus', *Journal of the American Musicological Society*, 32 (1979), 383–407.

KNIGHTON, T., 'A Day in the Life of Francisco de Peñalosa (c.1470–1528)', in Knighton and Fallows (eds.), *Companion*, 79–84.

——and FALLOWS, D. (eds.), *Companion to Medieval and Renaissance Music* (London, 1992).

KOOPS, W. R. H., KOSSMANN, E. H., and PLAAT, G. VAN DER (eds.), *Johan Huizinga 1872–1972* (The Hague, 1973).

KOSSMANN, E. H., 'Postscript', in Koops *et al.* (eds.), *Johan Huizinga*, 223–34.

KOSTOF, S. K., 'The Architect in the Middle Ages, East and West', in id. (ed.), *The Architect: Chapters in the History of the Profession* (Oxford, 1977), 59–95.

KUNTZ, M. L., 'Pythagorean Cosmology and its Identification in Bodin's *Colloquium Heptaplomeres*', in Kuntz and Kuntz (eds.), *Jacob's Ladder*, 253–66.

——and KUNTZ, P. G. (eds.), *Jacob's Ladder and the Tree of Life: Concepts of Hierarchy and the Great Chain of Being* (New York, 1987).

KUNTZ, P. G., 'A Formal Preface and an Informal Conclusion to *The Great Chain of Being*', in Kuntz and Kuntz (eds.), *Jacob's Ladder*, 3–14.

LA SALE, ANTOINE DE, *Jehan de Saintré*, ed. J. Misrahi and C. A. Knudson (Geneva, 1965).

LAWN, B. (ed.), *The Prose Salernitan Questions* (Auctores Britannici medii aevi, 5; London, 1979).

LECLERCQ, DOM J., *St Bernard* (Paris, 1990).

LEECH-WILKINSON, D., 'Ars Antiqua—Ars Nova—Ars Subtilior', in McKinnon (ed.), *Antiquity and the Middle Ages*, 218–40.

——*Machaut's Mass: An Introduction* (Oxford, 1990).

Bibliography

——'Machaut's *Rose, lis* and the Problem of Early Music Analysis', *Music Analysis*, 3 (1984), 9–28.

LE GOFF, J., *Les Intellectuels au moyen âge* (Paris, 1985).

——*Time, Work and Culture in the Middle Ages* (Chicago and London, 1980).

LEVY, K., 'A Dominican Organum Duplum', *Journal of the American Musicological Society*, 27 (1974), 183–211.

LEWIS, C. S., *The Discarded Image* (Cambridge, 1964).

LINDBERG, D. C., *The Beginnings of Western Science* (Chicago and London, 1992).

LYON, B., 'Was Johan Huizinga Interdisciplinary?', *Handelingen der Maatschappij voor Geschiedenis en Oudheidkunde te Gent*, 38 (1984), 181–8.

MACCAGNOLO, E., 'David of Dinant and the Beginnings of Aristotelianism in Paris', in P. Dronke (ed.), *A History of Twelfth Century Philosophy* (Cambridge, 1988), 429–42.

MCGEE, T. J., 'Medieval Dances: Matching the Repertory with Grocheio's Descriptions', *The Journal of Musicology*, 7 (1989), 498–517.

MACHAUT, GUILLAUME DE, *Œuvres*, ed. E. Hoepffner, 3 vols. (Paris, 1908–21).

——*Works*, ed. L. Schrade (Polyphonic Music of the Fourteenth Century, 2–3; Monaco, 1956; repr. 1977 as *Guillaume de Machaut: Œuvres complètes*).

MCKINNON, J. (ed.), *Antiquity and the Middle Ages: From Ancient Greece to the Fifteenth Century* (London, 1990).

MACY, L., 'Women's History and Early Music', in Knighton and Fallows (eds.), *Companion*, 93–8.

MANN, J., *Geoffrey Chaucer* (New York, 1991).

MARK, R., *Experiments in Gothic Structure* (Cambridge, Mass., 1982).

MATHIASSEN, F., *The Style of the Early Motet* (Copenhagen, 1966).

MENACHE, S., *The* Vox Dei: *Communication in the Middle Ages* (Oxford, 1990).

MILSOM, J., 'Recent Releases of Medieval Monody and Polyphony', *Plainsong and Medieval Music*, 1 (1992), 111–21.

MOORE, R. I., *The Formation of a Persecuting Society* (Oxford, 1987).

MORAND, F. (ed.), *Chronique de Jean le Févre*, 2 vols. (Paris, 1876 and 1881).

MORGAN, D., 'From a Death to a View: Louis Robessart, Johan Huizinga, and the Political Significance of Chivalry', in Anglo (ed.), *Chivalry*, 93–106.

MORRIS, C., *The Discovery of the Individual 1050–1200* (Toronto, 1987).

MOYER, A. E., *Musica Scientia: Musical Scholarship in the Italian Renaissance* (Ithaca, NY, and London, 1992).

VA, X., 'Vir quidem fallax et falsidicus, sed artifex praeelectus: Remarques sur l'image sociale et littéraire de l'artiste au Moyen Age', in Barral i Altet (ed.), *Artistes*, i. 53–72.

MURIS, JOHANNES DE, *Notitia artis musicae*, ed. U. Michels (Corpus Scriptorum de Musica, 17; American Institute of Musicology, 1972).

MURRAY, A., *Reason and Society in the Middle Ages* (corr. edn., Oxford, 1985).

NATHAN, H., 'The Function of Text in French Thirteenth-Century Motets', *Musical Quarterly*, 28 (1942), 445–62.

NORTH, J. D., 'The Astrolabe', *Scientific American*, 230 (1974), 96–106.

NORWOOD, P. P, 'Evidence Concerning the Provenance of the Bamberg Codex', *The Journal of Musicology*, 8 (1990), 491–504.

O'NEIL, W. M., *Time and the Calendars* (Manchester, 1975).

OESCH, H., *Berno und Hermann von Reichenau als Musiktheoretiker* (Berne, 1961).

PÄCHT, O., ' "La Terre de Flandres" ', *Pantheon*, 36 (1978), 3–16.

PAGE, C., 'Court and City in France, 1100–1300', in McKinnon (ed.), *Antiquity and the Middle Ages*, 197–217.

——'The English *a cappella* Heresy', in Knighton and Fallows, *Companion*, 23–9.

——'Going beyond the Limits: Experiments with Vocalization in the French Chanson, 1340–1440', *Early Music*, 20 (1992), 446–59.

——'Johannes de Grocheio on Secular Music: A Corrected Text and Translation', *Plainsong and Medieval Music*, 2 (1993). Forthcoming.

——'Machaut's "Pupil" Deschamps on the Performance of Music', *Early Music*, 5 (1977), 484–91.

——'Music and Chivalric Fiction in France, 1150–1300', *Proceedings of the Royal Musical Association*, 111 (1984–5), 1–27.

——*The Owl and the Nightingale: Musical Life and Ideas in France 1100–1300* (London, 1989).

——'The Performance of Ars Antiqua Motets', *Early Music*, 16 (1988), 147–64.

——'The Performance of Songs in Late Medieval France: A New Source', *Early Music*, 10 (1982), 441–50.

——'Polyphony before 1400', in H. M. Brown and S. Sadie (eds.), *Performance Practice*, 2 vols. (London, 1989), i. 79–104.

——'A Treatise on Musicians from ?c.1400: The *Tractatulus de differentiis et gradibus cantorum* by Arnulf de St Ghislain', *Journal of the Royal Musical Association*, 117 (1992), 1–21.

——*Voices and Instruments of the Middle Ages: Instrumental Practice and Songs in France 1100–1300* (London, 1987).

——(ed. and trans.) *The* Summa music*e: A Thirteenth-Century Manual j-Singers* (Cambridge, 1991).

PALISCA, C. V., *Humanism in Italian Renaissance Musical Thought* (New Haven, Conn., and London, 1985).

PANOFSKY, E., *Gothic Architecture and Scholasticism* (London, 1957).

PATTERSON, L., *Negotiating the Past: The Historical Understanding of Medieval Literature* (Madison, Wis., 1987).

PEARSALL, D., 'Chaucer and the Modern Reader: A Question of Approach', *Dutch Quarterly Review of Anglo-American Letters*, 11 (1981), 258–66.

PEIPER, R., 'Fortolfi Rhythmimachia', *Abhandlungen zur Geschichte der Mathematik*, 3 (1880), 169–227.

PERKINS, L. L., and GAREY, H. (eds.), *The Mellon Chansonnier*, 2 vols. (New Haven, Conn., and London, 1979).

PERNOUD, R., *Pour en finir avec le moyen âge* (Paris, 1977).

PESCE, D., 'A Revised View of the Thirteenth-Century Latin Double Motet', *Journal of the American Musicological Society*, 40 (1987), 405–42.

——'The Significance of Text in Thirteenth-Century Latin Motets', *Acta musicologica*, 58 (1986), 91–117.

PEVSNER, N., *An Outline of European Architecture* (7th rev. edn., Harmondsworth, 1963).

PIRROTTA, N., 'Dante *Musicus*: Gothicism, Scholasticism and Music', *Speculum*, 43 (1968), 245–57.

POIRION, D., and REGALADO, N. F. (eds.), *Contexts: Style and Values in Medieval Art and Literature* (Yale French Studies, Special Issue; New Haven, Conn., 1991).

PRICE, B. B., *Medieval Thought* (Oxford, 1992).

RADDING, C. M., 'Superstition to Science: Nature, Fortune and the Passing of the Medieval Ordeal', *The American Historical Review*, 84 (1979), 945–69.

——and CLARK, W. W., 'Abélard et le bâtisseur de Saint-Denis', *Annales, Economies, Sociétés, Civilisations*, 43 (1988), 1263–90.

REANEY, G., 'Fourteenth Century Harmony and the Ballades, Rondeaux and Virelais of Guillaume de Machaut', *Musica disciplina*, 7 (1953), 129–46.

——*Guillaume de Machaut* (London, 1971).

——'The Isorhythmic Motet and its Social Background', *Bericht über den internationalen musikwissenschaftlichen Kongreß Kassel 1962* (Kassel, 1963), 1–25.

——'The Part Played by Instruments in the Music of Guillaume de Machaut', *Studi musicali*, 6 (1977), 3–11.

——'Voices and Instruments in the Music of Guillaume de Machaut', *Revue belge de musicologie*, 10 (1956), 3–17 and 93–104.

Bibliography

REANEY, G., (ed.), *Early Fifteenth-Century Music*, ii (Corpus mensurabilis musicae, 11; American Institute of Musicology, 1959).

RECKOW, F. (ed.), *Der Musiktraktat des Anonymus IV*, 2 vols. (Wiesbaden, 1967).

REESE, G., *Music in the Renaissance* (New York, 1954).

RENÉ D'ANJOU, *Traité de la forme et devis d'un tournoi*, ed. E. Pognon (Paris, 1946).

RICHARDS, J., *Sex, Dissidence and Damnation: Minority Groups in the Middle Ages* (London and New York, 1990).

ROBERTSON, A. W., *The Service-Books of the Royal Abbey of Saint-Denis: Images of Ritual and Music in the Middle Ages* (Oxford, 1991).

ROBERTSON, D. W., *A Preface to Chaucer: Studies in Medieval Perspectives* (London, 1963).

ROBINSON, F. W., 'Medieval, the Middle Ages', *Speculum*, 59 (1984), 745–56.

ROESNER, E. H., AVRIL, F. and REGALADO, N. F. (eds.), *Le Roman de Fauvel in the Edition of Mesire Chaillou de Pesstain* (New York, 1990).

ROHLOFF, E. (ed. and trans.), *Die Quellenhandscrhiften zum Musiktraktat des Johannes de Grocheio* (Leipzig, 1972).

RUBIN, M., 'Religious Culture in Town and Country: Reflections on a Great Divide', in D. Abulafia *et al.* (eds.), *Church and City 1000–1500: Essays in Honour of Christopher Brooke* (Cambridge, 1992), 3–22.

SALTER, E., 'Medieval Poetry and the Visual Arts', *Essays and Studies*, NS, 22 (1969), 16–32. Repr. in *English and International: Studies in the Literature, Art and Patronage of Medieval England* (Cambridge, 1988), 245–55.

SANDERS, E., 'Consonance and Rhythm in the Organum of the Twelfth and Thirteenth Centuries', *Journal of the American Musicological Society*, 33 (1980), 264–86.

——'The Medieval Motet', in Arlt *et al.* (eds.), *Gattungen der Musik*, 497–573.

SCAGLIONE, A., *Knights at Court: Courtliness, Chivalry and Courtesy from Ottonian Germany to the Italian Renaissance* (Berkeley, Los Angeles, and Oxford, 1991).

SCHAPIRO, M., 'On the Aesthetic Attitude in Romanesque Art', in id., *Romanesque Art* (London, 1977), 1–27.

SCHRADE, L. (ed.), *Le Roman de Fauvel* (Polyphonic Music of the Fourteenth Century, 1; Monaco, 1956).

Scriptores de musica medii aevi, ed. E. de Coussemaker, 4 vols. (Paris, 1864–76).

Scriptores ecclesiastici de musica sacra, ed. M. Gerbert, 3 vols. (Saint–Blaise, 1784).

SEAY, A., *Music in the Medieval World* (2nd edn., Englewood Cliffs, NJ, 1975).

Bibliography

SHATZMILLER, J., *Shylock Reconsidered: Jews, Moneylending and Medieval Society* (Berkeley, Los Angeles, and Oxford, 1990).

SHORT, I. (ed.), *Comput* (London, 1984).

SIMSON, O. VON, *The Gothic Cathedral: The Origins of Gothic Architecture and the Medieval Concept of Order* (London, 1956).

SIRAISI, N. G., *Medieval and Early Renaissance Medicine* (Chicago and London, 1990).

SLAVIN, D., 'Questions of Authenticity in Some Songs by Binchois', *Journal of the Royal Musical Association*, 117 (1992), 22–61.

SMITH, C., '*Della tranquillità dell'animo*: Architectural Allegories of Virtue in a Dialogue by Leon Battista Alberti,' *Journal of Medieval and Renaissance Studies*, 19 (1989), 103–22.

SMITS VAN WAESBERGHE, J., *Cymbala* (Musicological Studies and Documents, 1; American Institute of Musicology, 1951).

——*et al.* (eds.), *The Theory of Music from the Carolingian Era up to 1400*, i (Répertoire International des Sources Musicales; München–Duisburg, 1961).

SOUTHERN, R. W., *Medieval Humanism* (Oxford, 1970).

STADELMANN, R., *Vom Geist des ausgehenden Mittelalters* (Halle, 1929).

STEVENS, J., *Music and Poetry in the Early Tudor Court* (corr. edn., Cambridge, 1979).

——'The "Music" of the Lyric: Machaut, Deschamps, Chaucer', in P. Boitani and A. Torti (eds.), *Medieval and Pseudo-Medieval Literature* (Cambridge, 1984), 109–29.

——*Words and Music in the Middle Ages: Song, Narrative, Dance and Drama, 1050–1350* (Cambridge, 1986).

STOCKMANN, D., '*Musica Vulgaris* bei Johannes de Grocheio', *Beiträge zur Musikwissenschaft*, 25 (1983), 3–56.

STROHM, R., 'The Close of the Middle Ages', in McKinnon (ed.), *Antiquity and the Middle Ages*, 269–312.

——*Music in Late Medieval Bruges* (rev. edn., Oxford, 1990).

STRONG, R., *Art and Power: Renaissance Festivals 1450–1650* (Woodbridge, 1984).

SWITTEN, M. L., *The Cansos of Raimon de Miraval* (Cambridge, Mass., 1985).

TANAY, D., 'Music in the Age of Ockham: The Interrelations Between Music, Mathematics and Philosophy in the 14th Century', Ph.D. diss. (University of California at Berkeley, 1989).

TAYLOR, H. O., *The Medieval Mind*, 2 vols. (Oxford, 1911).

THIBAULT, G., and FALLOWS, D. (eds.), *Chansonnier de Jean de Montchenu* (Paris, 1991).

THOMAS, W. (ed.), *Robin and Marion Motets*, 3 vols. (Newton Abbott, 1987–9).

Bibliography

THORNDIKE, L., *The Sphere of Sacrobosco and its Commentators* (Chicago, 1949).

—— 'Computus', *Speculum*, 29 (1954), 223–38.

——and Kibre, P., *A Catalogue of Incipits of Mediaeval Scientific Writings in Latin* (London, 1963).

TINCTORIS, JOHANNES, *The Art of Counterpoint*, trans. A. Seay (Musicological Studies and Documents, 5; American Institute of Musicology, 1961).

——*Opera theoretica*, ed. A. SEAY (Corpus scriptorum de musica, 22; American Institute of Musicology, 1975–8).

TISCHLER, H. 'Coordination of Separate Elements: Chief Principle of Medieval Art', *Orbis musicae*, 2 (1973–4), 67–82.

——'Intellectual Trends in Thirteenth-Century Paris as Reflected in the Texts of Motets', *The Music Review*, 29 (1968), 1–11.

——*The Style and Evolution of the Earliest Motets*, 4 vols. (Musicological Studies, 40; Henryville, Ottawa, Binningen, 1985).

——(ed.), *The Earliest Motets*, 3 vols. (New Haven, Conn., 1982).

——(ed.) with S. Stakel and J. C. Relihan, *The Montpellier Codex*, 4 vols. (Recent Researches in the Music of the Middle Ages and the Renaissance, 8; Madison, Wisc., 1985).

TOBLER, A., and LOMMATZSCH, E., *Altfranzösisches Wörterbuch* (Berlin, 1925; Wiesbaden, 1954–)

TOOMER, G. J., 'A Survey of the Toledan Tables', *Osiris*, 15 (1968), 5–174.

TREITLER, L., 'Troubadours Singing their Poems', in Baltzer *et al.* (eds.), *The Union of Words and Music*, 15–48.

TRILLMICH, W., and BUCHNER, R. (eds.), *Quellen des 9. und 11. Jahrhunderts zur Geschichte der Hamburgischen Kirche und des Reiches* (Darmstadt, 1961).

TUCHMAN, B., *A Distant Mirror: The Calamitous Fourteenth Century* (London, 1979).

VALE, J., *Edward III and Chivalry: Chivalric Society and its Context* (Woodbridge, 1982).

VALE, M., *War and Chivalry* (London, 1981).

VAN DER WERF, H., *The Chansons of the Troubadours and Trouvères* (Utrecht, 1972).

WAGENAAR-NOLTHENIUS, H., 'Estampie/Stantipes/Stampita', *L'Ars Nova italiana del Trecento, 2* (Certaldo, 1969), 399–409.

WALTHER, H., *Lateinische Sprichwörter*, 6 vols. (Göttingen, 1963–9).

WANGENSTEIN, O. H., and WANGENSTEIN, S. D., *The Rise of Surgery* (Folkestone, 1978).

WARD, B., *The Venerable Bede* (London, 1990).

WEINTRAUB, K. J., *Visions of Culture* (Chicago, 1966).

Bibliography

WENZEL, S., 'The Moor Maiden—A Contemporary View', *Speculum*, 49 (1974), 69–74.

WERNER, E., 'The Mathematical Foundation of Philippe de Vitry's *Ars Nova*', *Journal of the American Musicological Society*, 9 (1956), 128–32.

WILSON, C., *The Gothic Cathedral* (London, 1990).

WILSON, E., *The Gawain–Poet* (Leiden, 1976).

WIMSATT, J. I., 'Chaucer and Deschamps' "Natural Music"', in Baltzer *et al.* (eds.), *The Union of Words and Music*, 132–50.

——and Cable, T., 'Introduction' to Baltzer *et al.* (eds.), *The Union of Words and Music*, 1–14.

WOLF, R. E., 'The Aesthetic Problem of the "Renaissance"', *Revue belge de musicologie*, 9 (1955), 83–102.

WRIGHT, C., 'Leoninus, Poet and Musician', *Journal of the American Musicological Society*, 39 (1986), 1–35.

——*Music and Ceremony at Notre Dame of Paris 500–1550* (Cambridge, 1989).

——*Music at the Court of Burgundy 1364–1419: A Documentary History* (Musicological Studies, 28; Henryville, Ottawa, Binningen, 1979).

YUDKIN, J. (ed.), *De Musica Mensurata: The Anonymous of St. Emmeram* (Bloomington and Indianapolis, Ind., 1990).

——*Music in Medieval Europe* (Englewood Cliffs, NJ, 1989).

ZUMTHOR, P., 'From Hi(story) to Poem, or the Paths of Pun: The Grands Rhétoriqueurs of Fifteenth-Century France', *New Literary History*, 10 (1979), 231–63.

Index

Index

Index